CONTENTS

NICKY HENDERSON

What a season Nicky Henderson had: a career best 115 winners at a 23 per cent strike rate and prize-money of over £2.1 million made it a campaign to remember. Those are statistics that are unlikely to be matched this season as a result of the unfortunate, and highly controversial, three-month ban from making entries for his horses imposed on the trainer back in July. None of this matters a damn to punters, and it will be very much business as usual at Seven Barrows.

It's odd how some horses get praised to the heavens for relatively moderate achievements, and other genuine stars don't get the credit they deserve. So it is with the Champion Hurdle winner **Punjabi**, and if you look at his form it's even harder to understand why.

He started his season with a win in the Fighting Fifth at Wetherby, and then fell when upsides the leader in the Christmas Hurdle – that turned out to be one of the most expensive falls in jump racing, but more of

▲ **Punjabi (centre)**

that later. He was third in the Kingwell Hurdle in his 'prep' race for Cheltenham, but that was at a time when the Henderson horses had been held up by the weather. In the Champion he took the lead at the last and then just held on by a neck from Celestial Halo. His final run of the season was when he just lost out in a titanic struggle with Solwhit in the Irish Champion.

'He didn't do much wrong, did he. Except, I suppose, he fell in the Christmas Hurdle and there was a £1 million bonus for any horse winning the Fighting Fifth, the Christmas and then the Champion! Anyway, he's back in and in good form, and I suppose that his campaign will be exactly the same again – that's the plan, but as we all know it's not always as simple as that with horses!'

Binocular was 6/4 in the Champion, compared to his stable companion's 22/1, and that was on the back of hugely impressive wins in the Betfair Hurdle at Haydock and the Boylesports at Ascot. The fact that the weather had got in the way when Nicky was planning to step up Binocular's work was one of the reasons that some considered Punjabi a slightly fortunate winner. In the Champion Binocular came to win his race, but he was never quite finding enough. It was the interrupted preparation, or him not being quite good enough, or Cheltenham not being his ideal track – you pays your money and you takes your choice!

'In a perfect world he and Punjabi will meet again at Cheltenham in March, and not before. We set out a plan last year that he'd have only two races before Cheltenham, but then we got caught out by the weather and we had two weeks off, which I just couldn't afford – we'll probably campaign him differently this season. He was probably the horse we expected to be our number one in the Champion, but that's why it's so handy to have two going there! The Boylesports is the obvious place to start him, and he'll probably take in a trip to Ireland at some stage.'

Punchestowns won the Intermediate Hurdle at Cheltenham, and then Ascot's Long Walk, before coming second to Big Buck's in the Cleeve Hurdle. On World Hurdle day he had to settle for second best again, although he got the gap down to less than two lengths behind the Nicholls runner on that occasion.

'He'll almost certainly go novice chasing, which was the plan last season until we realised just how good he was over hurdles. We don't need to plan out a campaign for him as there are a lot more options than there would be if he stayed hurdling. He has always been a good jumper and I hope that he'll be very good over fences.'

▲ **Punchestowns**

The Queen's horse, **Barber Shop**, was fancied in some quarters for the Cheltenham Gold Cup, but he slightly disappointed, fading out of contention from three out. Prior to that he'd won a valuable Intermediate chase at Sandown, after coming an excellent second in the Paddy Power.

'I still hope that there's more to come from him, and I'm inclined to put his Gold Cup run down to weakness more than anything else. It's not going to be easy to place him as the options are limited off his handicap mark, but the ultimate aim is the Gold Cup once again, and with another year behind him, who knows?'

Zaynar had been placed twice on the Flat in France for Alain de Royer-Dupre, and started off his juvenile hurdle campaign by winning a Newbury event that Nicky has used several times before to introduce a good three-year-old hurdling prospect. After that he won an Ascot event at 5/1 on before winning the Triumph, with stamina seeing him home up the hill. He looked that day as though he was a horse who would be even better over a longer trip.

▲ **Barber Shop**

'He's unbeaten and long may it last! That second season for juvenile hurdlers is a very difficult one, so I'm not sure exactly where we'll go with him. We've always thought that stamina would be his longer suit, and he certainly doesn't want a sharp two miles – maybe a race like the Ascot Hurdle, over two and a half miles, would suit.'

Petit Robin won a decent Newbury handicap chase on his seasonal debut, and while he didn't manage to win again, he ran some smashing races – second in the Desert Orchid and the Victor Chandler, and third in the Champion Chase.

'Life's going to be pretty difficult from now on as he's got very high in the handicap as a result of running up the backsides of some good horses. Having said that, he's a good horse, and I think that we can run him over a bit further, which has the advantage of avoiding the likes of Master Minded. If all went well then the Ryanair would be a more likely Festival target than the Champion.'

'**Sentry Duty** got a horrible injury in the Scottish Champion Hurdle, and I thought he'd be out for a very long time, but they've done a great job and he's back cantering. He has to stay over hurdles as he's tiny – he couldn't jump a fence as he couldn't even see over the top of it! He was a stayer on the Flat in France so I'll almost certainly try going further with him.'

'**Jack The Giant** is back after injury but you won't be seeing him for a while, as he's a good-ground horse and I can't have him ready to run before the ground turns. The target last year was always going to be the Ryanair and that'll be the plan once again.'

'**Aigle D'Or** looked fantastic in his first run of the season, when he was second in the Greatwood. However, he ran poorly next-time out and then, with one thing and another, we didn't run him again until Liverpool. He runs really well fresh so I've got a few ideas about how we might campaign him – let's just say that you won't be seeing a lot of him. He will jump a fence if we want him to.'

My hunch is that Aigle D'Or will be brought along very steadily with the aim of having him fresh and well for the day that matters, whenever that may be.

'After **Afsoun** fell at Fakenham we put him back over hurdles, and he ran some decent races. However, we'll go back chasing as he absolutely has to jump fences – we'll take it one step at a time with him but as everyone knows, he has a lot of ability.'

'**Andytown** was a new arrival last season, and he had a good campaign, winning at Cheltenham in November, and then in the Martin Pipe Conditionals race at the Festival. We tried him over fences a couple of times, but we've got to try again and make a success of it, as the handicapper has him by the scruff of the neck over hurdles.'

'**Dave's Dream** won the Imperial Cup last season and will now be going novice chasing – you'd have to think he will be very good at it too. He's a lovely, big, strong horse with all of the scope in the world – he's a good one.'

'I'm going to try **Duc Du Regniere** back over fences. He went wrong two seasons ago but he came back with some good runs over hurdles last year.'

'**Mad Max** is a very, very good horse, but unfortunately his breathing isn't great – his season depends on whether that holds up. We've operated on it, again, but we'll just have to cross our fingers that it has worked. He won two novice hurdles last season despite his problems, and he's a horse with a lot of ability.'

'I think that **Mr Gardner** will be an exciting novice chaser – he was very impressive when he won his novice hurdle at Newbury. We changed tactics and rode him more prominently and that seemed to suit.'

'**Pepsyrock** joined us from France before last season, and he looked pretty good in handicap chases. He just kept on improving all season, and if that continues then he could be interesting.'

'I think you must include **Riverside Theatre**. He won

Nicky Henderson

Nicky Henderson had his best-ever season – what I call a 'Stable Cat' campaign because if he'd got round to entering it then it would probably would have won. It's a measure of just how good Nicky is, and the respect with which the bookmaking fraternity regard him, that a 23 per cent strike rate produced a miserly £2 level-stakes profit! The novice hurdlers were 29 per cent and produced a whopping loss, and only the handicap hurdlers showed a profit, courtesy of a couple of long-priced winners. Even the bumper horses, after the most marvellous season – see how good they were in the interview – couldn't get close to producing a profit. This is a proper old-fashioned National Hunt yard where summer jumping is virtually ignored, and where the start of the new season is round about mid-October. After that things kick off with a vengeance and the winners start to flow – last year October, November and December all showed sizeable level-stakes profits, as did March thanks to Punjabi's 22/1 success in the Champion. We should hold fast to the long-standing advice: if you fancy one of the stable's chasers, back it, and if it's fancied in the market, so much the better, as this is a stable that knows the time of day with its runners – more than 45 per cent of the stable's runners that were made favourite did the business, and that resulted in a modest profit. Winners come all through the year, and although April has sometimes been a disappointing month in the past, it certainly wasn't last year, being on a par with all of the other good months. With Mick Fitzgerald gone, Messrs McCoy and Geraghty shared the rides and very well it worked too, with both of them plus Felix De Giles showing decent profits. Among the courses, the profitable ones last season were Ascot – counter to the trend in some years – Newbury and Kempton, with Cheltenham and Ludlow getting honourable mentions. Old favourite Fakenham was two from seven and just turned a profit. However, when the Henderon horses are in form – and the *Racing Post* 'Today's Trainers' section is our friend here, as it should be with all trainers – don't be afraid to back one anywhere if you fancy it. Similarly, don't let the fact that it's a horse's first-time out put you off – Nicky knows how to get them ready at home.

his bumper and a couple of novice hurdles, and didn't run a bad race all season. We stepped him up to Grade Two and then Grade Once company at the end of the season, and he was third to Hurricane Fly at Punchestown. He's a pretty decent horse and he'll almost certainly be sent novice chasing – he could be good at it.'

'**Tasheba** is a horse that I've always liked, and he has done very little wrong for us, winning twice and running well on each of his starts. He's still only four and we'll be stepping him up in trip.'

'**Trabolgan** is back and in good form, but I can't tell you where we'd start out with him, or what he'd do, but he's sound at present.'

'**Zemsky** won two out of two for me right at the back-end, and I think he's pretty smart. He won point-to-points in Ireland and will go novice chasing.'

If there has ever been a time when a trainer had a stronger hand of former bumper horses ready to step up to novice hurdles, then I can't recall it! Some trainers are fans of bumpers, and some aren't, but Nicky clearly falls into the former category with 20 winners and a strike rate of around one in four in that sphere last season. There were a lot of them, and they were an exceptionally good bunch.

'**Bellvano** was two from two – we'll ignore the one where he got left at the start as that was just one of those things. He had a little problem after his final start or I would have taken him to Punchestown for their Champion bumper. JP Magnier did a good job on him last season, but it will be Tony McCoy from now on, as Bellvano is now owned by JP McManus.'

'It's a similar story with **Quantitativeeasing** who looked pretty good when he won his only start at Punchestown. That was a good performance from a baby having his first run.'

'**Candy Creek** wasn't with me last season [trained in Ireland by John Keily] but she won the Mares bumper at Liverpool – she's lovely. I'm looking forward to running her.'

'**Finian's Rainbow** looked pretty smart when he won at Kempton, and he is smart – he's a good horse. Exactly the same applies to **Flemmingsbond** – he won very easily but fractured his pelvis doing it, so I couldn't run him again.'

'**General Miller** was two out of two, and looked very impressive at Perth – I thought that was a very good performance.'

'**Lush Life** didn't have a clue what he was doing when he won at Kempton, but he's pretty smart.'

'**Madame Mado** won very well at Warwick but then picked up a problem. She's a good mare.'

'**Ryde Back** was only beaten a short head on her first start, but won well the second time, and I think she's a nice mare.'

'**Line Freedom** won her only start, at Cheltenham in April, and was very impressive.'

'**Zazamix** won a 'Junior' bumper at Newbury and certainly rates a mention.'

'Finally, there's **Oscar Whisky**, who won a 'Junior' bumper over a mile and a half at Newbury, and he could just be the best of the lot. I expected him to be seriously impressive there, and he was.'

'All of these will, touch wood, be going novice hurdling, and they're an exciting bunch.'

Nicky starts the new season with a tremendous team which shows strength in depth across the board. While beating last season's tally will be a very tall order, such is the quality of the ammunition available to him that anything other than another good campaign is inconceivable. ■

Chaser to follow: **Dave's Dream**
Hurdler to follow: **Binocular**
Dark Horse: **Oscar Whisky**

NICKY HENDERSON

	No. of Hrs	Races Run	1st	2nd	3rd	Unpl	Per cent	£1 Level Stake
NH Flat	*44*	*74*	*20*	*14*	*4*	*36*	*27.0*	*-23.03*
Hurdles	*96*	*307*	*73*	*39*	*33*	*162*	*23.8*	*+61.48*
Chases	*43*	*117*	*22*	*14*	*11*	*70*	*18.8*	*-35.44*
Totals	**155**	**498**	**115**	**67**	**48**	**268**	**23.1**	**+3.01**
07-08	*127*	*381*	*83*	*55*	*42*	*201*	*21.8*	*-65.48*
06-07	*104*	*317*	*73*	*39*	*37*	*168*	*23.0*	*-11.94*

BY MONTH

NH Flat	W-R	Per cent	£1 Level Stake
May	0-3	0.0	-3.00
June	0-0	0.0	0.00
July	0-0	0.0	0.00
August	1-1	100.0	+1.75
September	0-0	0.0	0.00
October	0-4	0.0	-4.00
November	5-16	31.3	+0.52
December	1-7	14.3	-3.75
January	2-10	20.0	-2.00
February	2-5	40.0	-1.77
March	3-10	30.0	-4.40
April	6-18	33.3	-6.37

Hurdles	W-R	Per cent	£1 Level Stake
May	3-16	18.8	+12.50
June	0-4	0.0	-4.00
July	0-1	0.0	-1.00
August	1-2	50.0	+3.00
September	0-1	0.0	-1.00
October	6-10	60.0	+17.00
November	14-43	32.6	+18.13
December	11-50	22.0	+14.75
January	8-28	28.6	-7.74
February	6-43	14.0	-29.55
March	16-66	24.2	+46.94
April	8-43	18.6	-7.55

Chases	W-R	Per cent	£1 Level Stake
May	0-5	0.0	-5.00
June	0-1	0.0	-1.00
July	0-1	0.0	-1.00
August	0-1	0.0	-1.00
September	0-2	0.0	-2.00
October	2-9	22.2	-2.75
November	7-22	31.8	-1.34
December	7-23	30.4	+10.17
January	0-10	0.0	-10.00
February	3-13	23.1	-5.28
March	0-18	0.0	-18.00
April	3-12	25.0	+1.75

Totals	W-R	Per cent	£1 Level Stake
May	3-24	12.5	+4.50
June	0-5	0.0	-5.00
July	0-2	0.0	-2.00
August	2-4	50.0	+3.75
September	0-3	0.0	-3.00
October	8-23	34.8	+10.25
November	26-81	32.1	+17.31
December	19-80	23.8	+21.17
January	10-48	20.8	-19.74
February	11-61	18.0	-36.60
March	19-94	20.2	+24.54
April	17-73	23.3	-12.17

DISTANCE

Hurdles	W-R	Per cent	£1 Level Stake
2m-2m3f	50-181	27.6	+30.19
2m4f-2m7f	17-90	18.9	+25.91
3m+	6-36	16.7	+5.38

Chases	W-R	Per cent	£1 Level Stake
2m-2m3f	10-34	29.4	-8.61
2m4f-2m7f	8-47	17.0	-11.08
3m+	4-36	11.1	-15.75

RACE CLASS

	W-R	Per cent	£1 Level Stake
Class 1	14-113	12.4	-22.27
Class 2	17-68	25.0	+41.41
Class 3	30-128	23.4	+23.66
Class 4	36-132	27.3	-33.49
Class 5	9-37	24.3	-9.61
Class 6	9-20	45.0	+3.31

FIRST TIME OUT

	W-R	Per cent	£1 Level Stake
Bumpers	15-44	34.1	-3.61
Hurdles	28-79	35.4	+56.31
Chases	9-32	28.1	-4.09
Totals	52-155	33.5	+48.61

JOCKEYS

	W-R	Per cent	£1 Level Stake
B J Geraghty	58-210	27.6	+12.75
A P McCoy	25-79	31.6	+21.17
Felix De Giles	14-60	23.3	+15.14
Andrew Tinkler	6-41	14.6	-2.50
Marcus Foley	4-63	6.3	-43.75
R J Killoran	3-20	15.0	-7.95
Mr J P Magnier	2-3	66.7	+0.23
C Wallis	1-2	50.0	+24.00
Richard Johnson	1-2	50.0	+0.25
Mr S Waley-Cohen	1-5	20.0	-3.33

COURSE RECORD

	Total W-R	Non-Hndcps Hurdles	Non-Hndcps Chases	Hndcps Hurdles	Hndcps Chases	NH Flat	Per cent	£1 Level Stake
Newbury	18-51	9-21	1-4	0-8	5-13	3-5	35.3	+17.00
Ascot	13-43	6-14	0-2	4-15	2-8	1-4	30.2	+12.39
Kempton	13-57	5-17	1-11	3-12	1-10	3-7	22.8	+13.36
Huntingdon	8-27	3-10	2-5	1-4	0-4	2-4	29.6	-5.42
Cheltenham	8-69	3-17	0-3	4-30	0-12	1-7	11.6	+14.13
Ludlow	7-18	3-7	0-0	3-6	0-0	1-5	38.9	+8.02
Sandown	6-32	2-10	1-2	2-16	1-2	0-2	18.8	+1.75
Hereford	4-10	3-5	0-0	0-3	0-1	1-1	40.0	+1.12
Towcester	4-19	1-8	1-2	0-1	1-2	1-6	21.1	-2.90
Wetherby	3-4	2-2	0-0	1-2	0-0	0-0	75.0	+2.98
Warwick	3-7	1-3	1-1	0-1	0-0	1-2	42.9	-1.02
Doncaster	3-8	2-4	0-1	1-1	0-0	0-2	37.5	-0.74
Perth	3-8	1-3	0-1	0-1	1-2	1-1	37.5	+1.38
Aintree	3-27	0-5	0-2	3-10	0-5	0-5	11.1	-1.50
Musselbgh	2-4	1-2	0-0	0-1	0-0	1-1	50.0	-0.13
Plumpton	2-6	1-4	1-1	0-0	0-1	0-0	33.3	-0.75
Ayr	2-7	0-1	0-0	1-4	1-2	0-0	28.6	+4.75
Fakenham	2-7	1-2	0-3	0-0	0-0	1-2	28.6	+0.44
Haydock	2-18	1-4	0-0	0-10	0-1	1-3	11.1	-14.79
Mrket Rsn	1-2	0-1	0-0	0-0	0-0	1-1	50.0	+0.75
Folkestone	1-3	0-0	1-2	0-0	0-0	0-1	33.3	-1.50
Leicester	1-4	0-0	1-3	0-0	0-1	0-0	25.0	+1.00
Chepstow	1-7	1-5	0-0	0-0	0-0	0-2	14.3	-2.50
Fontwell	1-7	0-2	0-1	0-1	0-0	1-3	14.3	-5.00
Bangor	1-8	0-2	0-1	1-3	0-0	0-2	12.5	-3.00
Stratford	1-9	0-1	0-0	1-3	0-3	0-2	11.1	-6.00
Taunton	1-9	1-5	0-0	0-1	0-0	0-3	11.1	-7.56
Wincanton	1-10	0-4	0-0	1-3	0-2	0-1	10.0	-6.25

PHILIP HOBBS

It was another typically excellent season for the admirable Philip Hobbs. The strike rate was up a little bit at nearly 18 per cent, and the century of winners was achieved for the eighth consecutive season. At his recent Owners' Day he commented that he was without 'any real star names', but a look at his list of horses shows a mix of high-class types and up-and-coming youngsters.

Snap Tie had a good season over hurdles, winning the WBX.com hurdle at Kempton on his reappearance, and then finishing second in the Christmas Hurdle and third in the Haydock Champion Hurdle Trial. He then ran well in the Champion itself, before running well under a huge weight in the Scottish equivalent.

'He's going novice chasing, and he should do well – the only worry is that he's not a horse who wants soft ground. He probably handles good to soft but not any worse than that. He was a little bit late coming back into training. The only worry would be if we had a really wet

▲ **Planet Of Sound**

▲ **Massini's Maguire**

autumn. I thought that he was possibly unlucky not to do even better in the Champion Hurdle, as he missed the break and got left – if he'd got away on level terms he might have finished fourth in that race. Obviously, if all went well we'd be hoping that he makes up into an Arkle horse.'

Planet Of Sound was Philip's Arkle horse last season, and he finished third in the big race. Prior to that he'd won twice at Newbury, and he rounded off his season with a third place at Liverpool, looking as though he didn't stay the two and a half miles there.

'Like Snap Tie I thought he was a bit unlucky not to finish closer at Cheltenham. He missed the break and then made a mistake which sent him even further back, but he finished really strongly and wasn't beaten that far. I'm not convinced that it was lack of stamina that found him out at Aintree, and we've always thought that he'd get further than two miles. The Haldon Gold Cup, over two and a quarter, is the obvious place to start him out as it's a limited handicap – if he went well there we can step him up to conditions races, otherwise it'll be handicaps.'

It's odd how we latch onto particular horses, and **Massini's Maguire** has always been a favourite of mine since he beat Wichita Lineman three years ago. Last season he went over fences, finishing second in the Feltham and the Scilly Isles, and third in the RSA Chase at the Festival.

'He's had an unusual injury – to a suspensory ligament on a hind leg – but he's now back cantering and so far it's all going well. That means, however, that he won't be back until around Christmas time. Like Planet Of Sound, he needs to step up on what he achieved as a novice or we'll just be running in decent handicaps. He's a horse who can be a bit inconsistent, but we don't know why that is. Ideally we'd like to start him over 2m 6f at one of the better tracks – maybe a Graduation chase if we can find one.'

Ballydub was hurdling last season, winning a Pertemps qualifier at Newbury.

'He's a very decent horse, but his jumping over hurdles sometimes wasn't the best. He's a great big, strong horse and he jumps well unless you really ask him a serious question – Richard Johnson would be the first to blame himself for his Cheltenham fall, asking him to stand off rather than fiddle the hurdle coming down the hill. The result was a pretty nasty fall which damaged his confidence. He's suited by three miles and soft ground and will be going novice chasing.'

Cockney Trucker won a novice hurdle at Newbury, but his best bit of form was when third in the County Hurdle at the Cheltenham Festival. **Copper Bleu** was second in the Supreme Novices, and then in an Aintree Grade Two. He finished his season with a win in a Punchestown novices event.

'I'd put the two together as we've always thought they were horses of very similar ability. Having said that, Cockney Trucker is rated 130 while Copper Bleu is off 143 – if I'm right then Cockney Trucker could just be a very well handicapped horse. They'll both start out in two-mile novice chases and will realistically end up needing two and a half. The main difference between them is that Copper Bleu will handle it soft, whereas Cockney Trucker needs good ground to show the best of his ability.'

In the light of his comments, I wonder whether Philip might be tempted to run Cockney Trucker over hurdles prior to going chasing? It would be a shame to waste his handicap mark if he is indeed well treated.

Kornati Kid won a Beginners chase at Exeter and then followed up in a Wetherby Grade Two. He then ran in the four-mile National Hunt Chase at Cheltenham, where he ran well until his stamina seemingly gave out after the third last.

'He had a good season, but was another one who disappointed at Cheltenham and I can't really explain what went wrong. I'm hoping in the back of my mind that the Welsh National might be the race for him, as he goes on soft ground and stays very, very well. I don't think it was lack of stamina that found him out at Cheltenham.'

Tarablaze won three of his four starts in novice hurdles, his only defeat coming in the Persian War at Chepstow just ten days after he made a successful debut. After that he won over the fixed brush hurdles at Haydock, and won again there in the Grade Two Albert Bartlett Hurdle in February.

Philip Hobbs

Another good season for Philip Hobbs with the strike rate up, but another level-stakes loss recorded. Winners came throughout the year, barring a barren August. Having told you in the past to avoid the yard's bumper runners, Philip almost doubled the number of winners in that sphere to nine, and produced another modest profit – that's two year's running and I think signifies a change of approach. Runners in non-handicap hurdles and chases are always worth a close look, and the yard's novice chasers are always well-schooled. The excellent Richard Johnson takes the lion's share of the rides and, accordingly, produces a huge level-stakes loss, but conditional Rhys Flint did well and showed a handsome profit. AP McCoy is, of course, a significant booking and while three from 11 wasn't as good as the previous season, it still ended up on the right side of the ledger. We were right in last year's *Guide to the Jumps* to predict that the previous season's 18 per cent strike rate at Cheltenham wouldn't be maintained, but Philip went and managed 17 per cent last season, making it a profitable venue! Course statistics vary from year to year, with old favourite Exeter falling from grace last season. Newbury was again very solid last season, as were Chepstow, Newton Abbot, Wincanton, Haydock and Hereford, but it could all be different next time around. Selectivity is the name of the game with Philip's yard, and novice hurdlers and chasers who are favoured in the market are always worth a look, as are runners in conditions races in general.

'He stays well, and we were going to run him in the three-mile novice hurdle at the Festival, but he got ill just before the race. We'll start him off in novice chases over two and a half to three miles – soft ground suits him well.'

'**Prince Taime** isn't that far off conditions-hurdle class. I suppose that he'll end up novice chasing, but he was improving so fast in the spring that I'm inclined to let him take his chance in a race like the Tote Silver Trophy. He's 145 now, and if he was to win that at Chepstow he'd probably be 155, and that's not too far off conditions races. I think he'd have to win there to persuade us to keep him over hurdles – you wouldn't want to be messing around all winter debating when he should go chasing.'

'We've always thought a lot of **Keki Buku**, but he hasn't really produced the goods yet. He has a great attitude and works very well at home, but once again he disappointed in his last run at Punchestown. I just feel that off a mark of 120 he's worth running in a handicap hurdle, but if he doesn't win it then I would think that he'll be chasing. He's suited by two and a half miles and handles most types of ground.'

'We didn't really have **Chance Du Roy** right all of last season, and then he ran a good race once it was all over. I think he's another who could run in a hurdle before we think about chasing, as he could just be well handicapped.'

'**Son Histoire** ran a remarkable race at Newton Abbot

▲ **Calusa Crystal (second right)**

on his final start – he really surprised us!. We stepped him up to 2m 6f and he finished really well and nearly got up. He hasn't had that much racing and was still rather green, so I'm very hopeful that he can show further improvement – we'll certainly start off by trying to win a novice hurdle.'

'**Mont Present** had an operation on his knee after he won at Fontwell on his first run for us, but he's fine now. He's another who'll probably start in a handicap hurdle and after that we can decide whether to go novice chasing. His mark of 125 might be high enough for what he has achieved so far, but the race he won has worked out pretty well. He had some decent form over hurdles in France before he joined us, and had a run over fences – he handles soft ground.'

'I think that **Giordano Bruno** was our best bumper horse last season, and I'm very hopeful that he'll be a high-class novice hurdler. He's a very keen sort so we'll definitely start at two miles to give him every chance to settle, but there's no reason why he shouldn't go further in time.'

Zakatal is a new arrival to Philip's team and runs in the colours of successful owner Terry Warner. A winner on the Flat in France for The Aga Khan, he's been bought with a juvenile hurdling campaign in mind.

'**Calusa Crystal** won four times over hurdles last season and was progressive. She looks the right sort for the mares novice chases and seems to be suited by good ground.'

'**Volador** won on his final start in a bumper, having been a bit unlucky the time before at Sandown when he didn't have the best of luck and ended up having just too much to do. We'll start him out at two and a half miles and you would hope that he'll do well over hurdles.'

'**Wishfull Thinking** wasn't healthy for most of last season, and then was very unlucky on his only start, in a Hereford bumper where he was trapped behind horses, and by the time he got out the winner had flown. I hope that there's a lot of improvement in him, and I think he'll start out in a two-and-a-half mile novice hurdle – he could be a very nice horse.'

'**Dare Me** had a problem over the summer. As a result he won't be out until around Christmas time, but he's a nice prospect who should do well over hurdles.'

Despite Philip's comment that his team is light on star names, he has a strong team in place for the new season, and I formed the view that he's very hopeful that last year's tally of winners can be surpassed. ■

Chaser to follow: **Snap Tie**
Hurdler to follow: **Son Histoire**
Dark Horse: **Zakatal**

PHILIP HOBBS

WITHYCOMBE, SOMERSET

	No. of Hrs	Races Run	1st	2nd	3rd	Unpl	Per cent	£1 Level Stake
NH Flat	*25*	*41*	*9*	*10*	*6*	*16*	*22.0*	*+1.36*
Hurdles	*91*	*303*	*53*	*36*	*29*	*185*	*17.5*	*+0.51*
Chases	*63*	*232*	*41*	*41*	*26*	*124*	*17.7*	*-65.91*
Totals	**147**	**576**	**103**	**87**	**61**	**325**	**17.9**	**-64.04**
07-08	*163*	*694*	*108*	*102*	*79*	*404*	*15.6*	*-95.35*
06-07	*160*	*606*	*115*	*91*	*66*	*334*	*19.0*	*-118.31*

BY MONTH

NH Flat	W-R	Per cent	£1 Level Stake
May	1-3	33.3	0.00
June	0-0	0.0	0.00
July	0-0	0.0	0.00
August	0-0	0.0	0.00
September	0-0	0.0	0.00
October	1-3	33.3	+1.50
November	2-5	40.0	+4.75
December	1-4	25.0	+13.00
January	0-5	0.0	-5.00
February	1-5	20.0	-2.13
March	3-7	42.9	-1.77
April	0-9	0.0	-9.00

Hurdles	W-R	Per cent	£1 Level Stake
May	5-16	31.3	+26.00
June	0-3	0.0	-3.00
July	1-2	50.0	+3.50
August	0-9	0.0	-9.00
September	1-7	14.3	-4.63
October	7-41	17.1	-1.50
November	8-49	16.3	-12.25
December	6-36	16.7	+8.00
January	3-34	8.8	-18.38
February	4-26	15.4	-5.75
March	9-42	21.4	-3.65
April	9-38	23.7	+21.17

Chases	W-R	Per cent	£1 Level Stake
May	2-16	12.5	-11.13
June	2-6	33.3	+2.75
July	1-3	33.3	+0.50
August	0-2	0.0	-2.00
September	1-3	33.3	+1.33
October	3-26	11.5	-7.50
November	5-37	13.5	-19.79
December	7-29	24.1	+1.83
January	5-24	20.8	-7.49
February	5-24	20.8	-3.38
March	5-29	17.2	-14.29
April	5-33	15.2	-6.75

Totals	W-R	Per cent	£1 Level Stake
May	8-35	22.9	+14.87
June	2-9	22.2	-0.25
July	2-5	40.0	+4.00
August	0-11	0.0	-11.00
September	2-10	20.0	-3.30
October	11-70	15.7	-7.50
November	15-91	16.5	-27.29
December	14-69	20.3	+22.83
January	8-63	12.7	-30.87
February	10-55	18.2	-11.26
March	17-78	21.8	-19.71
April	14-80	17.5	+5.42

DISTANCE

Hurdles	W-R	Per cent	£1 Level Stake
2m-2m3f	31-176	17.6	-37.93
2m4f-2m7f	16-91	17.6	+32.70
3m+	6-36	16.7	+5.75

Chases	W-R	Per cent	£1 Level Stake
2m-2m3f	14-64	21.9	-11.73
2m4f-2m7f	17-84	20.2	-26.05
3m+	10-84	11.9	-28.13

RACE CLASS

	W-R	Per cent	£1 Level Stake
Class 1	3-78	3.8	-61.50
Class 2	15-87	17.2	+2.45
Class 3	39-180	21.7	+1.56
Class 4	35-184	19.0	-5.98
Class 5	5-28	17.9	+1.34
Class 6	6-19	31.6	-1.89

FIRST TIME OUT

	W-R	Per cent	£1 Level Stake
Bumpers	5-25	20.0	-4.88
Hurdles	11-75	14.7	-0.25
Chases	8-47	17.0	-18.50
Totals	24-147	16.3	-23.63

JOCKEYS

	W-R	Per cent	£1 Level Stake
Richard Johnson	59-323	18.3	-39.69
R P Flint	17-48	35.4	+21.83
T J O'Brien	17-122	13.9	-34.76
A P McCoy	3-11	27.3	+0.50
T Molloy	2-8	25.0	+24.00
Darren O'Dwyer	2-31	6.5	-20.00
W T Kennedy	1-1	100.0	+0.83
Timmy Murphy	1-2	50.0	+1.25
Mr G Hawkins	1-2	50.0	+10.00

COURSE RECORD

	Total W-R	Non-Hndcps Hurdles	Non-Hndcps Chases	Hndcps Hurdles	Hndcps Chases	NH Flat	Per cent	£1 Level Stake
Cheltenham	10-59	0-7	1-6	4-24	4-20	1-2	16.9	+13.50
Newbury	9-35	3-8	2-4	2-9	1-11	1-3	25.7	+6.25
Taunton	9-36	2-22	3-5	3-5	0-2	1-2	25.0	-3.05
Chepstow	9-46	1-11	2-7	3-11	2-12	1-5	19.6	+15.42
Nton Abbot	8-24	3-7	0-0	2-9	2-6	1-2	33.3	+12.96
Haydock	7-21	2-4	0-0	4-10	0-6	1-1	33.3	+14.25
Wincanton	7-40	4-12	0-2	3-11	0-12	0-3	17.5	+12.63
Hereford	6-16	1-3	0-2	0-4	3-3	2-4	37.5	+14.27
Exeter	5-35	1-7	4-10	0-10	0-4	0-4	14.3	-20.17
Fontwell	4-11	3-4	0-2	0-2	1-3	0-0	36.4	+2.50
Huntingdon	3-9	1-1	0-2	1-3	1-2	0-1	33.3	+3.23
Perth	3-10	0-4	1-1	0-0	2-5	0-0	30.0	+3.08
Ascot	3-33	0-3	1-3	1-14	1-11	0-2	9.1	-19.42
Kempton	3-38	1-13	1-8	1-6	0-8	0-3	7.9	-26.25
Wetherby	2-6	0-1	1-2	1-1	0-2	0-0	33.3	+3.00
Bangor	2-12	1-2	1-2	0-3	0-4	0-1	16.7	-5.00
Ludlow	2-18	0-4	1-2	0-4	1-7	0-1	11.1	-10.75
Sandown	2-20	1-1	0-2	1-8	0-7	0-2	10.0	-4.00
Lingfield	1-2	0-0	0-0	0-1	1-1	0-0	50.0	+0.88
Leicester	1-4	0-1	1-1	0-0	0-2	0-0	25.0	-2.89
Plumpton	1-4	0-1	0-0	0-2	0-0	1-1	25.0	+2.00
Warwick	1-5	0-2	1-1	0-1	0-1	0-0	20.0	-3.09
Doncaster	1-6	0-3	0-1	0-1	1-1	0-0	16.7	+0.50
Mrket Rsn	1-8	0-0	0-1	0-5	1-2	0-0	12.5	-5.13
Towcester	1-8	1-4	0-3	0-0	0-1	0-0	12.5	-5.25
Uttoxeter	1-11	1-4	0-1	0-1	0-4	0-1	9.1	-8.00
Aintree	1-24	1-8	0-2	0-6	0-6	0-2	4.2	-20.50

ALAN KING

If there is to be a trainer who can, in the foreseeable future, challenge Paul Nicholls' domination of the National Hunt scene, then it is surely Alan King. Last season saw him notch up 136 winners at a strike rate of 17 per cent, and earn almost £1.9 million in prize-money for his owners. That was done against a background of a Cheltenham Festival that was barren until **Oh Crick** saved the day in the very last race of the meeting. A subtle change has taken place at Barbury Castle, with more ex-Irish point-to-pointers and potential chasers then in previous years. The team that Alan has assembled for the new season is a truly impressive one.

Voy Por Ustedes seems to have been around for a long time now, but he's still only an eight-year-old. Having been one of the very best two-milers around, Master Minded's arrival persuaded Alan to send Voy Por Ustedes over a longer trip. From his five starts he won two Grade Ones, the Betfair Chase at Ascot, and the Melling Chase at Aintree. The major disappointments of

▲ **Voy Por Ustedes (centre)**

▲ **Karabak (left)**

the season would have to be that he was beaten in the King George at Kempton and in the Ryanair at Cheltenham, on both occasions being let down by his normally excellent jumping.

'I'm not sure where we'll start him out: the Old Roan is an obvious possibility, but he'd be giving away a lot of weight there. The main target in the first half of the season will again be the King George, and thereafter I would think the same route as last season – Ascot, the Ryanair and Aintree. He was very good at Ascot last season, but in fairness it was probably one of his easier tasks – he won as he should have done. He had a very hard race at Cheltenham and did wonderfully well to finish second after the mistake that he made – I think that probably resulted in him running a few pounds below his best in the Melling Chase. He's had a good break, is back in, and seems to be in very good form – he's been a wonderful flag bearer for the yard.'

Katchit's year as reigning Champion Hurdler didn't go as well as Alan would have liked, but despite not recording a win, he ran well on a number of occasions. In the big one he ran creditably, staying on well up the hill to finish sixth behind Punjabi.

'I think that I made a huge mistake running him in the Elite Hurdle at Wincanton under 11st 10lb. He had a very hard race that day and I'm sure that it took the edge off him. Having said that, he ran well in the Champion, and he'd probably 'gone' for the season when he went to Liverpool. We're going to step him up to two and a half miles from the word go this season, with the view that he might even make up into a World Hurdle horse – I think that as he's got older he's just lost a little bit of his speed. He's had a good, long break this summer and is in fine form.'

As always in jumping yards there are those who are out of action through injury and it was disappointing to hear that we're unlikely to see the extremely promising Triumph Hurdle runner-up, **Walkon**, this season. The good news is that he will be back, but Alan fears that it would be so late in the season before he got him back on the racecourse, that it would be prudent to give the entire campaign a miss.

'**Karabak** has done very well. He was always a bit light last season but he's added a lot of condition over the summer. It'll be a similar route to Katchit, although we'll keep them apart – he'll start at two and a half and hopefully work up to three miles. I'd like to think that he too might become a World Hurdle horse. The trip won't be a problem for him, and he's a horse who ideally needs about six weeks between his races, so we'll work out a suitable campaign.'

Oh Crick was the Festival hero, and he had a cracking season, following up in the valuable Grade Three Red Rum Chase at Aintree. What was so noteworthy, was that those wins came in what was his novice chasing season.

'He's been a remarkable horse! We probably made a mistake in mid-season by trying to stretch him out to two and a half miles, but he clearly wasn't getting it – I think a fast-run two miles suits him down to the ground. I think we'll start him out in the Haldon Gold Cup at Exeter, and the top two-mile handicaps are where he'll be campaigned. He's rated 148, but I hope that we might squeeze a little bit more out of him.'

'**Nenuphar Collonges** was very consistent, and his jumping got better as the season went on. He's Hennessy bound, but I haven't yet decided whether he'll have a 'prep' race before then – he's a horse who does tend to run very well fresh. We established last season that he doesn't stay extreme distances, which was something that surprised me – I don't think he stayed in the Welsh National or, more accurately, he didn't on heavy ground. He's in very good nick at present.'

Tarotino went novice chasing last season, and after missing out on his first three starts, on ground softer than he likes, he notched up a hat trick. He won readily at Doncaster, and then had a battle with Soixante at Kempton before asserting three out. His final run was at Bangor, in what may just have been an average handicap chase, but he simply demolished his rivals, running them into the ground with a superb display of jumping.

'I was thrilled with Tarotino in the spring, and he was hugely impressive at Bangor in the third of his chase wins. He'll be aimed at the Paddy Power and he'll probably go straight there.'

Tarotino was progressing at a rate of knots last season, and he'll be a fascinating contender if he goes to post at Cheltenham. Although he acts on the soft, good ground is ideal, and if he gets his conditions he'll surely be a live contender.

Alan King

Another wonderful season for Alan King, but the bookies have learned their lesson and level-stakes profits are a thing of the past. The one area where this would have showed a profit was the bumper horses, and that's a traditional strength of this team. The stable's strike rate was consistent at 18 per cent, which is a highly creditable figure. This is a yard that is still getting better in terms of both numbers and quality of horses, and what we're seeing is the kind of improvement in the statistics that you get from a trainer who is right at the top of his game. The trend last season was for handicap runners over hurdles and fences to have a much lower strike rate than those in non-handicaps – novices are always worth a second look. This is a proper jumping yard, and the majority of the winners come between October and April (the February blip we've previously commented upon didn't happen). Don't be afraid to follow first-time out runners – indeed, go out of your way to support fancied runners on their seasonal debut. The excellent 'Choc' Thornton is firmly established as stable jockey and therefore likely to record a sizeable loss, and after two seasons of profit, last year Wayne Hutchinson's rides produced a loss. Not many mounts escape those two, although conditional Gerard Tumelty notched up a level-stakes profit for the second year on the trot. As with most yards, any outside bookings of big-name jockeys are worth a second glance – although 'Choc' won't let many get a look in! The record at Leicester and Warwick is outstanding over the years, and Huntingdon, Fontwell and Southwell are also worth a close look nowadays – they were joined last year by Towcester. Local course Newbury's statistics continue to be ones that don't inspire confidence. Behind Paul Nicholls this is the next strongest team in the land and close examination of its runners will pay rewards.

'The plan is to go novice chasing with **Bensalem**. He had a great season, winning his bumper and then three of his four novice hurdles. His one defeat came when he had a great battle with Diamond Harry – they were on opposite sides of the track and my fellow might have benefitted from having another horse to race against. In fact, he might run once over hurdles before going over fences, as he's quite fresh and keen – a hurdle run might just take a little bit of the fizz out of him. The Tote Silver Trophy at Chepstow might be a suitable race.'

Shalone made a big impression in his two races last season, winning a trifle fortuitously at Exeter when The Nightingale fell on the flat after the last, but then winning nicely at Kempton. That was in November, but sadly he wasn't seen out again.

'He's done nothing wrong in his entire career so far – he's only been beaten once and that was by Diamond Harry in a bumper. He got a touch of a 'leg' which wasn't much, but just enough to stop me. He might not be the easiest horse to place, as he's rated 145, but I'm not sure that he has the experience to go chasing – it's an interesting one.'

Chamirey is owned by Sir Robert Ogden, and is a fascinating new addition to Alan's team. Formerly trained in France, he has plenty of experience over both hurdles and fences, but is still a maiden.

'I don't know a huge amount about him, other than that he has some decent form in France. It's early days yet, but we like what we see and he'll go novice chasing. He's a straightforward kind of horse and has a bit of quality about him.'

'**Franchoek** had a difficult year, and I'm afraid we got in a bit of a muddle with him. We didn't really know what his trip was, but I think we established at Cheltenham's April meeting that he doesn't get three miles. The plan

▲ **Medermit**

is to go novice chasing and to drop him back to two and a half, or maybe even two miles. We haven't schooled him yet – I normally like to school them at the back-end of the season, but straight after Cheltenham the ground went like concrete.'

'**Bakbenscher** is another one who will go down the chasing route. He's always been a bit highly strung, but he seems to be much more relaxed this season. I might do the same as with Bensalem and give him a run over hurdles first. He's a decent horse who progressed very well last season, and ran a good race when second in the EBF Novices Final where he was a bit unlucky not to win – he got hampered at a crucial stage. He's another exciting prospect'.

'I think **Lidar's** extremely good. The best ones eat the hill on the Sharpridge gallop from day one, and he just sailed up there from the start. He was very unlucky not to win the Championship Bumper at Aintree where he didn't have much luck in running. Before that he'd won impressively at Doncaster. Everything he's done here has always been of the highest class and he'll go novice hurdling.'

'I'd also mention **Medermit**. He won twice over hurdles before finishing second in the Supreme Novices at the Festival. The plan is to go for the Greatwood Hurdle, and then to go chasing – we hope that he might just make up into an Arkle horse.'

'**Manyriverstocross** has been running well on the Flat – he's rated 98 which makes him a very high-class recruit to the jumping game. **The Betchworth Kid** won his last race off 104, and we don't get too many with that kind of a rating going jumping. When he arrives, he'll be novice hurdling at around two and a half miles.'

Alan King's Barbury Castle stables are stacked full of high-class jumping talent, and it's inconceivable that he'll have anything other than another highly successful season. As I said at the start, it's going to be virtually impossible for anyone to depose Paul Nicholls as Champion Trainer, but Alan's a strong bet to be runner-up, and if he had a great Cheltenham, who knows? ■

Chaser to follow: **Oh Crick**
Hurdler to follow: **Karabak**
Dark Horse: **Chamirey**

ALAN KING

BARBURY CASTLE, WILTS

	No. of Hrs	Races Run	1st	2nd	3rd	Unpl	Per cent	£1 Level Stake
NH Flat	*46*	*89*	*16*	*10*	*12*	*50*	*18.0*	*+1.79*
Hurdles	*130*	*485*	*84*	*78*	*58*	*265*	*17.3*	*-158.41*
Chases	*56*	*206*	*35*	*27*	*30*	*113*	*17.0*	*-62.85*
Totals	**208**	**780**	**135**	**115**	**100**	**428**	**17.3**	**-219.47**
07-08	*181*	*707*	*128*	*110*	*83*	*386*	*18.1*	*+28.55*
06-07	*120*	*409*	*87*	*73*	*50*	*198*	*21.3*	*+41.09*

BY MONTH

NH Flat	W-R	Per cent	£1 Level Stake
May	3-12	25.0	-1.88
June	0-3	0.0	-3.00
July	0-0	0.0	0.00
August	0-4	0.0	-4.00
September	0-0	0.0	0.00
October	0-2	0.0	-2.00
November	4-15	26.7	+14.25
December	4-11	36.4	+5.25
January	1-8	12.5	-2.50
February	1-9	11.1	-7.33
March	2-10	20.0	-3.00
April	1-15	6.7	+6.00

Hurdles	W-R	Per cent	£1 Level Stake
May	3-26	11.5	-17.63
June	2-7	28.6	-3.40
July	2-8	25.0	-1.30
August	4-11	36.4	-0.79
September	2-9	22.2	+1.38
October	10-46	21.7	-17.22
November	15-81	18.5	-34.61
December	10-64	15.6	-8.92
January	9-55	16.4	-0.50
February	12-51	23.5	+16.20
March	9-72	12.5	-51.44
April	6-55	10.9	-40.18

Chases	W-R	Per cent	£1 Level Stake
May	4-12	33.3	-2.51
June	1-5	20.0	-3.50
July	1-3	33.3	-1.43
August	0-2	0.0	-2.00
September	0-1	0.0	-1.00
October	2-16	12.5	+6.00
November	7-44	15.9	-14.29
December	5-32	15.6	-12.02
January	1-17	5.9	-11.50
February	3-25	12.0	-17.84
March	4-24	16.7	-9.42
April	7-25	28.0	+6.66

Totals	W-R	Per cent	£1 Level Stake
May	10-50	20.0	-22.02
June	3-15	20.0	-9.90
July	3-11	27.3	-2.73
August	4-17	23.5	-6.79
September	2-10	20.0	+0.38
October	12-64	18.8	-13.22
November	26-140	18.6	-34.65
December	19-107	17.8	-15.69
January	11-80	13.8	-14.50
February	16-85	18.8	-8.97
March	15-106	14.2	-63.86
April	14-95	14.7	-27.52

DISTANCE

Hurdles	W-R	Per cent	£1 Level Stake
2m-2m3f	53-270	19.6	-60.68
2m4f-2m7f	26-152	17.1	-58.61
3m+	5-63	7.9	-39.13

Chases	W-R	Per cent	£1 Level Stake
2m-2m3f	11-38	28.9	+16.37
2m4f-2m7f	18-89	20.2	-31.89
3m+	6-79	7.6	-47.33

RACE CLASS

	W-R	Per cent	£1 Level Stake
Class 1	11-117	9.4	-46.48
Class 2	7-77	9.1	-46.01
Class 3	35-214	16.4	-69.00
Class 4	63-273	23.1	-55.14
Class 5	15-62	24.2	+19.03
Class 6	4-37	10.8	-21.88

FIRST TIME OUT

	W-R	Per cent	£1 Level Stake
Bumpers	13-46	28.3	+35.13
Hurdles	20-111	18.0	-37.59
Chases	8-51	15.7	-15.08
Totals	41-208	19.7	-17.54

JOCKEYS

	W-R	Per cent	£1 Level Stake
Robert Thornton	92-466	19.7	-129.96
Wayne Hutchinson	19-130	14.6	-57.72
Gerard Tumelty	8-51	15.7	+13.50
Charlie Huxley	7-33	21.2	+8.44
Jack Doyle	4-27	14.8	+3.38
Christian Williams	4-29	13.8	-15.85
J A McCarthy	1-15	6.7	-12.25

COURSE RECORD

	Total W-R	Non-Hndcps Hurdles	Non-Hndcps Chases	Hndcps Hurdles	Hndcps Chases	NH Flat	Per cent	£1 Level Stake
Huntingdon	11-47	7-20	1-6	0-7	0-8	3-6	23.4	-13.75
Doncaster	10-29	5-14	2-3	2-6	0-2	1-4	34.5	+3.45
Fontwell	8-22	3-13	4-4	0-4	1-1	0-0	36.4	-1.55
Cheltenham	7-81	4-26	0-8	1-27	2-17	0-3	8.6	-35.86
Bangor	6-22	2-6	2-2	0-5	1-5	1-4	27.3	-1.97
Mrket Rsn	6-31	5-12	0-5	0-6	1-4	0-4	19.4	-7.16
Aintree	6-34	3-12	2-3	0-7	1-4	0-8	17.6	-12.22
Kempton	6-44	4-14	1-10	1-10	0-7	0-3	13.6	-16.27
Towcester	5-20	3-12	0-0	0-2	0-0	2-6	25.0	+20.40
Southwell	5-22	2-6	1-4	0-6	0-4	2-2	22.7	-7.38
Exeter	5-27	1-12	1-6	1-5	1-3	1-1	18.5	+13.00
Uttoxeter	5-31	1-13	0-1	1-7	1-2	2-8	16.1	-15.63
Ascot	5-32	4-11	1-6	0-8	0-5	0-2	15.6	-4.43
Wincanton	5-40	3-16	0-4	2-9	0-7	0-4	12.5	-14.68
Sandown	4-23	1-7	1-2	0-7	1-4	1-3	17.4	-6.00
Warwick	4-23	1-7	1-6	0-3	0-1	2-6	17.4	+6.00
Ludlow	4-24	3-9	0-3	1-8	0-1	0-3	16.7	-8.95
Chepstow	4-40	3-18	0-2	0-9	1-6	0-5	10.0	-27.00
Folkestone	3-6	1-3	1-1	1-1	0-1	0-0	50.0	+0.23
Plumpton	3-6	2-4	1-2	0-0	0-0	0-0	50.0	+0.10
Leicester	3-10	2-5	0-2	1-3	0-0	0-0	30.0	+0.08
Stratford	3-16	3-5	0-2	0-5	0-4	0-0	18.8	-8.95
Haydock	3-20	1-3	0-2	0-6	2-8	0-1	15.0	-5.00
Taunton	3-26	0-14	1-1	1-6	1-2	0-3	11.5	-11.50
Hereford	3-30	1-14	1-5	0-5	0-1	1-5	10.0	-21.17
Newbury	3-43	3-19	0-3	0-8	0-9	0-4	7.0	-22.50
Lingfield	2-7	2-4	0-0	0-2	0-1	0-0	28.6	-3.47
Nton Abbot	2-10	2-5	0-1	0-1	0-1	0-2	20.0	-4.80
Hexham	1-1	0-0	1-1	0-0	0-0	0-0	100.0	+0.50

FALLON

CHARLIE MANN

Last season saw former jump jockey Charlie Mann record his best ever tally of winners, with 63 notched up at an excellent strike rate of 21 per cent. That percentage was only bettered by Paul Nicholls and Nicky Henderson, so Charlie found himself in exalted company. After a number of seasons in the thirties, that number of winners represented a huge leap forward, but this is a yard that seems to be going places, with another 16 boxes recently opened to cope with an increased number of horses.

The star of the show, inasmuch as he's officially the best horse in the yard, is **Air Force One**, and he ran well last season without winning a race. A Grade One winner at Punchestown two seasons ago, on the form figures he bettered that performance when second to Madison Du Berlais in the Hennessy, carrying 11st 7lb. Air Force One is a German-bred, like a number of Charlie's horses, and he has found them to be a fruitful source of winners for the stables.

'I've got a good contact out there, and we go round the yards, buying privately. I'm out there three or four times a year, and I know the German form pretty well now – I think there tends to be more value there than there is in other countries.'

'We learned a fair bit about Air Force One last year. When he won his four novice chases the previous season he won on very soft ground, and I'd always believed that he handled it well, but then he won on a much quicker surface at Punchestown, and that's somewhat changed my view. Last season he ran two good races, at Ascot in the United House Gold Cup where he was second, and then in the Hennessy. He then picked up an injury when he ran in the King George, and it took him a while to get over that. He's off 158 now so we'll be mixing top handicaps and conditions races – if Denman turned up for the Hennessy that would be an obvious race for him as he'd have a decent weight. He's had quick jobs done on his wind before, but over the summer we had him hobdayed, and that seems to have helped. I'm hopeful that we can get him back on track, and we'll be picking his races carefully – if he was ready in time then the race at Ascot would be a good starting point, as we generally get some good ground at that time of the year.'

Gauvain is another ex-German horse and he ran nine times last season, winning four novice chases, including the Kingmaker at Sandown, and finishing a creditable sixth in the Arkle.

'He's a lazy little so-and-so who doesn't do a lot in his races, but he's a handy horse to have as you can run him ten times a year. In April he broke the track record at Plumpton, and four days later won at Cheltenham. As a result he's on a very high mark – 148 – but despite that, I can see him winning a decent handicap if things go his way. He doesn't do a tap in his races, and his final two wins were with blinkers on, so we'll probably keep them on. He goes on most types of ground, and he's best at a stiff two miles up to around two and a half – we could start him out in the Paddy Power.'

How's Business won three races last season, and ran sixth in the David Nicholson Mares Hurdle at the Festival.

'She's off 145, which must make her one of the highest-rated mares in training. She's enormous and the plan was always to go novice chasing with her, but she's still only five, and the opportunities in mares races are such

▲ **Moon Over Miami**

that it's worth keeping her over hurdles for another season, with the ultimate aim being the Cheltenham race once again. She ran well there last season, but I think that she has improved a fair bit – she stays two and a half miles well, and I think she could get three miles at somewhere like Kempton – there's a valuable mares race there in November.'

Moon Over Miami must have been a disappointment for his trainer last season. The horse clearly has a lot of ability, and won two novice chases the previous season, but in his seven starts he failed to trouble the scorer. After some disappointing runs he then put in a really good effort to be a close second in the Grand Annual at the Cheltenham Festival, but then followed it with a below-par run at Aintree.

'Like Air Force One he was frustrating last season, but he's well capable of winning a decent prize. He's a horse with a lot of talent – when things go right for him he's very good, but when they go wrong he's very bad. Cheltenham seems to suit him as he's a big horse who jumps very well, and he ran a good race at the Festival. He doesn't go right-handed, he wants either a stiff two miles or a bit further on an easy track, and he likes a bit of cut in the ground. He's on 146 right now but I hope he might be dropped a pound as there's a 0-145 handicap at Cheltenham in November.'

'**Shining Gale's** a gorgeous horse. I think he has improved since last season, and with a handicap mark of 143 he could start off in the Paddy Power if the ground was soft enough. Two and a half miles suits him on the soft, but he gets three miles on good ground as he showed when he broke the track record at Warwick, and was then second in an Aintree Grade Two. He lacks a bit of concentration so we put the cheek-pieces on him and they seemed to help – I'm hopeful that he might make up into a Betfair or a King George horse.'

'We were going to go novice chasing with **Wendel**, but we've had a change of heart and will have a go at the Stayers Hurdle route. He's still only five and was a bit weak last year, so we think there's a fair bit of improvement to come from him – currently he's off a

▲ **Shining Gale (right)**

mark of 140. He didn't do a lot wrong last season, winning three of his five starts, and he wants two and a half miles on soft ground to be seen at his best. I might start him off in the three-mile race at Newbury's Hennessy meeting.'

Red Admiral won twice in handicap hurdle company last season, and then in two novice chases over the summer, enabling him to retain his novice status for the whole winter campaign.

'He's been phenomenal! An ex-Godolphin horse who was good enough to win a Listed race at Salisbury, and was rated 94, he simply loves jumping and has won both his starts over fences, absolutely hosing up at Huntingdon in August. There are novice chases at Cheltenham in October over two, and two and a half miles, and I think he's good enough to jump round there. He's rated 139 which I think is crackers for a horse with so little experience, but we'll see how it goes.'

'**Sullumo** got a small hairline fracture at the end of his pelvis, which is why he wasn't out after November, but he's back cantering now. He was unbeaten in his two Flat starts in Germany, and he won two novice hurdles for us the season before last. He would have won his first race last season had it not been for a blunder at the last, and I think he's potentially very good. He looks more of a chaser than a hurdler, and I hope that he could be a SunAlliance Chase type – he's a gorgeous horse.'

'**Viva Colonia** was a useful horse on the Flat in Germany for Mario Hofer. We got him in mid-season, and he probably wasn't properly acclimatised as he came up quite light, but we got one run into him, and he won nicely at Fontwell. However, he has thrived over the summer and is quite forward – he might be all right. He's a novice all season so that gives us plenty of opportunities.'

'**Cast Cada's** a nice horse – a proper chaser. That's the job we bought him for – he's a winning point-to-pointer – and he's out of a mare who was beaten a short head in a four-mile chase at Cheltenham. He won his last two hurdle races, and stays all day. He'll need three miles-plus and is suited by a bit of cut – I'm hoping that he's the type for the National Hunt Chase at the Festival.'

'**Aqualung** will be going chasing – he jumped his hurdles like fences last season. He's had a big wind operation, and has been hobdayed and all sorts of things – short of taking his head off they couldn't have done much more! He needed it done as he won well at Ludlow but then disappointed, and it was all down to his wind. I think he's quite a decent horse and should make a good chaser.'

'**Montgermont** is now with us and he's a big, good-looking horse. He has some decent form a while back, and was favourite for the Hennessy three years ago, but got a 'leg' in that race and had a lot of time off. I remember seeing his first run of last season, at Newbury, where he never jumped a fence but still finished third. We'll see what we can do with him, but we'll need to get his jumping sorted out.'

'We've got some other nice horses in the yard for this season. **Ballinderry Park** will make a decent two-mile chaser – he ran well over hurdles including winning on the heavy at Folkestone. **King Brex** won a novice hurdle last season, but was a bit in and out – he'll be going novice chasing. **Kiribati King** has come from Mick Channon's and won three in a row on the Flat. Finally, we've got a very nice young horse called **Rebel Rebellion** who's worth looking out for in the months ahead.'

Last season saw a major step up for Charlie Mann, and matching last year's tally would be a considerable achievement and consolidate his position in the upper ranks of National Hunt trainers. He starts the season with a strong team, and as long as the horses can keep a clean bill of health, another good tally looks to be on the cards. ■

Chaser to follow: **Air Force One**
Hurdler to follow: **How's Business**
Dark Horse: **Viva Colonia**

Charlie Mann

A new addition to the *Guide to the Jumps* list of trainers on the back of an excellent season which saw the number of winners increase sharply, and the strike rate exceed 20 per cent. The challenge for Charlie now is to consolidate upon these numbers in the coming months. Winners came all through the season, barring a blip in December when the strike rate fell sharply. Whatever the problem was, it was soon fixed because January was business as usual. Noel Fehily rode the vast majority of the winners and achieved an excellent strike rate leading to a sizeable level-stakes profit. It will be interesting to see whether this can be repeated now that the bookies are alert to the threat posed by Charlie's runners. As far as courses go, Ludlow, Uttoxeter, Market Rasen, Southwell, Taunton and Plumpton all had strike rates in excess of one in three. Among the courses which featured less with the yard, Lingfield and Warwick caught the eye. Liverpool, Kempton and Cheltenham had less appealing statistics. This is a stable that knows the time of day with its runners, especially its chasers, where more than four in ten of all favourites won. Equally, no favourites in handicap hurdles went in!

CHARLIE MANN

UPPER LAMBOURN, BERKS

	No. of Hrs	Races Run	1st	2nd	3rd	Unpl	Per cent	£1 Level Stake
NH Flat	*9*	*16*	*1*	*6*	*0*	*8*	*6.3*	*-10.00*
Hurdles	*48*	*164*	*32*	*18*	*26*	*88*	*19.5*	*+21.63*
Chases	*30*	*117*	*29*	*21*	*14*	*53*	*24.8*	*+26.00*
Totals	**68**	**297**	**62**	**45**	**40**	**149**	**20.9**	**+37.63**
07-08	*66*	*227*	*35*	*30*	*22*	*140*	*15.4*	*-48.57*
06-07	*52*	*181*	*33*	*26*	*24*	*98*	*18.2*	*-29.23*

BY MONTH

NH Flat	W-R	Per cent	£1 Level Stake
May	0-1	0.0	-1.00
June	0-0	0.0	0.00
July	0-1	0.0	-1.00
August	0-0	0.0	0.00
September	0-0	0.0	0.00
October	0-1	0.0	-1.00
November	0-2	0.0	-2.00
December	1-4	25.0	+2.00
January	0-1	0.0	-1.00
February	0-3	0.0	-3.00
March	0-2	0.0	-2.00
April	0-1	0.0	-1.00

Hurdles	W-R	Per cent	£1 Level Stake
May	4-20	20.0	-11.42
June	3-9	33.3	-1.15
July	1-5	20.0	+3.00
August	1-3	33.3	+0.75
September	1-7	14.3	+6.00
October	2-13	15.4	+12.50
November	5-22	22.7	+2.25
December	1-16	6.3	-6.00
January	5-17	29.4	+29.50
February	4-17	23.5	-3.13
March	2-18	11.1	-7.00
April	3-17	17.6	-3.68

Chases	W-R	Per cent	£1 Level Stake
May	0-9	0.0	-9.00
June	2-5	40.0	+2.75
July	1-5	20.0	-1.00
August	2-3	66.7	+4.13
September	3-6	50.0	+14.50
October	2-9	22.2	+7.50
November	6-19	31.6	+12.60
December	0-12	0.0	-12.00
January	2-12	16.7	-4.50
February	3-14	21.4	+8.00
March	3-11	27.3	-0.42
April	5-12	41.7	+3.45

Totals	W-R	Per cent	£1 Level Stake
May	4-30	13.3	-21.42
June	5-14	35.7	+1.60
July	2-11	18.2	+1.00
August	3-6	50.0	+4.88
September	4-13	30.8	+20.50
October	4-23	17.4	+19.00
November	11-43	25.6	+12.85
December	2-32	6.3	-16.00
January	7-30	23.3	+24.00
February	7-34	20.6	+1.87
March	5-31	16.1	-9.42
April	8-30	26.7	-1.23

DISTANCE

Hurdles	W-R	Per cent	£1 Level Stake
2m-2m3f	23-100	23.0	+29.94
2m4f-2m7f	7-47	14.9	+3.50
3m+	2-17	11.8	-11.80

Chases	W-R	Per cent	£1 Level Stake
2m-2m3f	11-42	26.2	+12.55
2m4f-2m7f	14-35	40.0	+37.63
3m+	4-40	10.0	-24.17

RACE CLASS

	W-R	Per cent	£1 Level Stake
Class 1	3-30	10.0	-4.50
Class 2	4-35	11.4	-5.75
Class 3	14-74	18.9	+1.13
Class 4	39-135	28.9	+60.01
Class 5	2-17	11.8	-7.25
Class 6	0-6	0.0	-6.00

FIRST TIME OUT

	W-R	Per cent	£1 Level Stake
Bumpers	1-9	11.1	-3.00
Hurdles	6-40	15.0	-9.38
Chases	2-19	10.5	-11.75
Totals	9-68	13.2	-24.13

JOCKEYS

	W-R	Per cent	£1 Level Stake
Noel Fehily	51-212	24.1	+46.39
Paul Moloney	3-14	21.4	+12.50
Kevin Tobin	2-12	16.7	-4.50
Peter Toole	2-14	14.3	-2.00
Mr O Ellwood	1-1	100.0	+6.50
Jason Maguire	1-5	20.0	-2.00
Sam Thomas	1-6	16.7	+11.00
Dave Crosse	1-16	6.3	-13.25

COURSE RECORD

	Total W-R	Non-Hndcps Hurdles	Non-Hndcps Chases	Hndcps Hurdles	Hndcps Chases	NH Flat	Per cent	£1 Level Stake
Ludlow	6-16	2-5	3-3	1-3	0-3	0-2	37.5	+18.00
Uttoxeter	5-13	1-3	0-2	1-4	3-4	0-0	38.5	+10.75
Mrket Rsn	5-14	1-2	1-1	2-4	1-6	0-1	35.7	+16.75
Southwell	5-14	2-6	0-2	1-3	2-3	0-0	35.7	+2.55
Fontwell	5-20	3-7	0-3	0-3	2-6	0-1	25.0	+2.00
Taunton	4-11	1-4	1-3	0-1	2-3	0-0	36.4	+12.00
Huntingdon	4-14	2-5	1-1	0-2	1-3	0-3	28.6	-0.17
Plumpton	3-9	2-5	1-1	0-0	0-2	0-1	33.3	+6.07
Cheltenham	3-23	0-2	2-6	1-7	0-8	0-0	13.0	-2.25
Lingfield	2-4	0-0	1-2	1-2	0-0	0-0	50.0	+2.10
Worcester	2-5	1-1	1-1	0-1	0-2	0-0	40.0	+1.25
Bangor	2-8	0-0	0-2	1-3	1-3	0-0	25.0	+13.50
Exeter	2-9	0-4	0-1	2-3	0-1	0-0	22.2	+16.00
Folkestone	2-10	0-3	0-2	1-2	1-2	0-1	20.0	-2.25
Wincanton	2-11	1-5	0-0	0-5	1-1	0-0	18.2	-3.17
Ascot	2-12	1-3	0-0	0-5	1-4	0-0	16.7	-3.63
Sandown	2-12	0-2	1-4	1-4	0-1	0-1	16.7	+4.50
Warwick	1-3	0-0	1-1	0-1	0-1	0-0	33.3	+0.50
Doncaster	1-6	0-2	0-0	1-1	0-2	0-1	16.7	+6.00
Hereford	1-6	1-2	0-0	0-4	0-0	0-0	16.7	-3.38
Chepstow	1-7	0-2	0-0	0-3	1-1	0-1	14.3	-2.00
Newbury	1-7	0-2	0-0	0-1	0-2	1-2	14.3	-1.00
Kempton	1-14	1-6	0-5	0-1	0-2	0-0	7.1	-7.50

PAUL NICHOLLS

Has there ever been a National Hunt team like the one assembled by Paul Nicholls? In last season's Guide to the Jumps I questioned whether the feats of the previous season could ever be repeated, but we now know that they could, because Paul went and did it! It was another quite remarkable season and it was only the head by which Celestial Halo was beaten in the Champion Hurdle that prevented him making a clean sweep of the four major races at the Cheltenham Festival!

The obvious place to start is with the Gold Cup winner, the wonderful **Kauto Star**, who achieved what no horse had ever done before, by regaining his crown after missing out to Denman the previous season. Prior to Cheltenham he won the JNWine.com Champion Chase in Ireland, but then shocked his army of supporters by unseating his rider in the Betfair Chase at Haydock. It was back to business as usual in the King George where he won for a third time, before putting up an awesome performance in the Gold Cup – on paper his best ever run. There were none of the mistakes that had us holding our breath in the past, and he was simply the epitome of a top-class chaser. Throughout the season Paul was very bullish about Kauto Star and he made the point that the noseband the horse now wears seems to have improved his concentration, and he is firmly of the opinion that 'Kauto' needs time between his races to allow him to produce his absolute best.

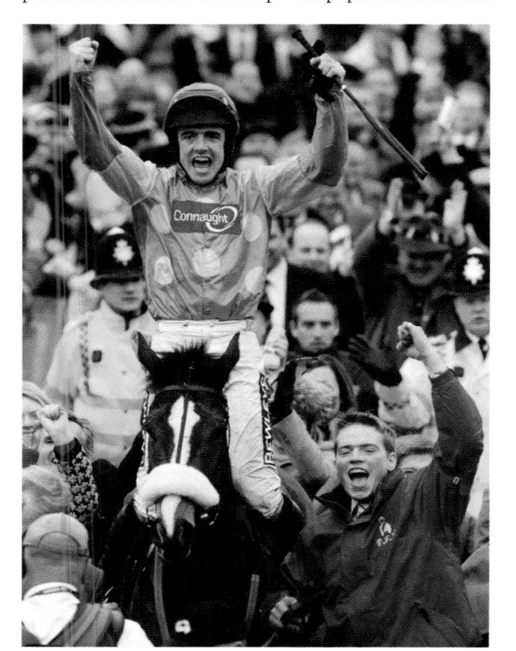

▲ **Kauto Star**

'The plan is one run before the King George, and then straight to the Gold Cup. That first run will be either the JNWine.com again, or the Betfair Chase. He's done half-speed work on the sand on our bottom gallop, and he's just like he was last year, fantastic.'

Denman's troubles last season are well documented, and he wasn't seen out until February as a result of his heart problem and the procedure to fix it. He was beaten by Madison Du Berlais in the Levy Board Chase at Newbury, and then ran tremendously well when second to Kauto Star in the Gold Cup. Madison Du Berlais then achieved the very rare double of beating Denman twice when he capitalised on the Nicholls horse's fall at Liverpool.

▲ **Denman (right, leading)**

'Denman has also done half-speed work and I'm much happier with him than I was at any stage last season – it's early days yet, but he shows all the signs of being back to his best. He'll start out, all being well, in either the Betfair or the Hennessy, depending on whether Kauto Star goes to Ireland – I suspect it will be the Hennessy as Newbury suits him, and Haydock might be on the sharp side. The long-term aim is, of course, to get both Kauto Star and Denman to Cheltenham in March for the Gold Cup, and in the form of their lives.'

With all of the focus on the Gold Cup winners, for many people **Master Minded** slips under their radar, but he is the most remarkable horse. Last season he was four from four, all in Grade Ones. After a workmanlike success in the Tingle Creek, he was devastating in the Victor Chandler, jumping brilliantly and cruising clear from three out, being eased after the last. He next won the Queen Mother Champion Chase, although on the book his performance was some way below what he achieved in the Victor Chandler, and more than a stone below the form of his success at the 2008 Festival. It was Liverpool next and he was given a fright by Big Zeb as he idled in front. Overall it was a flawless season, but the impression was that he had only once been at his imperious best.

'My honest view is that he was a bit over-rated the previous season because of his Champion Chase win, and his current mark is probably more realistic. I'd had a few issues with him and he got a little bit lazy in the spring. This might sound daft, and it's a bit hard to explain, but when they're four, going on five, to me they're like boys going through a growth spurt, and they can go a bit weak on you. After that they strengthen up as they mature, and for me Master Minded is a much more furnished and mature horse than he was at this time last year. He'll head for Cheltenham on the Sunday of the Paddy Power meeting for the Connaught Chase, the new two-mile race sponsored by the company that's our stable sponsor, and then for the Tingle Creek.'

Big Buck's was all the rage for the Hennessy last season, but he unseated his rider at the last when it was still all to play for. Put back over hurdles he showed that he was the best stayer around, with wins in the Unicoin Homes Hurdle on New Year's Day, followed by the Cleeve Hurdle, the World Hurdle and then the Liverpool Hurdle.

'He'll start out in the Long Distance Hurdle at Newbury on Hennessy day, and then the Long Walk at Ascot in December. The ultimate aim is, of course, the World Hurdle once again. I'm sure that we'll go over fences again some day, but while he's at the top of the tree over hurdles there's no need.'

The one who let the side down in the Cheltenham Festival Championship races was **Celestial Halo** – how dare he only finish second in the Champion Hurdle! He started out with second to Binocular in the Boylesports, and then won the Totepool Contenders at Sandown in January. Back at Cheltenham in March – he seems to be well suited by the course – he ran a blinder, being headed by the winner at the last, but refusing to go down without a fight.

'He's a more mature horse this season, which is sure to help him. In addition, he likes Cheltenham and the stiff uphill finish suits his style of running, so we'll stick with hurdles. The plan is a run somewhere before the Boylesports, and then another run before the Champion Hurdle. I think that the two-mile hurdlers is a very tough division, but Celestial Halo doesn't need to find much improvement to be right in there with a chance once again.'

Apart from these stars, there are plenty of others who will more than pay their way. **Big Fella Thanks** will be campaigned with the Grand National in mind, as will new arrival **Tricky Trickster**, while **Dear Villez** could be one for the Welsh equivalent. **Chapoturgeon** is one of the yard's Paddy Power possibles, along with **Kicks For Free** and **Tatenen.**

Twist Magic would be a star in any other yard, but Master Minded overshadows him to some extent at

▲ **Master Minded**

▲ **Big Buck's (leading)**

Manor Farm Stables, and he'll be aimed for the top two-mile chases where his stable mate doesn't run. **The Tother One** is back after injury and this talented horse will head for the Hennessy and is also eligible for Graduation chases. Old favourite **Star De Mohaison** is back, and you get the feeling that Paul feels that there are good races in him if he can be kept sound.

Paul Nicholls is always very strong in the novice chasing department, and this season looks to be no different, with around 50 waiting to take their chances.

'**American Trilogy** may well go over fences this season. The winner of last year's County Hurdle, he'll start out in the Elite Hurdle at Wincanton and we'll see where we go from there. If we decide on the chase route then he'll be an exciting two-mile novice chaser. Like most of mine he was schooled over fences before the summer.'

'**Alfie Sherrin** was two from two last season, winning a bumper and a novice hurdle. Previously he was a point-to-point winner for Richard Barber. We might give him a run over hurdles but he'll be chasing soon, and I think he could be useful.'

'**Beshabar** missed last season but he was useful for Nick Williams a couple of seasons ago, winning a valuable Sandown novices handicap. The plan has always been to go chasing and he's a horse to look out for.'

'**Definity** is an Irish point-to-point winner who joined us last season and won his first two hurdle races, before running well in a much better race at Cheltenham in April. He's from a chasing family and has the scope to do really well over fences.'

'**Forest Pennant** did well two seasons ago, but he ran

just once last season before sustaining an injury. He'll be going chasing and could be one to look out for over a staying trip.'

'**Meanus Dandy** was three from three in point-to-points for Richard Barber last season. He's a sound jumper who stays really well and is suited by soft ground.'

'**Michel Le Bon** was very impressive when he won over three miles at Newbury in March. He's always been a chaser in the making, and has schooled well at home. I hope that he's a horse with a very bright future.'

'**Nictory Vote** is a four-year-old who will be going chasing. He had some decent form over hurdles in France, and won a novice hurdle for us at Taunton in February. The plan was the Fred Winter Hurdle at the Festival, but he picked up an injury. He could be one to follow.'

'**Pride Of Dulcote** looks really exciting. He had a good season over hurdles, winning three races and coming second in the Albert Bartlett at the Festival. He has schooled really well and I'm looking forward to getting him out over fences.'

'**Qozak** won four AQPS bumpers in France before joining us, and then won two novice hurdles for us at Taunton. He's very much a chaser in the making and he could be good over the bigger obstacles.'

'I like **Rivaliste**. He's ex-French, and came to us after winning over hurdles at Compeigne in May. He's had a good break over the summer and will go straight over fences – he's got plenty of scope about him.'

'**Tataniano** won his bumper and then a novice hurdle over two and a half miles. Ruby [Walsh] kept telling me that he'd be better over two miles, and when we dropped him back in trip he bolted up at Cheltenham in April. I'm sure that he will get further, but we'll start him out over fences at two miles. Obviously with a horse like him you hope that he might be good enough for the Arkle.'

'**The Nightingale** is one where whatever he did over hurdles was a bonus, and he did well, winning one at Taunton. I expect him to come into his own over fences.'

The novice hurdle team also looks typically strong, with some fascinating new arrivals among them.

Paul Nicholls

Champion Trainer for the fourth time in a row and the strike rate maintained at over 25 per cent, but a stonking level-stakes loss; do you think the men with deep satchels are running scared? Every statistic is good with this stable but it's still not possible to follow the horses blindly. The fact is that the way you make money out of Paul's runners is to study the form and take note of what he says in the interview in the *Guide to the Jumps*, and in what he says in the *Racing Post* during the year. He's incredibly open about his horses, and you probably don't need to be an expert judge to do well following the stable. Ruby Walsh is the main man among the Ditcheat jockeys, and with Gold Cup-winning Sam Thomas off to pastures new, Christian Williams is back as his number two. Whenever the yard puts an amateur up it's worth taking note. Over the years Wincanton, Fakenham, Folkestone, and Newbury have all been especially good, and last season Worcester and Uttoxeter had strike rates of around 50 per cent. Haydock and Ascot have traditionally been less profitable, and were poor once again last season, but I would't put you off backing a runner there if Paul gives it a good mention and you fancy it. Perhaps the most profitable time to catch many of the chasers is on their seasonal reappearance, where a most impressive strike rate over the years can still usually return a profit. Winners come at all times of the year, and even in the summer when there are far fewer runners, the strike rate holds up. The advice remains the same: if you've got a good reason to fancy a runner from this yard – either on the basis of form or what Paul says – then don't be afraid to back it.

'**Al Amaan** won twice on the Flat in France for John Hammond, and was a staying-on fourth at Kempton on his only start for us. He's had a good summer and will be novice hurdling again.'

'**Benarchat** is a chaser in the making, as so many of mine are, but he will have a season in novice hurdles – he's an excellent jumper.'

'**Bold Addition** ran in a bumper at Liverpool in May, and will now go over hurdles – he has schooled well at home.'

'**Forlovenormoney** is a winning Irish point-to-pointer. He's another chasing type but he jumps well enough to have done well over hurdles for John Hales.'

'**Highest Start** is an exciting ex-French recruit. He won twice on the Flat over there, and was third in a Listed race on his final start. We've given him a break and he should be hurdling before Christmas.'

'**Jump City** also won on the Flat in France and, like Highest Start, was bought at the Saint-Cloud sales by Anthony Bromley. He's a big, strong horse who should make a hurdler, and again will be out around Christmas.'

'**King's Legacy** won his bumper at the second attempt. He's from the family of Hors La Loi III and Cyborgo, and can do well in novice hurdles. He's one I've always liked.'

'**Organisateur** is another who was bought at Saint-Cloud by Anthony Bromley. Trained in France by Carlos Laffon-Parias for whom he won once and was placed several times on the Flat, he has, like Jump City, been gelded and will be out around Christmas time.'

'**Pendower** won his bumper at the first time of asking and will now be going hurdling – he has schooled well and is one to look out for.'

'**Pepe Simo** ran well in two bumpers before winning at Taunton. I like him and he should do well over hurdles.'

'**Quideo De Touzaine** was a backward type who was out the back in his bumper until the penny dropped and he did really well to come through and win – that was a very encouraging run. He'll have learned a lot from that and can win races over a trip – he has schooled well.'

'**Royal Charm** finished second in a decent Sandown novice hurdle on his only start for us. We then put him away to retain his novice status, and that should pay dividends. He's a horse I've always liked.'

'**The Begrudger** is from Denman's family and owned by the same connections. Because of that he'll attract plenty of attention but I think he'll take time and will come into his own over fences.'

'**The Minack** is a winning Irish point-to-pointer and is a half-brother to Definity. He's an exciting horse who will stay well and should do well over hurdles.'

'**Tito Bustillo** won twice in France for Carlos Laffion-Parias. He's an exciting horse who has schooled well over hurdles and should do well this season.'

'Finally, **Valbuena** was very green so did well to win her bumper at Newton Abbot. That will have taught her a lot and she could do well in mares races over hurdles.'

As I said at the start, what a team! They say that success breeds success, and year-on-year Paul's team seems to get stronger. The headlines will all be focused on his Champions, but there are a host of others who are only lesser lights by comparison with the superstars – in other stables they'd be the headliners. It's almost inconceivable that Paul won't be Champion Trainer again and we should just sit back and enjoy watching him campaign his team. ■

Chaser to follow: **Kauto Star**
Hurdler to follow: **Big Buck's**
Dark Horse: **Beshabar**

PAUL NICHOLLS

DITCHEAT, SOMERSET

	No. of Hrs	Races Run	1st	2nd	3rd	Unpl	Per cent	£1 Level Stake
NH Flat	*30*	*46*	*17*	*4*	*4*	*21*	*37.0*	*+14.78*
Hurdles	*105*	*303*	*73*	*60*	*30*	*139*	*24.1*	*-33.48*
Chases	*73*	*264*	*65*	*37*	*26*	*136*	*24.6*	*-50.31*
Totals	**175**	**613**	**155**	**101**	**60**	**296**	**25.3**	**-69.01**
07-08	*174*	*615*	*150*	*97*	*69*	*299*	*24.4*	*-60.12*
06-07	*150*	*537*	*125*	*99*	*67*	*246*	*23.3*	*-117.49*

BY MONTH

NH Flat	W-R	Per cent	£1 Level Stake
May	1-2	50.0	-0.09
June	1-2	50.0	+1.75
July	0-0	0.0	0.00
August	0-0	0.0	0.00
September	0-0	0.0	0.00
October	2-6	33.3	-0.75
November	3-11	27.3	-0.25
December	2-6	33.3	-0.58
January	1-5	20.0	-2.00
February	2-3	66.7	+4.20
March	2-6	33.3	+8.50
April	3-5	60.0	+4.00

Hurdles	W-R	Per cent	£1 Level Stake
May	6-18	33.3	-6.46
June	6-10	60.0	+17.34
July	1-5	20.0	-3.64
August	1-5	20.0	+7.00
September	0-1	0.0	-1.00
October	8-33	24.2	+14.19
November	11-52	21.2	-24.86
December	7-43	16.3	-25.12
January	9-27	33.3	-7.21
February	9-35	25.7	-6.29
March	7-37	18.9	+8.91
April	8-37	21.6	-6.33

Chases	W-R	Per cent	£1 Level Stake
May	6-17	35.3	+4.06
June	2-7	28.6	0.00
July	3-7	42.9	-0.04
August	2-4	50.0	-0.75
September	0-1	0.0	-1.00
October	10-19	52.6	+7.25
November	10-46	21.7	-10.27
December	10-34	29.4	-3.44
January	5-21	23.8	-3.25
February	9-34	26.5	-1.85
March	4-33	12.1	-18.05
April	4-41	9.8	-22.97

Totals	W-R	Per cent	£1 Level Stake
May	13-37	35.1	-2.49
June	9-19	47.4	+19.09
July	4-12	33.3	-3.68
August	3-9	33.3	+6.25
September	0-2	0.0	-2.00
October	20-58	34.5	+20.69
November	24-109	22.0	-35.38
December	19-83	22.9	-29.14
January	15-53	28.3	-12.46
February	20-72	27.8	-3.94
March	13-76	17.1	-0.64
April	15-83	18.1	-25.30

DISTANCE

Hurdles	W-R	Per cent	£1 Level Stake
2m-2m3f	43-156	27.6	-6.56
2m4f-2m7f	18-85	21.2	-3.45
3m+	12-62	19.4	-23.47

Chases	W-R	Per cent	£1 Level Stake
2m-2m3f	30-81	37.0	-1.91
2m4f-2m7f	18-84	21.4	-23.45
3m+	17-99	17.2	-24.95

RACE CLASS

	W-R	Per cent	£1 Level Stake
Class 1	26-180	14.4	-43.25
Class 2	17-104	16.3	-37.12
Class 3	39-128	30.5	+0.28
Class 4	48-143	33.6	-9.79
Class 5	13-35	37.1	+11.61
Class 6	12-23	52.2	+9.26

FIRST TIME OUT

	W-R	Per cent	£1 Level Stake
Bumpers	12-30	40.0	+15.16
Hurdles	27-91	29.7	+7.77
Chases	17-54	31.5	-6.74
Totals	56-175	32.0	+16.19

JOCKEYS

	W-R	Per cent	£1 Level Stake
R Walsh	65-230	28.3	-30.35
Sam Thomas	38-150	25.3	-36.94
Harry Skelton	16-64	25.0	+11.82
Christian Williams	11-50	22.0	-11.38
A P McCoy	8-21	38.1	-1.59
Nick Scholfield	7-38	18.4	+6.71
Timmy Murphy	3-13	23.1	+7.75
Mr O Greenall	2-3	66.7	+0.73
Ian Popham	2-7	28.6	-3.09
Liam Heard	2-16	12.5	-6.67
Daryl Jacob	1-4	25.0	+11.00

COURSE RECORD

	Total W-R	Non-Hndcps Hurdles	Non-Hndcps Chases	Hndcps Hurdles	Hndcps Chases	NH Flat	Per cent	£1 Level Stake
Wincanton	19-46	11-23	1-2	2-8	4-8	1-5	41.3	+25.62
Taunton	15-33	9-17	2-6	1-6	0-0	3-4	45.5	+0.49
Chepstow	14-54	7-23	1-6	0-12	2-5	4-8	25.9	+6.49
Cheltenham	14-85	3-18	6-25	4-16	1-21	0-5	16.5	-10.56
Fontwell	9-25	5-11	2-4	0-2	0-3	2-5	36.0	-2.22
Nton Abbot	9-25	2-4	5-6	2-8	0-6	0-1	36.0	-8.37
Kempton	9-41	2-14	4-12	1-5	1-8	1-2	22.0	-15.55
Worcester	8-17	2-4	0-1	2-6	3-5	1-1	47.1	+14.32
Exeter	8-26	3-10	4-9	0-2	1-4	0-1	30.8	-6.61
Sandown	8-29	1-4	5-12	1-7	0-4	1-2	27.6	-3.55
Aintree	6-48	4-10	2-10	0-6	0-19	0-3	12.5	-31.83
Stratford	5-21	0-6	2-6	1-3	1-5	1-1	23.8	-1.68
Newbury	5-35	2-13	1-4	1-6	1-11	0-1	14.3	-6.10
Uttoxeter	4-7	0-1	2-2	1-1	0-2	1-1	57.1	+5.33
Doncaster	4-15	0-5	2-2	0-1	2-7	0-0	26.7	+0.25
Ascot	4-30	0-8	2-7	0-5	0-7	2-3	13.3	-17.00
Fakenham	2-5	0-1	2-2	0-0	0-2	0-0	40.0	+1.75
Warwick	2-5	1-3	1-2	0-0	0-0	0-0	40.0	-1.07
Bangor	2-6	0-1	1-1	1-2	0-1	0-1	33.3	+7.50
Ludlow	2-6	1-3	0-0	1-1	0-2	0-0	33.3	+1.33
Towcester	1-1	0-0	1-1	0-0	0-0	0-0	100.0	+2.25
Huntingdon	1-3	0-1	1-2	0-0	0-0	0-0	33.3	-1.64
Lingfield	1-4	1-2	0-0	0-0	0-2	0-0	25.0	-2.67
Wetherby	1-4	0-1	0-1	0-1	1-1	0-0	25.0	+4.00
Hereford	1-7	1-2	0-2	0-3	0-0	0-0	14.3	0.00
Haydock	1-16	0-3	0-2	0-5	1-6	0-0	6.3	-10.50

JONJO O'NEILL

Last season was another good one for the Jonjo O'Neill team, with the yard ending up just three short of the century of winners, and more than £1 million earned in prize-money. Jonjo has kept things going over the summer and he heads into the serious part of the season with his team seemingly in good form.

The yard experienced the lowest of low spots last season after the Totesport Bowl at Aintree, when Exotic Dancer suffered a heart attack and died after finishing in second place, and another when Wichita Lineman was killed at Fairyhouse. To lose such stable stalwarts leaves a big gap in Jonjo's team.

Albertas Run finished third behind Madison Du Berlais and his stable-mate in that Aintree event, and that was one of his better performances in an in-and-out season. The high spot was his second place to Kauto Star in the King George, but there were also a few moderate efforts. It isn't unknown for Royal & SunAlliance winners to have a less successful campaign the following year, and

▲ **Albertas Run (left)**

▲ **Don't Push It**

the hope must be that Albertas Run can bounce back this winter.

'He was disappointing, and we'd hoped for better after such a good novice season. However, as you said, it's not that unusual for the Royal & SunAlliance to leave a mark, so we're hopeful he'll do better this time around. He's certainly come back in looking well and in good form. The current plan is the Charlie Hall at Wetherby.'

Can't Buy Time started out in a Southwell novices handicap chase off a mark of 100, and ended his season when he fell in the Grand National, running off 143 – if we'd known then what we know now, he was some good thing at Southwell! After that he followed up at Huntingdon, and made it a hat-trick at Ascot. After a good third in the Tommy Whittle at Haydock, he got back on the winning trail at Sandown in a valuable handicap chase. Favourite for the four-mile handicap chase at the Festival, he ran well until his stamina gave out up the Cheltenham hill. In the National he was behind when he fell on the second circuit.

'He improved a lot last season, but he'll need to improve a lot more this time too, as he's gone up a fair way in the weights. However, he's a good jumper, touch wood, and should make a decent long-distance chaser. He didn't get the four miles at Cheltenham, but Aintree's a very different track and the National a very different race – it certainly won't put me off trying him there again.'

Don't Push It pulled up in the Paddy Power on his seasonal debut, and was then put back over hurdles to help him regain his confidence. He ran some decent races, finishing second at Cheltenham in December and January, before finishing seventh in the Pertemps Final at the Festival. None of that really indicated that he was about to hit peak form, but, put back over fences at Aintree, he romped home in the valuable John Smith's Handicap Chase.

'We've always thought a lot of the horse, and he came back to his old form at the end of last season. He's come back in and is in great shape – I hope that there's a bit more improvement to come from him. Better going left-handed, he's suited by three miles and some cut.'

Isn't That Lucky came good in the second half of the season, winning a Stratford novice chase, and then running a cracker to be second in the Jewson Novices

Handicap Chase at the Festival. He rounded off his season with a confidence-boosting win at Carlisle.

'We had his wind done prior to the Stratford race and it made a big difference to him, and he was also suited by being stepped up in trip. He really enjoyed himself in the Jewson, and galloped all the way up the hill. We might just take him back to Cheltenham for the Paddy Power – I'm very pleased with him at present.'

Sunnyhillboy had a great novice season over hurdles, winning four of his six starts. After winning at Exeter in October, he won a better race at Cheltenham five weeks later, but then surpassed that effort by landing a valuable handicap at Sandown in early December. Off for three months after that, he came back in the County Hurdle where he ran too keenly and weakened quickly, despite being well supported in the market. That may well have been the case as he bolted up at Aintree in a race worth £34,000. Still only six, will he try to progress further over hurdles or be sent chasing?

'I'd say that he'll go novice chasing, but he'll need to be good as there seem to be an awful lot of good hurdlers stepping up this time! We did school him over fences last season, so let's hope he'll be as good over them as he was over hurdles. He's not over-big but he's a nice horse and a decent prospect. Two and a half miles suits him, but I'd say that he has the pace and the class to run over two.'

Supreme Keano won his novice hurdle on his fourth attempt over the smaller obstacles, but was then sent into handicap company on his chasing debut. Ridden with great confidence by Tony McCoy, he won readily. His final run of the season was in a handicap chase at Sandown, where he unseated his rider at the fourth last.

'He's a full brother to Keen Leader who I had a few years ago – hopefully he's a better jumper than him! I see him as a staying horse who'll be suited by soft ground, but he's still inexperienced over fences, so we'll be starting out steadily with him before Christmas, and then we can see where we'll go.'

Synchronised disappointed on his seasonal debut, but after a break of nearly three months came back a different horse. He won two handicap hurdles, before falling at the last in the Pertemps Final at the Cheltenham Festival.'

'Hopefully he's a progressive horse – we like him anyway. The plan is to go chasing with him, and he's suited by three miles and he handles soft ground.'

Saphir Des Bois joined Jonjo's team during the season, having previously won over fences in France – he was also a multiple winner over hurdles there. He won on his debut for his new trainer, jumping well and running his rivals into the ground. On his next start, at Haydock, he blundered at the first and seemed to lose confidence thereafter, but his final start saw him finish second at Cheltenham's April meeting.

'He's a good little horse who jumps well, and is another who could be a Paddy Power type. Suited by two and a half miles, I don't think he quite gets three. We never got to the bottom of why he ran badly at Haydock, but he bounced back well at Cheltenham and I can't see why he wouldn't go on from that.'

'**Fresh Air And Fun** is a grand horse who seems to like the quicker ground. He is a bit of a character but when he's on form he's not too bad – he jumps well. We might just start him back over hurdles to build up his confidence before we go chasing again.'

'**Rate Of Knots** is a mare who likes cut, stays well, and jumps for fun. She won a couple of novice chases very easily, and then ran well on ground that was too quick for her in the Mares Final at Newbury. She'll be running in mares races and we hope that is a decent prospect.'

'**Kia Kaha** is a horse that doesn't stand a lot of racing, and seems to go well fresh. However, he's a fair horse on his day if you can just catch him right.'

Bearing in mind what Jonjo has said, the best time to catch Kia Kaha is when he's fresh, and he seems to be suited by two and a half miles and a bit of cut in the ground.

Forty Five took a couple of races to get the hang of novice hurdling, but once he got his act together he was progressive. He won a handicap hurdle at Ludlow in December off 93, followed up off 100, and then was one of the easiest winners of the season at Fakenham off 107, looking as though there was a fair bit of further improvement in him. However, Jonjo didn't seem to share my enthusiasm for him!

Jonjo O'Neill

I'm sure that somebody knows the time of day with Jonjo's horses, but I very much doubt it's anyone outside of Jackdaws Castle's inner circle! Last season saw the horses running more consistently throughout the year, bar a quiet time in April and May – accordingly, I wouldn't worry over-much about runners who disappointed at Aintree. The problem with the yard is, as always, the lack of pattern: last year the bumper runners were a disaster area, but the handicap hurlders showed a profit – next year, who knows?, Following favourites is one angle, and just as the year before, this was a lucrative seam last season – this confirms my view that someone knows what's going on! The 'Trainers In Form' section in the *Racing Post* can also be your ally here; when the stable is out of form give the yard's runners a sidestep, but when they are hot, watch the market and if they're supported, step in. Runners generally improve for a run so avoiding first-time out runners can help to minimise losses. Having said last year that AP McCoy, who takes most of the rides, produces a stonking level-stakes loss, you guessed it, he produced a profit! We got one thing right in that Noel Fehily's mounts again did OK, but next year, who knows! Exeter and Fontwell have historically been poor, but showed profits last year – aagh again! Three years ago Towcester leapt to prominence, and that was repeated the season before last. The most recent campaign saw a 19 per cent strike rate and another decent profit. That's probably as close as we get to a trend with this stable. Ludlow and Carlisle saw strike rates of over 35 per cent so it's worth keeping a close eye on them. However, the advice as always is to treat each runner from this team on its merits and take note if there's market support.

'I think the handicapper has got him now – he was very well handicapped when he won his three. As a result, I think we'll have to go chasing with him.'

'**Donaldson** is better on good ground, and he's won a couple of novice chases over the summer. He's having a break but will be coming back, and I think there's a decent little race in him if his jumping holds up.'

Among last season's bumper horses, **Aberdale**, **City Theatre** and **Get Me Out Of Here** stood out.

'Aberdale won for us at Uttoxeter and is a potentially pretty good. He'll be hurdling and I hope that he can turn out to be a really nice horse. City Theatre is similar: he's a lovely looking horse who'll be going over hurdles and it will be interesting to see how far he can progress. Get Me Out Of Here goes OK – I like him. He was backward and went weak on us after his win at Uttoxeter, so we couldn't run him again, and he may well run in another bumper before going hurdling.'

Jonjo's horses ran well over the summer, and that surely has to be a sign that things are in good shape for the serious part of the season. It's hard to foresee anything other than a steady stream of winners from his state-of-the-art training base at Jackdaws Castle, and another good season seems assured. ■

Chaser to follow: **Isn't That Lucky**
Hurdler to follow: **Fresh Air And Fun**
Dark Horse: **Aberdale**

JONJO O'NEILL

CHELTENHAM, GLOUCS

	No. of Hrs	Races Run	1st	2nd	3rd	Unpl	Per cent	£1 Level Stake
NH Flat	*31*	*50*	*2*	*2*	*5*	*41*	*4.0*	*-40.50*
Hurdles	*103*	*292*	*42*	*28*	*21*	*201*	*14.4*	*-23.86*
Chases	*87*	*281*	*53*	*33*	*34*	*161*	*18.9*	*+0.29*
Totals	**178**	**623**	**97**	**63**	**60**	**403**	**15.6**	**-64.07**
07-08	*201*	*724*	*107*	*84*	*67*	*465*	*14.8*	*-203.79*
06-07	*193*	*818*	*125*	*112*	*96*	*484*	*15.3*	*-136.66*

BY MONTH

NH Flat	W-R	Per cent	£1 Level Stake
May	0-0	0.0	0.00
June	0-1	0.0	-1.00
July	0-0	0.0	0.00
August	0-1	0.0	-1.00
September	0-3	0.0	-3.00
October	0-6	0.0	-6.00
November	0-10	0.0	-10.00
December	0-7	0.0	-7.00
January	0-3	0.0	-3.00
February	0-5	0.0	-5.00
March	2-4	50.0	+5.50
April	0-10	0.0	-10.00

Hurdles	W-R	Per cent	£1 Level Stake
May	3-27	11.1	-5.00
June	2-3	66.7	+4.50
July	1-15	6.7	-4.00
August	2-18	11.1	-6.17
September	4-23	17.4	+0.50
October	6-41	14.6	+10.25
November	4-39	10.3	-6.25
December	6-33	18.2	+12.50
January	3-19	15.8	-4.50
February	5-19	26.3	+1.33
March	4-32	12.5	-16.27
April	2-23	8.7	-10.75

Chases	W-R	Per cent	£1 Level Stake
May	2-29	6.9	-20.50
June	4-7	57.1	+16.83
July	5-21	23.8	-4.22
August	6-23	26.1	+4.83
September	2-14	14.3	+0.50
October	6-36	16.7	-12.72
November	4-32	12.5	-3.25
December	4-26	15.4	-5.88
January	7-20	35.0	+22.50
February	3-24	12.5	-13.60
March	7-28	25.0	+20.42
April	3-21	14.3	-4.64

Totals	W-R	Per cent	£1 Level Stake
May	5-56	8.9	-25.50
June	6-11	54.5	+20.33
July	6-36	16.7	-8.22
August	8-42	19.0	-2.34
September	6-40	15.0	-2.00
October	12-83	14.5	-8.47
November	8-81	9.9	-19.50
December	10-66	15.2	-0.38
January	10-42	23.8	+15.00
February	8-48	16.7	-17.27
March	13-64	20.3	+9.65
April	5-54	9.3	-25.39

DISTANCE

Hurdles	W-R	Per cent	£1 Level Stake
2m-2m3f	15-143	10.5	-65.52
2m4f-2m7f	19-101	18.8	+34.16
3m+	8-48	16.7	+7.50

Chases	W-R	Per cent	£1 Level Stake
2m-2m3f	9-50	18.0	-0.63
2m4f-2m7f	24-118	20.3	-0.12
3m+	20-113	17.7	+1.04

RACE CLASS

	W-R	Per cent	£1 Level Stake
Class 1	3-43	7.0	-22.50
Class 2	3-46	6.5	-19.00
Class 3	27-154	17.5	+23.82
Class 4	55-271	20.3	+7.35
Class 5	7-80	8.8	-32.25
Class 6	2-29	6.9	-21.50

FIRST TIME OUT

	W-R	Per cent	£1 Level Stake
Bumpers	1-31	3.2	-26.00
Hurdles	7-79	8.9	-20.67
Chases	7-68	10.3	-33.42
Totals	15-178	8.4	-80.09

JOCKEYS

	W-R	Per cent	£1 Level Stake
A P McCoy	63-303	20.8	+25.27
Noel Fehily	11-66	16.7	+15.25
R P McLernon	11-133	8.3	-60.25
Mr A J Berry	5-35	14.3	-10.25
Richard McGrath	4-24	16.7	+4.03
Timmy Murphy	1-3	33.3	-0.13
Miss Jenny Carr	1-3	33.3	+3.00
Dominic Elsworth	1-19	5.3	-4.00

COURSE RECORD

	Total W-R	Non-Hndcps Hurdles	Non-Hndcps Chases	Hndcps Hurdles	Hndcps Chases	NH Flat	Per cent	£1 Level Stake
Bangor	10-40	0-7	3-5	4-14	3-13	0-1	25.0	+7.03
Ludlow	8-22	1-3	1-8	3-4	3-6	0-1	36.4	+36.25
Towcester	7-36	1-9	1-3	3-9	2-12	0-3	19.4	+12.08
Mrket Rsn	7-38	1-10	0-2	2-11	4-13	0-2	18.4	-8.75
Southwell	6-31	0-9	0-1	1-6	5-12	0-3	19.4	-14.44
Hereford	4-20	1-8	0-0	1-4	2-4	0-4	20.0	+0.88
Exeter	4-22	0-6	0-2	3-5	1-7	0-2	18.2	+13.00
Worcester	4-22	0-2	1-3	2-8	1-8	0-1	18.2	+4.50
Chepstow	4-30	0-7	3-3	0-5	1-10	0-5	13.3	-5.13
Stratford	4-33	1-11	1-3	1-7	1-9	0-3	12.1	-14.83
Carlisle	3-8	0-0	3-4	0-0	0-4	0-0	37.5	-0.90
Leicester	3-10	0-2	0-2	0-0	3-6	0-0	30.0	+7.50
Wincanton	3-12	0-2	1-1	2-6	0-2	0-1	25.0	+2.50
Sandown	3-15	0-0	0-1	1-7	2-6	0-1	20.0	-1.00
Nton Abbot	3-20	1-3	0-2	1-8	1-7	0-0	15.0	-1.25
Fontwell	3-21	1-4	0-1	1-5	0-9	1-2	14.3	-10.67
Huntingdon	3-31	1-6	0-2	0-13	2-8	0-2	9.7	-3.80
Uttoxeter	3-42	2-12	0-5	0-9	0-12	1-4	7.1	-27.25
Fakenham	2-8	0-2	1-3	1-2	0-1	0-0	25.0	-4.46
Warwick	2-9	0-2	1-1	1-2	0-2	0-2	22.2	-2.33
Ascot	2-12	0-0	0-1	1-5	1-4	0-2	16.7	+4.50
Aintree	2-13	0-1	0-2	1-3	1-6	0-1	15.4	+6.00
Haydock	2-16	0-2	0-4	1-3	1-7	0-0	12.5	+6.00
Cheltenham	2-40	0-3	0-4	1-15	1-16	0-2	5.0	-19.00
Lingfield	1-2	0-0	0-1	1-1	0-0	0-0	50.0	+0.75
Newbury	1-22	0-7	0-2	0-4	1-5	0-4	4.5	-7.00
Kempton	1-23	0-6	0-3	0-3	1-9	0-2	4.3	-19.25

David Pipe

While last season wasn't vintage for the Pipe team, with the number of winners and the strike rate down, there were plenty of highlights, and there are good grounds for believing that the new season will see things firmly on the up. There were periods when it was clear from the statistics that the horses simply weren't firing, and sadly one of those was during March, when the Festival takes place. As long as the horses retain a clean bill of health – and the signs over the summer are very, very good – I foresee a cracking year for David's team, with prospects further enhanced if **Well Chief** could manage a full campaign.

It's hard to overstate just how good Well Chief is, and how difficult he is to train. Since 2005, he has run just four times, falling in the 2007 Queen Mother Champion Chase when the Form Book suggested that he was the best horse in the race That may have been his best chance of landing the two-mile championship, but he managed a cracking run in last season's equivalent, on his only start of the campaign, finishing

▲ **Well Chief**

▲ **Madison Du Berlais**

second to the outstanding Master Minded. It was with some trepidation that I asked David about Well Chief's health!

'He's back in, and is cantering. It's the same old story which is that we have to take every day as it comes with him. He's now a ten-year-old but he hasn't got many miles on the clock, and isn't showing his age. We got just the one run into him last year, but what a run it was – he ran a blinder and just showed everyone what a great horse he is. I've got my fingers, and everything else, crossed that we get a fuller season with him this time around. With a horse like him the options are strictly limited as to his races, and we'll look at all of the top two-mile chases.'

The stable star last season was undoubtedly **Madison Du Berlais**. After a blank winter, it was hard to predict the dramatic improvement the horse would find last season. After a somewhat lifeless initial run in the United House at Ascot, David put cheek-pieces on Madison Du Berlais and the affect was dramatic. He won the Hennessy in game style, finding plenty under pressure, but even that win didn't prepare us for what came next. His win in the Levy Board Chase at Kempton was another leap up in form, but what made the headlines was that he beat the Gold cup winner Denman, who was, admittedly, below his best after his heart scare. On the basis of that run he was well fancied in the market for the Cheltenham Gold Cup, but he ran well below his best. However, back on a flat track at Aintree, he put up a wonderful performance to win the Totesport Bowl, once again beating Denman. However you interpret the form, Madison Du Berlais is now a very serious chaser.

'For me he was disappointing in the Gold Cup – I'd thought he'd run better than that – but you can't fault the way that he bounced back at Liverpool. He was off the bridle a long way out that day, but he battled up the long straight at Aintree and ran his rivals into the ground. So far he seems to be better on a flatter track, but I'm not yet absolutely convinced that is the case – back in 2006 he was third in the Grand Annual, staying on well at the end of his race. I'm sure that we'll try Cheltenham again at some stage and I wouldn't be afraid to do that. At eight he's young enough to improve again so we're really looking forward to the season ahead.'

Comply Or Die, the 2008 Grand National winner, put up a valiant effort to repeat the feat off a 15lb higher mark, only losing out to the well-handicapped Mon Mome, but winning more than £190,000 in the process! Prior to Liverpool he'd run three times: twice without blinkers when he ran poorly, and then once with the headgear that he would wear in the big race when he showed much better form.

'He put up a great performance in the National, and it was a better performance than when he won. It looked like a repeat of the year before, and jumping the last I thought we'd win again until he came up against a better-handicapped horse. He's ten now, so he isn't getting any younger, but he'll be aimed at long-distance chases, with the National once again his main aim.'

Ashkazar won the Kingwell Hurdle at Wincanton, with the eventual Champion Hurdle winner, Punjabi, 11 lengths away in third place. However, come the big day,

▲ **Comply Or Die**

Ashkazar, in first-time blinkers, ran poorly, finishing tailed-off.

'He disappointed in the Champion, and we decided to call it a day after that – his season hadn't been straightforward. Looking back at the Kingwell, I'm not sure that it was a true result. There was a lot of snow around and Nicky Henderson couldn't get a lot of his horses out, whereas we'd been able to keep going. Having said that, Ashkazar's a smart horse who will, I'm sure, be stepped up in trip at some stage. He's a good jumper, and while plans aren't yet confirmed, he'll probably go novice chasing this season.'

'**Pablo Du Charnil** has a similar profile each season, where he runs well fresh. He was good at Cheltenham in November, and then in his next race at Kempton, but then his form tailed off a bit, until he ran a really good race at Uttoxeter in May. He seemed to get the three miles that day which opens up a few more options for us. I'm sure that he'll be entered at from two to three miles this season, and we'll try to find the right races for him.'

Lough Derg is a stable stalwart and a horse who has a legion of fans. What people admire most in racehorses is first and foremost talent, but after that it's bravery and will to win – Lough Derg has plenty of ability, but he also has more than his fair share of the latter two qualities. Jockey Tom Scudamore loves the horse, saying: 'All he ever wants to do is battle, please you, and give you more'. Last season Lough Derg ran ten times, winning three times over two and a half miles, although he gets three miles well.

'He's another stable star and is wonderfully tough. Last season was as good as any, and arguably his best. Tom gets on with him really well, and knows perfectly the pace that Lough Derg can go – once he's into his rhythm he'll keep going all day. It'll be a similar campaign once again – he loves Ascot so that will be on the agenda, but we may bypass the World Hurdle at the Festival.'

Consigliere won three chases on the bounce for David, before running disappointingly over the National fences in the Topham Trophy. That race was very different from those where he recorded his successes, as, apart from being a step up in class, it was run on faster ground, and there was a field of 29 runners.

'He jumped well that day, and we wouldn't be afraid of

David Pipe

Last season was a tough one for David's team. There were periods when the horses were clearly running well below par – October saw one winner from 56 runners, and December, March and April were well below what we've come to expect from Pond House. This just goes to show that even the best are at the mercy of bugs striking their string. As a result, forming a view on the patterns in David's training methods has to be further delayed. What we do know is that, like his father, he's a trainer of the highest calibre – look at the way that the fragile Well Chief has been handled if you want evidence of that. As a result of whatever malaise was affecting the horses, statistics last winter meant next to nothing, so the best thing to do is to ignore last season and look at previous years. Watch out for a 'hot streak' as, when that happens, the statistics can be simply awesome, and non-handicap chases are a good area on which to focus – I've always done better with the Pipes' chasers than hurdlers in general. Timmy Murphy takes the mounts on David Johnson's horses but last year the strike rate was down and he showed a level-stakes loss. The booking of AP McCoy continues to be significant and he had a 30 per cent strike rate last season. Stable jockey, the excellent Tom Scudamore did well with 43 winners, but as tends to be the case with retained jockeys, he rides a lot that are unfancied as well as those that are. The pattern of doing well with runners travelling to the north didn't pay dividends last season – bar at Sedgefield which was three from seven – but I have a hunch that it will in a more normal year. Ascot and Fontwell have generally been good tracks, and both did OK last season, and will probably do better this time around. Hereford seemed to be joining them as a favourite, but it was zero from 18 last winter so let's put that one on hold!

taking on those fences again. However, I think we'd placed him well to win his first three starts, and he was probably suited by the smaller fields. Having said that, he's still only six and is open to further improvement – he's a lovely young horse.'

'**Mr Thriller** won his first two starts for us, and he had some really good form in France where he had been second to Long Run, who's very good. He loves soft ground, which makes his fourth place in the Imperial Cup read even better, as the ground was pretty quick that day. He then was sixth in the Fred Winter just four days later, which was another good effort. He has summered well and he's one we're really looking forward to running again – it hasn't yet been decided whether he sticks to hurdles or goes over fences.'

'**Mr Bennett** had a slight injury after his run at Chepstow, so wasn't out again. However, he's back in now and is looking really well. The form of that race has worked out, which is encouraging. He'll be a three-mile chaser, but we'll probably start him out over hurdles.'

'**Great Endeavour** won three races for us and, like Mr Bennett, looks to have grown and filled out his frame over the summer. He jumps his hurdles really well, and is an Irish point-to-point winner, so I would imagine he'll go chasing – fences won't be a problem for him. Two and a half to three miles will be his trip.'

American Art is a fascinating new arrival at Pond House. Rated 88 on the Flat for Barry Hills, he had one run over hurdles for Venetia Williams, winning nicely at Cartmel in May.

'We bought him at the sales and we're hoping that he can progress from that decent win in a small race – he's a likeable sort.'

Dan Breen won a couple of bumpers over the summer, both at Newton Abbot.

'That probably wasn't a bad run when he won carrying his penalty – the Irish horse that was second was very well fancied, and we beat him giving him 7lb. He'll almost certainly be hurdling and is promising.'

'**Over The Creek** is back although you probably won't see him until later in the year. Long-distance chases are his game.'

Finally, I had to ask David about **The Package**, as in last year's Guide the the Jumps it was clear that he held him in some regard. Last season he ran seven times, four over fences before being switched back to hurdles and, although he didn't win, he showed a fair amount of ability – his second to New Little Bric in a valuable Newbury event makes him one of the higher-rated novice chasers.

'That run was at the end of February and we thought we might as well keep him a novice over fences, so we put him back over hurdles. We thought he had a great chance at Newbury but he came up against a rejuvenated New Little Bric, who was well in on his old form. However The Package ran well that day, and he's a horse who shows a lot of potential even though he hasn't quite fulfilled it yet – mind you, he's still only six.'

I reckon The Package is headed for a good season and he will be right up there on my list of horses to follow.

As I said in the introduction, as long as the Pipe horses stay healthy this season, I expect David to better comfortably last season's score, and to land some big prizes. The one caveat is that a number of the stable's stalwarts aren't getting any younger, and David needs some of the promising younger horses to step up and make a name for themselves, but it would be a brave man who bet against that happening. ■

Chaser to follow: **Madison Du Berlais**
Hurdler to follow: **Mr Bennett**
Dark Horse: **The Package**

DAVID PIPE

NICHOLASHAYNE, DEVON

	No. of Hrs	Races Run	1st	2nd	3rd	Unpl	Per cent	£1 Level Stake
NH Flat	*16*	*20*	*3*	*0*	*2*	*15*	*15.0*	*-2.33*
Hurdles	*140*	*455*	*51*	*42*	*40*	*322*	*11.2*	*-170.09*
Chases	*69*	*187*	*22*	*16*	*24*	*125*	*11.8*	*-33.17*
Totals	**181**	**662**	**76**	**58**	**66**	**462**	**11.5**	**-205.59**
07-08	*178*	*698*	*99*	*76*	*80*	*443*	*14.2*	*-95.50*
06-07	*178*	*757*	*133*	*89*	*76*	*459*	*17.6*	*-233.26*

BY MONTH

NH Flat	W-R	Per cent	£1 Level Stake
May	2-7	28.6	+1.67
June	0-0	0.0	0.00
July	0-1	0.0	-1.00
August	0-1	0.0	-1.00
September	0-0	0.0	0.00
October	0-1	0.0	-1.00
November	0-0	0.0	0.00
December	0-1	0.0	-1.00
January	0-4	0.0	-4.00
February	1-3	33.3	+6.00
March	0-1	0.0	-1.00
April	0-1	0.0	-1.00

Hurdles	W-R	Per cent	£1 Level Stake
May	4-47	8.5	-17.76
June	6-32	18.8	-4.50
July	4-20	20.0	-7.63
August	4-21	19.0	+5.00
September	7-19	36.8	+8.38
October	1-45	2.2	-36.50
November	4-38	10.5	-22.59
December	0-28	0.0	-28.00
January	5-33	15.2	-1.00
February	7-46	15.2	-19.50
March	5-72	6.9	-26.00
April	4-54	7.4	-20.00

Chases	W-R	Per cent	£1 Level Stake
May	2-14	14.3	-7.90
June	5-16	31.3	-5.60
July	0-10	0.0	-10.00
August	1-11	9.1	-6.00
September	0-4	0.0	-4.00
October	0-10	0.0	-10.00
November	4-25	16.0	+40.50
December	2-20	10.0	-9.00
January	2-15	13.3	-3.00
February	3-15	20.0	+8.75
March	2-21	9.5	-13.92
April	1-26	3.8	-13.00

Totals	W-R	Per cent	£1 Level Stake
May	8-68	11.8	-23.99
June	11-48	22.9	-10.10
July	4-31	12.9	-18.63
August	5-33	15.2	-2.00
September	7-23	30.4	+4.38
October	1-56	1.8	-47.50
November	8-63	12.7	+17.91
December	2-49	4.1	-38.00
January	7-52	13.5	-8.00
February	11-64	17.2	-4.75
March	7-94	7.4	-40.92
April	5-81	6.2	-34.00

DISTANCE

Hurdles	W-R	Per cent	£1 Level Stake
2m-2m3f	25-256	9.8	-136.01
2m4f-2m7f	17-130	13.1	-13.25
3m+	9-69	13.0	-20.83

Chases	W-R	Per cent	£1 Level Stake
2m-2m3f	11-44	25.0	+15.35
2m4f-2m7f	3-57	5.3	-49.60
3m+	8-86	9.3	+1.08

RACE CLASS

	W-R	Per cent	£1 Level Stake
Class 1	7-83	8.4	-5.67
Class 2	3-58	5.2	-34.00
Class 3	13-115	11.3	-44.92
Class 4	39-302	12.9	-87.91
Class 5	13-96	13.5	-29.42
Class 6	1-8	12.5	-3.67

FIRST TIME OUT

	W-R	Per cent	£1 Level Stake
Bumpers	3-16	18.8	+1.67
Hurdles	11-114	9.6	-43.00
Chases	3-51	5.9	-35.25
Totals	17-181	9.4	-76.58

JOCKEYS

	W-R	Per cent	£1 Level Stake
Tom Scudamore	43-348	12.4	-107.82
J W Farrelly	11-102	10.8	-12.65
Timmy Murphy	9-68	13.2	-26.83
Danny Cook	7-47	14.9	+6.83
A P McCoy	3-10	30.0	-4.62
O Dayman	1-1	100.0	+9.00
Andrew J McNamara	1-4	25.0	+3.50
Hadden Frost	1-30	3.3	-21.00

COURSE RECORD

	Total W-R	Non-Hndcps Hurdles	Non-Hndcps Chases	Hndcps Hurdles	Hndcps Chases	NH Flat	Per cent	£1 Level Stake
Nton Abbot	11-63	4-26	1-2	3-22	3-10	0-3	17.5	+0.25
Uttoxeter	6-36	4-16	0-4	1-8	1-6	0-2	16.7	-4.66
Fontwell	5-24	2-8	0-2	0-7	2-6	1-1	20.8	-6.17
Towcester	5-25	2-7	1-2	1-8	0-6	1-2	20.0	+10.71
Worcester	5-26	4-10	1-3	0-9	0-3	0-1	19.2	-14.23
Taunton	4-50	1-27	0-1	2-15	1-7	0-0	8.0	-19.00
Sedgefield	3-7	2-2	0-2	1-3	0-0	0-0	42.9	+7.58
Sandown	3-13	2-3	0-0	1-9	0-1	0-0	23.1	+0.17
Ascot	3-18	1-4	0-2	1-7	1-5	0-0	16.7	+0.91
Stratford	3-20	0-6	1-2	2-8	0-3	0-1	15.0	-6.25
Wincanton	3-43	1-15	0-0	2-16	0-11	0-1	7.0	-24.67
Folkestone	2-6	1-3	0-0	0-2	1-1	0-0	33.3	+4.50
Warwick	2-7	0-4	0-0	1-2	1-1	0-0	28.6	+21.00
Plumpton	2-13	1-7	0-1	0-3	1-2	0-0	15.4	-6.17
Bangor	2-15	1-4	0-1	0-4	0-3	1-3	13.3	-1.50
Kempton	2-15	0-4	1-5	0-3	1-3	0-0	13.3	+0.75
Newbury	2-16	0-3	0-1	0-3	2-9	0-0	12.5	+13.75
Aintree	2-26	1-2	1-2	0-12	0-8	0-2	7.7	-10.38
Cheltenham	2-70	1-14	0-5	0-33	1-18	0-0	2.9	-52.50
Wetherby	1-5	1-2	0-0	0-2	0-1	0-0	20.0	-3.20
Doncaster	1-7	1-1	0-0	0-3	0-2	0-1	14.3	-0.50
Perth	1-7	1-2	0-0	0-4	0-1	0-0	14.3	-3.50
Huntingdon	1-10	0-1	0-1	0-6	1-2	0-0	10.0	-3.50
Southwell	1-11	1-4	0-2	0-2	0-3	0-0	9.1	-8.00
Mrket Rsn	1-12	0-2	0-0	1-6	0-4	0-0	8.3	-7.50
Ludlow	1-14	1-7	0-1	0-3	0-2	0-1	7.1	-9.50
Chepstow	1-21	0-9	0-0	1-6	0-6	0-0	4.8	-6.00
Exeter	1-35	0-11	0-0	1-16	0-7	0-1	2.9	-31.00

NICKY RICHARDS

Last season wasn't a vintage one for Nicky Richards' Greystoke team, with winners down to 38, and the strike rate also down a fraction at 14 per cent. This is a period of rebuilding with owner Duncan Davidson's horses now being trained by his daughter, Rose Dobbin. But Nicky starts the year with a team of around 65 horses, made up of solid, experienced types and promising youngsters.

Money Trix has always been held in the highest regard by Nicky, but injuries have restricted the nine-year-old to just nine starts in four seasons. Last term he ran three times, falling in a Newbury Graduation chase when still bang in contention, then finishing second at Ayr, before winning readily at Kelso.

'We didn't run him again after that Kelso win, but it was just because the ground went against him. He's back and in full training – I'm looking forward to a good year with him, hopefully. It was a crying shame that he tipped up at Newbury as that just shook his confidence a bit – his other two runs were about rebuilding that. Three miles is his trip, and it can't be soft enough for him, which is one reason why we might just campaign him in Ireland from time to time – I hope we're not flying too high in thinking about a race like the Lexus Chase, which is run at Leopardstown just after Christmas. He'll need a run before that, but I haven't yet got anything specific in mind.'

Monet's Garden started out with a respectable effort in the Old Roan Chase at Liverpool in October, before going on to win the Peterborough Chase at Huntingdon in game style. His third and final run of the season was after a three-month break when finishing sixth in the Ryanair Chase.

'I wasn't able to run him again after Cheltenham as he just tweaked a tendon, but he seems to be fine now, and is back in nice work. It'll be a similar programme I suppose, although he may go for the Charlie Hall rather than the Old Roan, but it's ground dependent, as it was far too soft for him at Liverpool last year. After that the Peterborough is the obvious next step. I got him in a bit earlier this year, as he seems to take a bit more getting fit as he gets older – despite being 11 now he seems to be in great shape at present.'

Noble Alan was second at Cheltenham in October in the Jewson Final, and then ran poorly at Ascot in the Ladbroke Hurdle. He was off for four months after that but bounced back with a vengeance when he won the Scottish Champion Hurdle in impressive style, coming to hit the front at the final hurdle and then quickening away.

'He's a horse we've always liked and it was smashing to round the year off by winning such a nice prize. He's ready to run and he'll be starting out on the novice chase route, and I see two miles being his trip – he has a lot of speed – and to get the best out of him he needs good ground. We've been looking forward to putting him over fences for a while now, and he's an exciting prospect. As I do with all of mine I'll start him out small in the north, and hope that he proves good enough to go south one day.'

Palomar was another to manage just three runs: wins at Kelso and Catterick, and then a fall when stepped up to two and a half miles at Musselburgh.

'He sprained his hock when he fell, but he's back in work now and is fine. After his fall he went back to Sir

▲ **Monet's Garden**

Robert Ogden's Sickling Hall Stud where they gave him plenty of time and brought him back very steadily – I've got him in full training now. Like Noble Alan, two miles is probably his best trip, although he may get two and a half. He was going the right way on his first two starts so I hope he can continue to progress – I've run him three times at Musselburgh now, and they were his three worst performances, so I'll think twice before sending him back there.'

Merrydown ran six times in his novice hurdling season, winning at Kelso and at Newcastle – the form of both races has worked out remarkably well – and then running with credit in an Aintree Grade One, and a valuable event at the Punchestown Festival.

'He's a nice horse who had a good season, and his owner let me bring him along steadily. We've always seen him as a potential steeplechaser and hopefully this season will be the start of things for him. He's a horse with a fair measure of ability, and it's going to be very interesting to see how far up the ladder he can climb. Two and a half to three miles will be his trip.'

Grand Theatre was novice hurdling last season, and won three of his five starts, looking like a progressive sort.

'A nice horse: another one that, like Merrydown, his owner let me bring along steadily. He rounded off his season with a good win up at Ayr, and we've started to school him over fences – it's gone well so far. He'll be a three-mile chaser, and like Merrydown will probably want decent ground – neither of them would want extremes.'

According To John is a very talented horse, but one that has been plagued by problems in recent seasons. If you go back, he won his first six races for Nicky, four over hurdles and then two novice chases, and in 2007 was third behind Denman in the Royal & SunAlliance Chase. He ran just once the following season, but came back at the end of January and ran three times between then and May. He started out in a Sandown handicap chase where he ran with great promise, and he then disappointed at Aintree. His final run was at Punchestown, but he got no further than the first fence, where he unseated his rider.

'He ran a nice race at Sandown and the plan was to go to Cheltenham, but he didn't get into the handicap. The track just didn't seem to suit him at Aintree, as they were just going a little bit too sharp for him, but he stayed on and finished fourth. I then took him over to Ireland, and we thought we'd never had him better, but he unfortunately unshipped his jockey early on, so it was a bit of a wasted journey. However, he had showed us that he retains the ability to be able to win a nice race, so hopefully he'll manage to do that this season.'

Sadly, the excellent Len Lungo announced in June that he'd decided to hand in his training licence, citing the economic downturn as the reason. One of my favourite horses, **Skippers Brig**, has moved a few miles south to join Nicky's team. Last season he ran four times, winning on his chasing debut at Carlisle, and then following up there six weeks later – both of those runs being on heavy ground. Stepped up in trip and class, he then seemed to be found out at Wetherby – it might have been that he didn't get three miles, or that he simply wasn't up to the task, but for me it's more likely that the officially soft conditions just weren't testing enough for him, as all of his six career wins have been on heavy ground. Back on his favoured surface at Newcastle in February, he ground out a win in a moderately run three-mile event, appearing to stay the distance.

'He's a big, beautiful, proper old-fashioned type of horse. I don't know how well handicapped he is, but we'll find that out as we go along. His season will probably revolve around December, January and February when we will hopefully get his ground – he may be one that doesn't get a lot of racing, but when he does run it will be in decent races.'

'**Double Default** is back after injury. It's a shame, as he was a nice novice hurdler and we thought he'd make a good novice chaser, but he has just been plagued with injuries. Anyway, Sir Robert Ogden gave him plenty of time, as he always does, and we're hopefully on the way back. Three-mile novice chases on soft ground will be the plan, and with luck he'll still prove himself a good horse.'

'**Harmony Brig** has been a good old campaigner, and we'll probably mix hurdles and chases with him, just as we did last season. He won a nice hurdle race up at Ayr, and he ran well over fences on a couple of occasions. We'll work away with him, but we might try him again over extreme distances – I ran him in the Eider Chase

Nicky Richards

It was a tough season for Nicky Richards' team, with the number of winners and the strike rate both down. In addition, the loss of the Duncan Davidson horses as daughter Rose, now married to Nicky's former jockey, Tony Dobbin, starts her training career, is another hurdle to overcome. However, Nicky rebuilt things after he took over from his late father, and he's sure to do so once again. Things weren't right with the horses for some periods of the season: October, December and January showed disappointing strike rates. So, as is the case with stables that strike such problems, the advice is to revert to type. This is one of those yards that is made up of chasers, and potential chasers. That's not to say that there isn't hurdle race success, but you always feel that hurdles are a means to an end and the strike rate reflects that. The chasers have a great strike rate, and even in a poor year, those competing outside of handicap company recorded a 29 per cent strike rate. Watch out for the novices and don't be put off backing them first-time out. With stable jockey Davy Condon having headed back to Ireland, Brian Harding and Fearghal Davis seem likely to share the majority of the rides. Look out for Nicky's pattern of placing his good horses to win a sequence of races in the north before he takes them south – prices may be modest but a winner is a winner! Wherever Nicky sends his horses they are worthy of support, and he never sends them south just for the fun of it – Ayr, Carlisle, Hexham, Kelso, Newcastle and Perth are generally lucrative tracks for the yard, and probably will be again. This is an important season for Nicky Richards and, as is clear in the interview, he has some good young horses coming through – I'm sure that it will be a gradual restoring of fortunes but I expect it to start this season.

over four miles, but he was just a bit too keen to be able to stay.'

'**Native Coral** is a grand old horse who has had the odd leg problem, but in the main he's very consistent, and he's a nice horse to have. He's another who'll have a similar campaign to last season – handicap chases at around two and a half to three miles.'

'**Houston Dynimo** is a nice, consistent little horse who finished second three times last season. When he came to me he'd had a long, hard Flat season in Ireland, but he's now had a nice holiday, and that will hopefully pay dividends.'

'**Steady Tiger's** not a bad sort of a horse. He ran some decent races over hurdles, but he'll be going novice chasing and I hope that he can make up into a decent staying chaser.'

'**The Whisperer** only ran twice last season, but he finished off with a good effort at Carlisle under a big weight. I think he'll go on from that, and more than pay his way this season.'

'I've got a nice bunch of young horses this season, and **Premier Sagas** is very exciting. He won a bumper at Kelso, and I think that he can prove himself to be well above average.'

It's clear from last season's statistics that there were periods last season – October, December and January – when Nicky's horses were somewhat out of form. Given a clear run, I would confidently expect last year's number of winners to be comfortably eclipsed. ■

Chaser to follow: **Noble Alan**
Hurdler to follow: **Harmony Brig**
Dark Horse: **Premier Sagas**

NICKY RICHARDS

GREYSTOKE, CUMBRIA

	No. of Hrs	Races Run	1st	2nd	3rd	Unpl	Per cent	£1 Level Stake
NH Flat	*7*	*11*	*1*	*2*	*2*	*6*	*9.1*	*-8.75*
Hurdles	*57*	*160*	*20*	*17*	*9*	*114*	*12.5*	*-1.79*
Chases	*36*	*99*	*17*	*11*	*8*	*63*	*17.2*	*-10.97*
Totals	**78**	**270**	**38**	**30**	**19**	**183**	**14.1**	**-21.51**
07-08	*98*	*308*	*48*	*44*	*28*	*188*	*15.6*	*-70.95*
06-07	*96*	*318*	*63*	*61*	*41*	*153*	*19.8*	*-96.85*

BY MONTH

NH Flat	W-R	Per cent	£1 Level Stake	Hurdles	W-R	Per cent	£1 Level Stake
May	0-2	0.0	-2.00	May	2-16	12.5	-8.63
June	0-2	0.0	-2.00	June	0-6	0.0	-6.00
July	0-0	0.0	0.00	July	2-9	22.2	+2.33
August	0-0	0.0	0.00	August	0-3	0.0	-3.00
September	0-0	0.0	0.00	September	1-3	33.3	+4.00
October	0-0	0.0	0.00	October	1-20	5.0	-13.50
November	0-3	0.0	-3.00	November	3-23	13.0	-9.75
December	0-1	0.0	-1.00	December	0-12	0.0	-12.00
January	0-0	0.0	0.00	January	2-14	14.3	+12.75
February	0-0	0.0	0.00	February	2-16	12.5	-7.75
March	1-2	50.0	+0.25	March	3-23	13.0	+7.25
April	0-1	0.0	-1.00	April	4-15	26.7	+32.50

Chases	W-R	Per cent	£1 Level Stake	Totals	W-R	Per cent	£1 Level Stake
May	1-5	20.0	+0.50	May	3-23	13.0	-10.13
June	0-2	0.0	-2.00	June	0-10	0.0	-10.00
July	2-5	40.0	-0.09	July	4-14	28.6	+2.24
August	0-0	0.0	0.00	August	0-3	0.0	-3.00
September	0-1	0.0	-1.00	September	1-4	25.0	+3.00
October	1-11	9.1	-5.50	October	2-31	6.5	-19.00
November	4-16	25.0	+7.25	November	7-42	16.7	-5.50
December	2-17	11.8	-7.75	December	2-30	6.7	-20.75
January	0-7	0.0	-7.00	January	2-21	9.5	+5.75
February	2-10	20.0	+4.00	February	4-26	15.4	-3.75
March	2-10	20.0	+5.00	March	6-35	17.1	+12.50
April	3-15	20.0	-4.38	April	7-31	22.6	+27.12

DISTANCE

Hurdles	W-R	Per cent	£1 Level Stake	Chases	W-R	Per cent	£1 Level Stake
2m-2m3f	5-50	10.0	-21.00	2m-2m3f	7-17	41.2	+16.41
2m4f-2m7f	10-69	14.5	+21.58	2m4f-2m7f	8-43	18.6	-0.13
3m+	5-41	12.2	-2.38	3m+	2-39	5.1	-27.25

RACE CLASS

	W-R	Per cent	£1 Level Stake
Class 1	2-22	9.1	-6.50
Class 2	4-30	13.3	+9.50
Class 3	7-56	12.5	-2.25
Class 4	19-122	15.6	-29.09
Class 5	3-29	10.3	+7.33
Class 6	3-11	27.3	-0.50

FIRST TIME OUT

	W-R	Per cent	£1 Level Stake
Bumpers	0-7	0.0	-7.00
Hurdles	8-47	17.0	-7.29
Chases	5-24	20.8	+6.75
Totals	13-78	16.7	-7.54

JOCKEYS

	W-R	Per cent	£1 Level Stake
D J Condon	21-126	16.7	+3.75
Brian Harding	5-45	11.1	-3.72
Mrs R Dobbin	4-31	12.9	-6.63
Fearghal Davis	3-40	7.5	-10.67
Miss J R Richards	2-10	20.0	-1.75
Noel Fehily	1-1	100.0	+2.00
B J Geraghty	1-1	100.0	+5.00
Harry Haynes	1-10	10.0	-3.50

COURSE RECORD

	Total W-R	Non-Hndcps Hurdles	Non-Hndcps Chases	Hndcps Hurdles	Hndcps Chases	NH Flat	Per cent	£1 Level Stake
Kelso	8-26	2-8	2-3	1-6	2-7	1-2	30.8	+15.50
Perth	6-31	1-6	2-4	2-11	1-8	0-2	19.4	-2.76
Newcastle	4-23	2-7	0-0	1-12	1-3	0-1	17.4	+10.00
Ayr	4-32	1-10	0-3	3-14	0-4	0-1	12.5	+19.75
Carlisle	3-16	0-0	2-7	0-0	1-9	0-0	18.8	-1.50
Bangor	2-11	1-5	0-0	1-4	0-2	0-0	18.2	+2.75
Mrket Rsn	2-13	0-1	2-4	0-6	0-2	0-0	15.4	-4.75
Musselbgh	2-20	1-6	1-3	0-4	0-6	0-1	10.0	-3.00
Huntingdon	1-3	0-0	1-2	0-1	0-0	0-0	33.3	+3.00
Cartmel	1-4	1-2	0-0	0-2	0-0	0-0	25.0	+1.00
Catterick	1-6	0-2	1-2	0-2	0-0	0-0	16.7	-2.75
Southwell	1-6	0-1	0-1	1-4	0-0	0-0	16.7	+9.00
Haydock	1-7	0-1	0-0	1-4	0-2	0-0	14.3	-1.00
Sedgefield	1-12	0-6	1-3	0-1	0-0	0-2	8.3	-9.13
Hexham	1-13	1-6	0-2	0-4	0-1	0-0	7.7	-10.63

Trainers' Tips

A trio to follow from each trainer interviewed

Nicky Henderson

Chaser: **Dave's Dream**
Hurdler: **Binocular**
Dark Horse: **Oscar Whisky**

Paul Nicholls

Chaser: **Kauto Star**
Hurdler: **Big Buck's**
Dark Horse: **Beshabar**

Philip Hobbs

Chaser: **Snap Tie**
Hurdler: **Son Histoire**
Dark Horse: **Zakatal**

Jonjo O'Neill

Chaser: **Isn't That Lucky**
Hurdler: **Fresh Air And Fun**
Dark Horse: **Aberdale**

Alan King

Chaser: **Oh Crick**
Hurdler: **Karabak**
Dark Horse: **Chamirey**

David Pipe

Chaser: **Madison Du Berlais**
Hurdler: **Mr Bennett**
Dark Horse: **The Package**

Charlie Mann

Chaser: **Air Force One**
Hurdler: **How's Business**
Dark Horse: **Viva Colonia**

Nicky Richards

Chaser: **Noble Alan**
Hurdler: **Harmony Brig**
Dark Horse: **Premier Sagas**

IRISH SCENE Alan Sweetman

At the end of the 2008-09 Irish jumps-season there was no dispute about the identity of its dominant figures. At the Punchestown Festival Willie Mullins and Ruby Walsh set the seal on a terrific campaign, sharing in a series of performances that opens up an attractive vista for the season ahead.

In winning the Evening Herald Champion Novice Hurdle **Hurricane Fly** cemented his status as a prime Champion Hurdle contender for 2010. After winning Grade One events at Fairyhouse and Leopardstown the five-year-old Montjeu gelding was forced to miss Cheltenham because of a setback. However, his clear-cut superiority over the Supreme Novices Hurdle winner **Go Native** on the two occasions that they clashed provides an idea of how he stands apart from his contemporaries.

With the old guard of hurdlers fading into the background, the emergence of the Charles Byrnes-trained **Solwhit** breathed significant new life into the scene. He ended the season with Grade One wins at Aintree and Punchestown where he beat the reigning champion Punjabi, with the Mullins-trained **Quevega**, winner of the David Nicholson Mares Hurdle, taking an honourable third to confirm her position as the best mare currently on the scene.

Muirhead, the Noel Meade-trained gelding who was best of the Irish-trained runners when fifth in the Champion Hurdle, did not reproduce that form at Punchestown but has overtaken stablemates such as **Jered** and the ageing **Harchibald** in the stable's hurdling pecking-order. **Kempes**, second to stablemate Hurricane Fly at Punchestown, and last season's leading Irish juvenile hurdler **Jumbo Rio**, from the Edward O'Grady stable, also look capable of winning good races over hurdles.

The Mullins-trained **Mikael D'Haguenet** was last season's outstanding novice hurdler over staying distances. Unbeaten in six starts since arriving from France, the six-year-old proved that he was not just a heavy-ground specialist when winning the Ballymore Novices Hurdle, and went out on a high by proving much too strong for stablemate **Cousin Vinny** at Punchestown.

▲ **Harchibald (leading)**

Go Native (right, leading)

Blessed with a rich amalgam of speed and stamina, Mikael D'Haguenet looks an exceptional prospect for staying novice chases. His trainer's fine record in the RSA Chase means that there is be no doubt about his ultimate objective, and it is going to take something special to lower his colours in the main Irish staying novice chases through the winter. His most significant opponents may include the Noel Meade-trained **Pandorama** and **Venalmar**, due back in action for the Mouse Morris yard after a lengthy absence.

Fiveforthree, the Mulllins-trained 2008 Ballymore winner, is also earmarked for chasing. During an abridged campaign he was a fine second to Solwhit in the John Smith's Aintree Hurdle and won the Ladbrokes.com World Series Hurdle at Punchestown. If connections opt to keep the seven-year-old over hurdles he would represent the main Irish hope in the staying division, in which there has been a relative dearth of talent in the country in recent seasons.

Cousin Vinny, the previous season's top bumper performer, has the makings of a smart two-mile chaser. Another talented sort for the two-mile novice chasing scene is the former AIG winner **Sizing Europe**. He has given trainer Henry de Bromhead plenty of heartache, so it was reassuring to see him get off the mark over fences in good style at Punchestown in May before being given a break. Edward Harty's 2008 Supreme Novices winner **Captain Cee Bee** is another top-class candidate for novice chases after a spell on the sidelines.

The Albert Bartlett winner **Weapon's Amnesty** can be expected to make a mark as a staying chaser along with the Willie Mullins-trained **The Midnight Club**, who finished third to Weapon's Amnesty at Cheltenham and was unbeaten in four races on home territory. **Jessies Dream**, unbeaten in three starts last season, is another promising chasing type in the Mullins yard.

The only major blot for the Mullins team at Punchestown was the eclipse of the RSA Chase winner **Cooldine** in the Boylesports.com Champion Novice Chase. However, he was found to be suffering from a chest infection, and the run can be ignored. The manner of his Cheltenham victory makes the seven-year-old a credible Cheltenham Gold Cup hope.

The Jim Dreaper-trained **Notre Pere** emerged as a

high-class staying chaser last season. Victories in the Troytown and the Welsh National provided the launch-pad for an assault on the major conditions chases, and a second placing behind Neptune Collonges in the Hennessy Cognac Cup confirmed his improvement. A superb jumper and a thorough stayer, he won the Punchestown Guinness Gold Cup in tremendous style. It should be stressed that the ground would need to be very soft for him to be considered a genuine Cheltenham Gold Cup hope, and his campaign will be geared around the main domestic prizes. These races will also be the natural target for the likes of the Noel Meade-trained **Aran Concerto**, who delivered on his tall reputation by landing the Powers Gold Cup at Fairyhouse, and **Rare Rob**, who had the similarly promising **Joncol** back in third when winning the Boylesports.com Novice Chase at Punchestown

If the likes of Cooldine and Notre Pere provide hope that British raiders can be repelled in the major staying chases, the performance of **Big Zeb** in giving the dual two-mile champion Master Minded a massive scare in the Kerrygold Champion Chase at Punchestown offers a similar level of anticipation. Perhaps the Colm Murphy-trained eight-year-old may never be entirely cured of the jumping frailties that have blighted his career, and which crucially surfaced at the final fence in the Punchestown race. However, that reservation apart, he is a genuine class-act in the two-mile division.

Forpadydeplasterer will be a powerful recruit to the senior ranks among the two-milers. After being put in his place by Cooldine over two miles and five furlongs in the Dr PJ Moriarty Chase at Leopardstown the Tom Cooper-trained gelding proved he is best suited by a strong-run two miles when winning the Arkle Trophy at Cheltenham. He maybe had done enough for the season by Punchestown where he was no match for **Barker** from the rampant Mullins team. A former winner of the Pierse Hurdle when trained by James Barrett, Barker did not initially take well to chasing but was revitalised by his transfer to Mullins. His short-head second in the Powers Gold Cup proved that he stays two and a half miles, extending the range of options for him.

In customary fashion the Mullins stable produced a stream of bumper winners through last winter, sparking the inevitable speculation in advance of the bumper at Cheltenham. This time all the talk was supremely relevant, since the season found one of its most exciting stars in the shape of the Philip Fenton-trained **Dunguib**. The Presenting gelding earned rave reviews in establishing a four-race winning sequence that culminated in brilliant victories in the Grade One events at Cheltenham and Punchestown.

That Dunguib tested positive for a prohibited substance after his Punchestown triumph was deeply regrettable, but is unlikely to have any significant effect on his prospects which remain a cause for genuine excitement. By common consent, there has not been a bumper horse like him in the past two decades with the possible exception of Montelado, who returned to Cheltenham 12 months after his bumper victory to capture the Supreme Novices Hurdle. Dubguib looks a rare talent.

There was strength-in-depth in the bumper division as well. **Luska Lad**, beaten 13 lengths by Dunguib at Navan last December and third in the Punchestown race, achieved the rare feat of winning four bumpers and should make his mark as a novice hurdler for John Joseph Hanlon, a rising star of the training ranks. **Sweeps Hill**, the main beneficiary of Dunguib's Punchestown disqualification, won his only other start at Leopardstown in impressive fashion and looks a fine long-term prospect for trainer John Kiely whose team of novice hurdlers will also include **Liss Na Tintri** who dominated the Listed bumper at Aintree.

The Mullins bumper horses may have been outshone in the season's two Grade One races, but a number of them are more than likely to make the grade as novice hurdlers. Among the most interesting are **Quel Spirit**, fourth at Cheltenham and the winner of his other two starts, **Fionnegas**, an unbeaten winner of two bumpers who was quickly off the mark with a maiden hurdle win at Ballinrobe in May, and the mare **Morning Supreme**, fifth at Cheltenham and third to Candy Creek at Aintree.

Tom Mullins has charge of a smart hurdling prospect in **Some Present**, who was appearing for the first time since a debut success at Punchestown last November when second to Dunguib at Cheltenham, and Dermot Weld has a good sort for novice races in Cheltenham third **Rite Of Passage**.

These complete the aforementioned attractive vista of Irish hopefuls for the winter ahead. ■

QUIET ACHIEVERS Brian Morgan

A level-stakes profits for followers of Quiet Achievers last season.

BOLD RANSOM (Keith Reveley)

This seven-year-old son of Lord of Appeal out of a Roselier mare lives right up to the hoary old cliché of staying longer than the in-laws. Placed on his only bumper outing, he tried hurdles just four times, winning on the last of these starts over three miles at Newcastle with a dour staying performance from the front. His chasing debut at Carlisle saw him jump nicely enough, but the trip was too short for him to bring his stamina into play. Taken on for the lead at Ayr next time out, he had nothing left when the winner went past, but posted improved form over a marathon 3m 4f at Carlisle in his third chase, showing great courage and fighting back when looking beaten, at a time when he could have been forgiven for downing tools. His reward came on his last appearance, at Kelso, where he again displayed plenty of heart to land the spoils in testing conditions. I'd be tempted to say that no trip is too far and no going too taxing for Bold Ransom, and he's the type to continue improving with age. If, like me, you admire a horse who can relentlessly gallop the hooves off his rivals, then this has to be one for your shortlist. ■

BURTON PORT (Nicky Henderson)

A winning Irish pointer, he's only finished out of the frame once in six appearances under Rules. Justifying favouritism on his bumper debut at Hereford, he followed up next time over hurdles at the same course, making most under a typical AP McCoy ride. Turned over at Fontwell when odds-on, Burton Port was then outpaced over the minimum trip at Sandown. Upped in trip next time by half a mile at the Esher track, he was noticed steaming up the hill in the closing stages to finish fourth, already looking as if he needed further. His debut UK season ended with the runner-up spot in a well-contested fixed-brush hurdle at Haydock, and he seemed really to relish the more challenging obstacles. I see no reason why he shouldn't stay three miles, he acts well with cut in the ground, and whatever he achieves over hurdles will be just a nice addition on the way to success as a chaser. Keep a close eye on this one. ■

CAOBA (Victor Dartnall)

Consistent, determined and improving – three words which, taken together, sum up my favourite type of horse. This five-year-old mare is already one of them. A winner of two and placed five times in ten hurdle runs, she won a long-distance Flat handicap at Nottingham in May, backed heavily as a result of improvements since last running on the level in France. While with Philip Hobbs she ended a sequence of seconds with a novice victory over 2m 3f at Newton Abbot, before having almost a year off and reappearing at her current yard.
A decent runner-up spot confirmed her wellbeing and she duly went one better next-time out, landing a staying novice event at Wincanton by all of 16 lengths, even after making a hash of the final flight. Still on the upgrade she finished her first NH campaign with third place in a valuable mares handicap at Cheltenham. Caoba acts on any ground but may prefer a sound surface; she'll get three miles for sure; she can run well fresh; and, should connections choose that route, they could have a very exciting novice chaser on their hands. ■

DARKSIDEOFTHEMOON (Tim Vaughan)

A horse I'd always noticed because of his name, he was highly regarded yet rather frustrating in his time with Nick Gifford, with just one long-distance maiden win on the Flat to show for 14 runs under both codes. Sold for £10,000 in May this year he had a small break before resuming his hurdles career – it had brought him three placings from eight starts – at Market Rasen in mid-August. There was plenty of market confidence in the gelding that day, and he justified the faith despite looking as though he may still have a few ideas of his own about the job. The trip was 2m 3f and he'll have no problem in getting quite a bit further than that. Darksideofthemoon likes decent jumping ground and may even make up into a chaser at some point. ■

DOUBLE DASH (George Baker)

Sir Harry Lewis is fast becoming a very decent NH sire, and his reputation won't be done any harm by this fine five-year-old hurdling prospect. On the evidence of his four bumper outings, Double Dash may be able to live up to the promise of his name. Sent off at 66/1 on his debut at Bangor he looked to benefit greatly from the experience and came a very respectable third. Next-time out he won a hands-and-heels race at Ludlow in most determined fashion, beating Nicky Henderson's promising Acordeon by over three lengths. A visit to Chepstow saw him claim the runner-up spot on pretty wet ground (just couldn't raise his game when the winner went past). On his final start to date he was quite simply outclassed in the Weatherbys Champion Bumper at the Cheltenham Festival. George Baker has made a great start to his training career and he's sure to place Double Dash to good effect in his first year over obstacles. ■

HELPSTON (Pam Sly)

Another Sir Harry Lewis owner-bred five-year-old: but this time there's a difference, as the owner is the trainer too. Helpston showed a modicum of promise in both his bumpers, and then raced a bit too freely on his hurdling debut at Lingfield, pressing the long odds-on Charity Lane hard on heavy going. This was a good performance so it was somewhat surprising to see him go off at 11/2 next time out at Leicester. Upped in trip to two and a half miles he hurdled well for a big horse and proved a real battler as he ground out a four-length win.

Placed efforts at Kempton and Huntingdon were a reward for honest effort, and to be fair anything achieved over hurdles was always going to be a bonus, as chasing is surely destined to be Helpston's game. With another winter behind him and the expert care he'll have received from his owner, he should be a most welcome recruit to the novice chasing ranks. He should stay the full three miles-plus, likes plenty of cut, and will be fun to follow. ■

MIDSUMMER MAGIC (Nicky Henderson)

The Queen's five-year-old Muhtarram mare is a sister to First Love, and looks as if she will reach at least the same level of form. Her three bumper runs yielded two placings, and she lost her maiden tag on her second hurdling attempt, on New Year's Day, making all at Fakenham and staying on very stoutly indeed. She was tried with the same tactics on her next run over 2m 5f at Towcester, a totally different prospect, but had to settle for second, ten lengths or so adrift of the winner but almost 20 clear of the other contenders. Back at the same track over the minimum trip on her final run of the last campaign, she led until Calusa Crystal took it up two out, but then stuck most pleasingly to her task and made her rival pull out all the stops before finishing a short head adrift at the line. A gutsy individual with an admirable attitude, she'll probably get three miles and enjoys good jumping ground, although her breeding suggests she'll cope with it on the soft side too. Midsummer Magic is one of those horses who'll always give you a full run for your money. ■

SKIPPERS BRIG (Nicky Richards)

The oldest (at eight) and most successful (six wins from 11 races) of this year's Quiet Achievers, Skippers Brig has recently moved south of the border due to Len Lungo's departure from the training ranks. I would hope this won't affect him too much, as he's in the right hands and right company as a talented chaser. Skippers Brig won his second of two bumpers in facile fashion at Carlisle and, after unseating his pilot on his hurdling debut, doubled up with decisive victories at Ayr and Haydock. Just two more hurdle runs followed, with a midfield finish in the Brit Insurance Novices at the 2007 Festival, his final one to date. Off the track for over 18 months with a strained tendon, he returned in great heart to win a 2m 5f novice chase at Carlisle without really noticing he'd been in a race. Jumping beautifully out of the heavy ground he looked every inch a classy long-distance chaser. Back at the same course in similar conditions next time out he kept to his task nicely to outpoint Chief Dan George, and then ended the campaign with a fair fourth in a Grade Two novice at Wetherby. The ground was 'only' soft that day, which may have hindered him a touch, as he's a real old-fashioned mudlark. I'm convinced he'll stay three miles and perhaps more, and he's going to be a tough nut to crack up north when the going gets bottomless. ■

SPEED BONNIE BOAT (Henry Daly)

A consistent and versatile Alflora mare, Speed Bonnie Boat was placed in one of her two bumpers and has made the frame on all five hurdle starts. On her debut over the sticks she didn't have the look of a natural, but her technique has improved a lot since. Runner-up on her next two outings over 2m 5f at Ludlow, on each occasion fresh after a break, she then found them going a bit too quickly for her when dropped in trip at Doncaster. Everything fell nicely for her in March, though, with the stiff track at Towcester over 2m 5f proving ideal, and she ran out a cosy winner of a mares novice event. Now she's tasted success she can go on to better things, and given her yard's fine record with chasers, there's every chance she'll graduate to those ranks soon enough. I'd expect her to get supporters singing her praises more than once in the coming campaign. ■

STOW (Venetia Williams)

A winner on the Flat for Hughie Morrison over ten furlongs at Bath, this four-year-old Selkirk gelding stayed a mile and a half and looked a fair deal at his 26,000 guineas sales price. After a first jumping season which brought two wins from five hurdle starts, the deal looks even better. He made a confident debut at Hereford, taking it up two out and keeping on well despite running a touch green. Next time he lost any chance at Ascot with an error two out, and was then put firmly in his place by Mr Thriller at Fontwell – but when the victor came fourth in the Imperial Cup that didn't look so bad a place. Stow was next seen in a six-runner event at Haydock, making all in grand style, before taking on the big boys in the JCB Triumph Hurdle, his 50/1 price reflecting his prospects, which were anyway undone by a significant blunder. Dropped into more modest company over the coming months, he can make up into a nice, consistent hurdler. He should stay two and a half miles and beyond, acts well on the soft and ran nicely on firm on the Flat, so his astute trainer will have plenty of options open to her. ■

IRISH TEN TO FOLLOW Alan Sweetman

Big Zeb (Colm Murphy)

Master Minded's reputation as a two-mile chaser in a league of his own was challenged on his final start of the season when the Colm Murphy-trained Big Zeb gave him an almighty fright at Punchestown. The result might have gone the other way, but for Big Zeb's blunder at the final fence. The uncomfortable truth is that the strapping eight-year-old has fallen in four of his ten races over fences, and remedial work on his technique is still required. However, in terms of natural ability, he is well ahead of the other principal Irish two-milers. ■

Sweeps Hill (John Kiely)

One of the best trainers of mares in the business, and particularly skilled with bumper horses, John Kiely combined those aspects of his talent when sending out Candy Creek to win two bumpers on either side of a fourth placing behind the brilliant Dunguib at Navan. Sadly for the trainer, Candy Creek has switched to Nicky Henderson's yard. But Sweeps Hill was impressive at Leopardstown and looks a fine long-term prospect. ■

Cousin Vinny (Willie Mullins)

The outstanding bumper horse of the season before last, Cousin Vinny was overshadowed by stablemates Mikael D'Haguenet and Hurricane Fly during last year's novice hurdling season. However, the doubts raised by a tame effort at Cheltenham, which may well have been attributable to the fact that he travelled badly, were largely erased by his run behind Hurricane Fly at Punchestown. He should make the grade as a novice chaser, appealing as a type who will stay well but who will also be suited by a strong-run two miles. ■

Dunguib (Philip Fenton)

Such was the impression created by Dunguib on last season's bumper scene that several experienced judges ventured the opinion that he could be good enough to make the grade as a Cup horse on the Flat. His form relative to Luska Lad, who likewise won four bumpers, offers an insight into the scale of his achievements, and he won three high-class bumpers with any amount in hand. If he jumps hurdles with fluency he could be a novice to compare with the great Golden Cygnet. Quite simply, the most exciting novice hurdling recruit for many a year. ■

Fionnegas (Willlie Mullins)

One of a number of horses taken over by Willie Mullins last season when trainer James Barrett handed in his licence, Fionnegas was not ready in time for the bumper at Cheltenham. However, the Accordion gelding proved himself as one of the stable's best young prospects by winning two bumpers. He also got a maiden hurdle win under his belt before being given a break, and could take a leading position in the ranks of the Irish novice hurdlers. ■

Hurricane Fly (Willie Mullins)

Though prevented by injury from contesting the Deloitte at Leopardstown and the Supreme Novices Hurdle, Hurricane Fly established himself as the season's top two-mile novice during a three-race campaign that came in the aftermath of a sole defeat over hurdles in the Prix Alain du Breil at Auteuil. With the names of Hardy Eustace, Brave Inca and Harchibald now taking their rightful place in hurdling folklore, the spotlight will turn on the rising stars of the Irish hurdling scene, and Hurricane Fly is poised to lead the Irish charge for the 2010 Champion Hurdle. ■

Mikael D'Haguenet (Willie Mullins)

The star of Ireland's novice hurdling scene, Mikael D'Haguenet was beaten on his only venture over fences in France as a four-year-old. As it transpires, that was a fortunate outcome since he would otherwise have been ineligible for the novice ranks. He enjoyed a flawless six-race campaign last winter, embracing three Grade One wins, and looks tailor-made for the season's main staying novice chases. Despite concerns raised by a high knee-action and a reputation as a soft-ground specialist, he handled drying ground at Cheltenham. ■

Notre Pere (Jim Dreaper)

Patience and an acute sense of realism have always been the hallmarks of Jim Dreaper's training career, and those qualities have been evident in his careful handling of Notre Pere. Graduating from the handicap ranks after winning the Welsh National, the French-bred eight-year-old ended the season with a smart performance at Punchestown to announce his arrival in chasing's major league. He is much too dependent on very soft ground to be a prime Cheltenham Gold Cup contender, but is an ideal type for a typical Irish winter. ■

Quevega (Willie Mullins)

Just under than three weeks after beating stablemate and subsequent Ebor winner, Sesenta, at Punchestown, Quevega blitzed the opposition in the second running of the David Nicholson Mares Hurdle at Cheltenham. She went on to finish third behind rising star Solwhit and reigning champion hurdler Punjabi at Punchestown, and will set the standard among the mares for the season ahead, providing that she comes back suffering no ill-effects from a below-par run in France on her final start. ■

Weapon's Amnesty (Charles Byrnes)

Having initially made his name as a trainer adept at landing gambles with modest animals, Charles Byrnes has moved his career up several notches in the past year or so, getting better-class horses into his yard, such as top-class hurdler Solwhit. He tasted Cheltenham Festival success for the first time with Weapon's Amnesty in the Albert Bartlett Novices Hurdle, and this Presenting gelding should mature into a very capable chaser. It is likely that he will win his share of novice races over staying distances. ■

TEN TO FOLLOW Colin Boag

Cockney Trucker (Philip Hobbs)

Read Philip Hobbs' comments about this one. What's more, I know that one of the big tipping services sees Cockney Trucker as extremely well handicapped. The plan is to go novice chasing but I'll be surprised if Philip can resist testing out Cockney Trucker's handicap mark over hurdles first. If he does, we could enjoy an early dividend ahead of winnings over the bigger obstacles. ■

Dave's Dream (Nicky Henderson)

Last season's Imperial Cup winner is obviously a classy hurdler. Now he is destined to be sent over fences and can be expected to hit the heights as well. Described by his trainer as big, strong and scopey, he's just the sort to make a name for himself over the larger obstacles. It is early days, of course, but he may even be good enough to become an Arkle contender. ■

Don't Push It (Jonjo O'Neill)

Don't Push It won a valuable Aintree handicap chase when switched back to fences from hurdles, and is expected to go on from that. With that experience added to his obvious ability, I fully expect him to land a big handicap at some stage this season. Indeed, maybe we will not have to wait too long. ■

Lidar (Alan King)

Lidar is held in high regard, and has been from day one. Alan King describes the horse's work as being of 'the highest class', and that will do for me. When a trainer of Alan's standing says as much you can be sure the horse has every chance to make a name for himself, in this case at novice hurdling. ■

Noble Alan (Nicky Richards)

Nicky Richard's style is to start them out low, build a sequence, and then send them south only if they show themselves to be good enough. I strongly suspect that this is the case with Noble Alan. He is made for chasing and his trainer can't keep his enthusiasm out of his voice when discussing the future. ■

Oscar Whisky (Nicky Henderson)

This could be the best of an exceptional crop of bumper winners that the stable housed last season. Now Oscar Whisky is being sent over hurdles. Clearly his highly impressive win at Newbury was no sort of a surprise to his trainer and I can't wait to see him over the smaller obstacles. The best of a talented bunch, potentially. ■

Royal Charm (Paul Nicholls)

When Paul Nicholls takes care to preserve a future chaser's novice hurdler status, he's doing it for a reason, and in the case of the ex-French Royal Charm, it's clearly because he thinks he's rather good. After talking with the trainer, I'd expect this one to be in the picture for next year's Supreme Novices Hurdle. ■

Shining Gale (Charlie Mann)

This is one of the apples of his trainer's eye. Shining Gale was progressive last season and has done exceptionally well over the summer. The Paddy Power's a possible starting point, but Charlie Mann thinks Shining Gale could improve enough to go beyond handicap company. ■

Skippers Brig (Nicky Richards)

This gelding moved to Nicky Richards from Len Lungo, and is a 'tool' when he gets his ideal conditions. Suited by heavy – and I don't mean namby-pamby soft ground, I mean redolent of the Somme – he goes through that better than most other horses. Nicky knows that and will place him accordingly. Keep an eye on conditions and strike when they are in Skippers Brig's favour.■

The Package (David Pipe)

David Pipe has always been very good at picking horses to follow from his team, and in last year's Guide to the Jumps he singled out The Package. It didn't work out last season for the six year-old, but he has time on his side and I reckon we'll see a different horse this time around. Keep the faith, this one should deliver this winter. ■

RACING POST RATINGS TEN TO FOLLOW Steve Mason

Ainama (Nicky Henderson)

Not many horses break the 130-barrier at the first time of asking over hurdles, but this former smart Flat handicapper ran to a Racing Post Rating of 134+ when brushing aside the decent Hebridean on his jumping debut at Kempton in January. That run marked him down as an obvious contender for the big spring festivals and he took his chance at all three, respectable runs at Cheltenham and Punchestown being split by a career best effort in Grade Two company at Aintree. That run was worth a RPR (Racing Post Rating) of 148, a figure that compares very favourably with his current official mark of 139. Ainama should make his mark in decent handicap company. ■

Babe Heffron (Tom George)

This is not one of Tom George's stable stars, but nevertheless has won two out of four starts since joining the yard. This enthusiastic front-runner created a good impression when running away from a modest field at Cartmel in May. Admittedly his handicap mark has risen by 30lb since his earlier win at Lingfield, but a handicap mark of 110 still looks to underestimate him and, given that this former winning pointer is open to further improvement, he should be good enough for further successes before the handicapper catches up with him. ■

Cape Tribulation (Malcolm Jefferson)

Malcolm Jefferson transferred Cape Tribulation's smart bumper/Flat form to hurdles, and recorded impressive victories in his first two starts, most notably when thrashing a decent field of novices in Grade Two company at Doncaster in February. The RPR of 155 Cape Tribulation earned that day secured him fourth spot in the list of the season's top novice hurdlers and, although the gelding then failed to match that level of form on better ground at Cheltenham and Aintree, those below-par runs did see his official mark come down by 10lb. It's far too soon to write off a horse his shrewd trainer has compared to Dato Star and an official mark of 145 looks ripe for exploiting en route to tackling the leading staying hurdlers. ■

Carruthers (Mark Bradstock)

Still really to convince at Cheltenham, there is nevertheless no doubting the talent of this hugely likeable front-runner who confirmed himself one of last season's leading novice chasers with an emphatic success in the Grade Two Reynoldstown Chase at Ascot in February. Carruthers was surprisingly dropped in the handicap after a respectable run behind Cooldine in the RSA. Still, it will be disappointing if his current official mark of 149 doesn't prove very lenient. A RPR of 158 suggests he could easily end up conpeting with the best around and a decent handicap win this winter looks a given. ■

Clova Island (Philip Hobbs)

This six-year-old is lightly raced with just the one win over hurdles to date, but with the potential to rate an awful lot higher than his start of season mark of 120. Clova Island beat the well-touted Thundering Star in December in good style at Taunton and was in the process of giving the well-handicapped Indian Blood a real fight when falling at the last at Newbury on his return to action in late February. Clova Island is a sort who looks sure to develop into a smart handicapper this season and his trainer can be relied upon to get the best out of him. ■

Doctor David (Caroline Bailey)

Doctor David reportedly lives on his nerves a bit and got worked up at the start prior to opening his account over fences at Kempton. The gelding seems to reserve his best efforts for Haydock where the flat, left-handed track and easy ground seem to play to his strengths. Twice a winner at the track over hurdles, he made it three wins from three visits when slamming subsequent Arkle runner-up/Aintree winner Kalahari King in December. That run was worth a RPR of 153 (official rating 147) and, granted similar conditions, he could develop into a 160+ two-miler chaser this season. ■

Horner Woods (Jessica Harrington)

A long-term plan to go for the Jewson at the Festival was scuppered when Horner Woods failed to make the cut, but a run in the RSA proved to be a highly satisfactory consellation as the 66/1 shot beat all bar the hugely impressive Cooldine. The latter could easily turn out to be an outstanding winner of that race and an Anglo-Irish Classifification mark of 142 for Horner Woods would appear to represent a very conservative evalulation of the value of that RSA form. The better ground he encountered at Cheltenham probably helped and he looks nailed on to pick up a decent handicap this season. ■

Isn't That Lucky (Jonjo O'Neill)

Isn't That Lucky's problems with his wind have had a negative impact on his career to date, but he has looked an improved performer after a tie back, with wins at Stratford and Perth being split by a career-best run behind the impressive Chapoturgeon in Jewson Novices Handicap Chase at the Cheltenham Festival. His handler will be looking to improve on last season's top-ten place among British-based jumps trainers and this improving six-year-old looks set to make a valuable contribution with the Paddy Power Gold Cup an obvious early-season target. ■

Medermit (Alan King)

Medermit ran below expectations when sent off favourite for the Scottish Champion Hurdle on his final start, but prior to that had been most progressive, landing a Grade Two at Ascot prior to beating all bar Go Native in the Supreme Novices Hurdle at the Festival. The time of that race stood up well compared with the Champion Hurdle and it will be surprising if an official rating of 146 is bar to this lightly-raced five-year-old plundering a decent two-mile handicap hurdle prior to fences. ■

Quartz De Thaix (Venetia Williams)

This French import impressed on his first two starts over in Britain, most notably when thrashing a trio of subsequent winners in testing ground at Bangor in February. The gelding subsequently twice disappointed when stepped up in trip in competitive heats at Sandown and Cheltenham, but, from a point of view of handicapping, an official mark of 125 does look very generous. One to keep on the right side. ■

RACING POST RATINGS TOP 600 CHASERS

A New Story (IRE) 138 [3] (3m 5f, Fair, Gd, Apr 13)
Abbeybraney (IRE) 151 [2] (3m 110y, Sand, GS, Dec 5)
Abragante (IRE) 138 [5] (3m 110y, Chel, GS, Mar 11)
According To John (IRE) 137 [4] (3m 110y, Sand, GS, Jan 31)
According To Pete 146 [4] (3m, Donc, Sft, Jan 24)
Afistfullofdollars (IRE) 159 [1] (3m 1f, Fair, Yld, Feb 23)
Aggie's Lad (IRE) 138 [2] (3m, Pert, GF, Jul 2)
Agus A Vic (IRE) 142 [2] (3m 1f, Punc, Hvy, May 2)
Air Force One (GER) 165 [2] (3m 2f 110y, Newb, GS, Nov 29)
Akilak (IRE) 144 [2] (2m 5f, Chel, Hvy, Jan 24)
Albanov (IRE) 149 [2] (2m, Naas, Sft, Jan 6)
Albertas Run (IRE) 172 [2] (3m, Kemp, Gd, Dec 26)
Alderburn 146 [3] (3m, Asco, GS, Dec 20)
Aleron (IRE) 136 [1] (3m 1f, Live, GS, May 15)
Alexander Taipan (IRE) 147 [2] (2m 2f, Thur, Sft, Mar 6)
Almaydan 143 [1] (2m 110y, Donc, Sft, Jan 23)
Alphabetical (IRE) 137 [1] (2m 3f, Asco, Gd, Nov 21)
Alright Now M'lad (IRE) 140 [1] (2m 6f 110y, Newb, GS, Nov 27)
Always Waining (IRE) 147 [1] (2m 6f 110y, Mark, Gd, Sep 27)
Ambobo (USA) 150 [1] (3m 1f, Punc, Hvy, May 2)
Amicelli (GER) 142 [1] (3m 2f 110y, Chel, Gd, Apr 16)
An Accordion (IRE) 156 [1] (3m 110y, Chel, GS, Mar 11)
An Siorrac (IRE) 144 [1] (2m 6f 100y, Fair, Sft, Feb 21)
Andreas (FR) 160 [1] (2m, Sand, Gd, Apr 26)
Ansar (IRE) 147 [3] (2m 6f, Galw, Yld, Jul 30)
Antonius Caesar (FR) 137 [1] (3m 110y, Carl, Gd, Apr 11)
Araldur (FR) 155 [1] (2m, Sand, GS, Dec 6)
Aran Concerto (IRE) 145 [1] (2m 4f, Fair, Gd, Apr 12)
Aranleigh (IRE) 137 [3] (2m 4f, Punc, Hvy, Nov 16)
Arbor Supreme (IRE) 150 [3] (3m 1f, Punc, Hvy, May 2)
Archie Boy (IRE) 141 [1] (2m 110y, Newt, GF, Jun 23)
Armaturk (FR) 142 (2m 4f 110y, Bang, Hvy, Feb 8)
Arnold Layne (IRE) 137 [1] (3m 5f, Warw, Gd, Feb 22)
Arturio (FR) 140 [1] (2m 5f, Chel, GS, Jan 26)
Ashley Brook (IRE) 159 [1] (2m 1f 110y, Devo, GS, Nov 4)
Ashwell (IRE) 137 [1] (3m, Kemp, GS, Nov 12)
Atouchbetweenacara (IRE) 151 [1] (2m 5f, Chel, Gd, Apr 15)
Au Courant (IRE) 149 [1] (2m 4f 110y, Kemp, Gd, Apr 20)
Auroras Encore (IRE) 139 [1] (3m 1f, Ayr, Gd, Apr 18)
Baby Run (FR) 144 [1] (3m 1f, Punc, Hvy, May 2)
Back On Line (IRE) 140 [3] (2m 6f 110y, Newb, Sft, Mar 29)
Backbeat (IRE) 145 [1] (3m 110y, Sand, GS, Jan 5)
Backstage (FR) 154 [1] (3m 1f 110y, Ffos, Gd, Aug 28)
Bagan (FR) 143 [1] (2m 4f 110y, Warw, GS, Feb 9)
Ballistraw (IRE) 153 [1] (2m 4f, Gowr, Sft, Feb 16)
Ballycullen Boy (IRE) 138 [3] (3m 1f, Punc, Gd, Apr 22)
Ballyfitz 156 [2] (3m 1f 110y, Chel, GS, Dec 12)
Ballyfoy (IRE) 137 [3] (3m 5f, Warw, Gd, Feb 22)
Ballyholland (IRE) 150 [1] (2m 6f, Galw, Sft, Jul 29)
Ballytrim (IRE) 139 [1] (3m 6f, Punc, Hvy, May 1)
Bambi De L'orme (FR) 141 [4] (2m 110y, Donc, Gd, Feb 2)
Barbers Shop 165 [1] (3m 110y, Sand, GS, Dec 5)
Barker (IRE) 163 [1] (2m, Punc, Hvy, Apr 30)
Barna Bay (IRE) 145 [2] (2m 1f, Ball, Sft, Aug 10)
Battlecry 154 [2] (3m 1f, Live, Gd, Apr 4)
Beat The Boys (IRE) 140 [3] (3m 3f 110y, Chel, Sft, Nov 15)
Beef Or Salmon (IRE) 147 [5] (3m, Leop, Sft, Feb 10)
Beggars Cap (IRE) 142 [1] (2m, Live, Gd, May 8)
Bella Mana Mou (IRE) 142 [1] (3m, Nava, Hvy, Mar 15)
Benefit Night (IRE) 142 [2] (2m, Naas, Sft, Feb 24)
Best Actor (IRE) 148 [1] (3m 110y, Sout, GS, Feb 17)
Bewleys Berry (IRE) 138 [5] (4m 4f, Live, Gd, Apr 5)
Bible Lord (IRE) 144 [1] (2m 3f 110y, Devo, GS, Feb 10)
Big Buck's (FR) 164 (3m 2f 110y, Newb, GS, Nov 29)
Big Fella Thanks 156 [3] (3m, Kemp, Gd, Feb 21)
Big Zeb (IRE) 166 [2] (2m, Punc, Sft, Apr 28)
Bill's Echo 137 [1] (2m 5f 110y, Stra, GF, Oct 25)
Billyvoddan (IRE) 150 [4] (3m 1f 110y, Chel, GS, Jan 26)
Bishop's Bridge (IRE) 146 [1] (2m 4f 110y, Hunt, Gd, Nov 22)
Black Apalachi (IRE) 164 [1] (3m 1f, Fair, Sft, Feb 21)
Black Hills 140 [6] (3m, Kemp, Gd, Feb 23)
Blaeberry 141 [3] (2m 4f, Live, Gd, Apr 5)
Blueberry Boy (IRE) 144 [1] (2m, Punc, Hvy, Apr 30)
Bluesea Cracker (IRE) 136 [1] (3m, Lime, Sft, Apr 5)
Bobs Pride (IRE) 138 [1] (2m 1f, Galw, Sft, Aug 2)
Boomshakalaka (IRE) 136 [3] (2m 1f, Asco, GS, Dec 19)
Bothar Na (IRE) 140 [3] (3m 6f, Punc, Hvy, May 1)
Boychuk (IRE) 144 [1] (3m 1f 110y, Chel, Gd, Apr 15)
Brave Rebellion 136 [1] (3m, Muss, Gd, Feb 20)
Breaking Silence (IRE) 144 [2] (2m 6f 110y, Mark, Gd, Sep 27)
Breedsbreeze (IRE) 154 (3m, Asco, Hvy, Feb 14)
Briareus 162 (2m, Chel, GS, Mar 11)
Briery Fox (IRE) 139 [2] (3m, Asco, Gd, Apr 11)
Bring Me Sunshine (IRE) 141 [1] (2m 3f 110y, Chep, GS, Feb 14)
Bringbackthebiff (NZ) 140 [1] (2m 2f, Gowr, Hvy, Feb 14)
Brooklyn Breeze (IRE) 137 [2] (3m, Pert, GS, Apr 24)
Brooklyn Brownie (IRE) 143 [2] (2m 5f 110y, Live, Sft, Nov 23)
Buck The Legend (IRE) 150 [1] (2m 2f 110y, Newb, GS, Nov 28)
Butler's Cabin (FR) 147 [7] (4m 4f, Live, GS, Apr 4)
Cailin Alainn (IRE) 148 [1] (2m 4f, Thur, Hvy, Jan 29)
Calatagan (IRE) 152 [3] (2m 110y, Chel, GS, Mar 14)
Calgary Bay (IRE) 154 [2] (2m 1f, Asco, GS, Jan 17)
Callow Lake (IRE) 138 [1] (2m 4f, List, Fm, Jun 1)
Can't Buy Time (IRE) 146 [1] (3m 110y, Sand, GS, Jan 31)
Candy Girl (IRE) 140 [1] (3m, Lime, Sft, Apr 6)
Cane Brake (IRE) 147 [3] (3m, Leop, Sft, Dec 28)
Cappa Bleu (IRE) 147 [1] (3m 2f 110y, Chel, GS, Mar 13)
Captain Conflict (IRE) 139 [2] (2m 2f, Gowr, Hvy, Feb 14)
Caribou (FR) 144 [1] (3m, Newb, Sft, Mar 29)
Carrigeen Kalmia (IRE) 140 [2] (2m 6f, Thur, Sft, Nov 6)
Carronhills (IRE) 138 [2] (3m, Leop, Sft, Feb 15)
Carruthers 158 [1] (3m, Asco, Hvy, Feb 14)
Carthalawn (IRE) 153 [1] (2m, Naas, Sft, Feb 22)
Casey Jones (IRE) 152 [1] (3m, Leop, Sft, Dec 28)
Celestial Gold (IRE) 146 [7] (3m 1f, Live, Gd, Apr 4)
Central House 146 [3] (2m 3f, Leop, Hvy, Jan 25)
Cerium (FR) 139 [5] (4m 4f, Live, GS, Apr 4)
Chapoturgeon (FR) 158 [1] (2m 5f, Chel, GS, Mar 12)
Character Building (IRE) 150 [1] (3m 1f 110y, Chel, GS, Mar 12)
Cheating Chance (IRE) 143 [1] (2m 1f, Asco, Gd, Nov 22)
Checkpointcharlie (IRE) 145 [1] (2m 5f, Fair, Hvy, Mar 4)
Chelsea Harbour (IRE) 162 [2] (3m, Gowr, Hvy, Jan 22)
Chief Dan George (IRE) 143 [1] (2m 6f 110y, Kels, Gd, Mar 20)
Chief Yeoman 136 [5] (3m 110y, Sand, GS, Jan 5)
Christy Beamish (IRE) 139 [2] (2m 5f 110y, Live, Gd, Apr 2)
Church Island (IRE) 150 [2] (3m 5f, Fair, Gd, Apr 13)
Clarified (IRE) 138 [3] (2m 2f, Gowr, Hvy, Feb 14)
Classic Fiddle 146 [1] (2m 4f, Newb, GS, Nov 29)

Clew Bay Cove (IRE) 143[3] (2m 110y, Donc, GS, Jan 31)
Clew Bay Lodge (IRE) 136[1] (2m 4f, Tipp, GF, Jun 19)
Clopf (IRE) 149 (2m, Nava, Sft, Feb 17)
Cloudy Lane 165[1] (3m, Hayd, Sft, Jan 17)
Coe (IRE) 142[2] (3m 4f, Hayd, Hvy, Feb 14)
Companero (IRE) 141[1] (3m 110y, Carl, GS, Nov 2)
Comply Or Die (IRE) 160[2] (4m 4f, Live, GS, Apr 4)
Conna Castle (IRE) 154[3] (2m, Punc, Sft, Apr 28)
Consigliere (FR) 137[1] (2m 1f, Asco, Hvy, Feb 14)
Cool Operator 136[1] (2m 4f, Sedg, Gd, Sep 30)
Cool Roxy 136[1] (2m 5f 110y, Fake, GS, Feb 27)
Cooldine (IRE) 170[1] (3m 110y, Chel, GS, Mar 11)
Coq Hardi (FR) 140[1] (2m 6f 110y, Utto, Gd, May 10)
Cornas (NZ) 151[4] (2m, Live, GS, Apr 4)
Cornish Sett (IRE) 150[1] (3m 1f 110y, Winc, Sft, Nov 8)
Crescent Island (IRE) 151[3] (2m 5f, Chel, GS, Mar 12)
Crystal D'ainay (FR) 145[1] (2m 7f 110y, Devo, GS, Feb 10)
Cuan Na Grai (IRE) 136[1] (2m 1f, Kill, Gd, May 11)
D'argent (IRE) 147[1] (3m 5f, Warw, Hvy, Jan 12)
Dante Hall (IRE) 145[1] (2m, Punc, Hvy, Nov 15)
Dark Artist (IRE) 140[2] (2m, Nava, Sft, Feb 17)
Darkness 156[1] (3m 2f 110y, Newb, Gd, Feb 28)
Dashing George (IRE) 149[1] (2m 4f, Tral, Hvy, Oct 1)
Davenport Democrat (IRE) 141[2] (2m 1f, Galw, Yld, Aug 1)
Dbest (IRE) 151[2] (2m 1f, Cork, GF, Jun 5)
De Soto 137[1] (3m 110y, Bang, Gd, Aug 15)
Dear Villez (FR) 154[4] (3m 110y, Chel, GS, Mar 10)
Decoy Daddy (IRE) 136[1] (2m, Gowr, Sft, Mar 20)
Deep Purple 153[1] (2m 4f, Ayr, Gd, Apr 18)
Denman (IRE) 184[1] (3m 2f 110y, Chel, GS, Mar 14)
Desert Quest (IRE) 145[2] (2m 110y, Hunt, Gd, Feb 21)
Deutschland (USA) 144[4] (2m, Punc, Hvy, Apr 30)
Dev (IRE) 137[2] (2m, Live, Gd, Apr 3)
Dix Villez (FR) 136[1] (3m 7f, Chel, Sft, Nov 14)
Doctor David 153[1] (2m, Hayd, Sft, Dec 20)
Don't Be Bitin (IRE) 140[4] (2m, Naas, Sft, Feb 24)
Don't Push It (IRE) 156[1] (3m 1f, Live, GS, Apr 4)
Donaldson (GER) 139[2] (2m 4f 110y, Worc, GS, Aug 7)
Dosco (IRE) 140[1] (2m 1f, Fair, Yld, Mar 25)
Dream Alliance 144 (2m 7f 110y, Devo, GS, Feb 10)
Dreamy Gent (IRE) 136 (2m, Rosc, Yld, Sep 29)
Drumconvis (IRE) 145[2] (4m, Chel, GS, Mar 11)
Drunken Disorderly (IRE) 143[2] (2m 1f, Fair, Sft, Mar 22)
Duc De Regniere (FR) 139[1] (2m 4f 110y, Ling, Sft, Jan 4)
El Vaquero (IRE) 137[7] (2m, Sand, GS, Jan 5)
Emma Jane (IRE) 148[1] (3m, Naas, Sft, Mar 14)
Emotional Article (IRE) 136[4] (2m 4f, Nava, Gd, Mar 28)
Endless Power (IRE) 153[1] (2m 5f 110y, Live, Sft, Nov 23)
Enlightenment (IRE) 142[5] (2m, Live, Gd, Apr 2)
Equus Maximus (IRE) 145[1] (2m 5f, Punc, Hvy, May 1)
Eric's Charm (FR) 150[3] (3m 5f 110y, Sand, GS, Dec 6)
Ever Present (IRE) 137[3] (2m 4f 110y, Kemp, Sft, Jan 12)
Exmoor Ranger (IRE) 144 (2m 5f, Chel, GS, Mar 12)
Exotic Dancer (FR) 178[1] (3m, Leop, Sft, Dec 28)
Faasel (IRE) 137[1] (2m 5f, Carl, Hvy, Nov 10)
Fair Along (GER) 156[4] (2m 5f 110y, Asco, Gd, Feb 16)
Fair Point (IRE) 140[1] (2m 7f 110y, Taun, Hvy, Feb 5)
Fiepes Shuffle (GER) 156[1] (2m, Kemp, Gd, Dec 27)
Fier Normand (FR) 140[1] (2m 4f, Ludl, Gd, Apr 9)
Financial Reward (IRE) 141[1] (2m 3f 120y, Lime, Sft, Dec 26)
Finger Onthe Pulse (IRE) 150[3] (2m 5f, Leop, Sft, Jan 11)
Fire And Rain (FR) 137[1] (3m 4f, Utto, Gd, Jun 28)
First Look (FR) 136[1] (2m 4f, Ayr, GS, Nov 24)
Fisher Bridge (IRE) 142[1] (2m 4f, Kilb, Hvy, Sep 11)
Fix The Rib (IRE) 141[1] (2m, Kemp, Gd, Feb 28)
Fleet Street 147[1] (3m, Kemp, Gd, Dec 27)
Flintoff (USA) 146[2] (3m 4f 110y, Hayd, GS, Feb 16)
Florida Express (IRE) 150[2] (3m, Naas, Sft, Mar 14)
Flying Falcon 138[1] (2m 4f, Utto, Sft, Apr 12)
Follow The Plan (IRE) 152[1] (2m 1f, Leop, Sft, Dec 26)
Foreman (GER) 139[2] (2m 110y, Chep, Sft, Feb 21)
Forest Green (FR) 138[6] (2m 5f, Chel, Gd, Apr 17)
Forest Leaves (IRE) 138[1] (3m 4f, Punc, Hvy, Feb 1)
Forget The Past 147[6] (2m 5f, Leop, Yld, Mar 2)
Forpadydeplasterer (IRE) 161[1] (2m, Chel, GS, Mar 10)
Freds Benefit (IRE) 136[4] (2m 1f, Fair, Sft, Nov 30)
Free World (FR) 153[2] (2m, Kemp, Gd, Feb 28)
French Accordion (IRE) 139[3] (2m 1f, Kill, Yld, Jul 14)
French Opera 149[3] (2m 110y, Chel, GS, Mar 13)
Fundamentalist (IRE) 153[1] (3m 1f, Live, GS, Oct 25)
Garde Champetre (FR) 160[1] (3m 7f, Chel, GS, Mar 10)
Gauvain (GER) 151[6] (2m, Chel, GS, Mar 10)
Gemini Lucy (IRE) 146[5] (2m, Punc, Gd, Apr 22)
Gidam Gidam (IRE) 139[2] (3m 2f, Donc, Gd, Feb 28)
Glasker Mill (IRE) 143[2] (3m, Hayd, Sft, Jan 17)
Glencove Marina (IRE) 152[1] (2m 5f, Leop, Hvy, Jan 13)
Glenfinn Captain (IRE) 157[1] (2m 4f, Gowr, Hvy, Feb 14)
Go For One (IRE) 142[1] (3m 2f 110y, Newb, Sft, Dec 17)
Gods Token 144[5] (2m 4f 110y, Chel, GS, Mar 13)
Gold Medallist 136[5] (2m 5f, Chel, Gd, Apr 17)
Golden Silver (FR) 150[1] (2m 1f, Leop, Hvy, Jan 25)
Gone To Lunch (IRE) 159[2] (4m 110y, Ayr, Gd, Apr 18)
Good Company (IRE) 140[2] (2m, Worc, Gd, Jul 28)
Gungadu 162[1] (3m, Kemp, Gd, Feb 23)
Gwanako (FR) 159[5] (2m 5f, Chel, GS, Mar 12)
Gypsy George 141[2] (3m 1f, Ayr, Sft, Jan 10)
Halcon Genelardais (FR) 171[3] (3m 5f 110y, Chep, Sft, Dec 27)
Hasty Prince 146[2] (2m, Sand, GS, Jan 5)
Hear The Echo (IRE) 158[1] (3m 5f, Fair, Yld, Mar 24)
Hedgehunter (IRE) 152[2] (3m 1f, Fair, Yld, Feb 23)
Hello Bud (IRE) 145[1] (4m 110y, Ayr, Gd, Apr 18)
Hennessy (IRE) 143[1] (3m 5f 110y, Sand, Gd, Apr 25)
Herecomestanley 138[1] (3m, Kemp, GS, Feb 8)
Herecomesthetruth (IRE) 153[1] (2m 4f 110y, Kemp, Gd, Feb 21)
Hi Cloy (IRE) 156[1] (2m 4f, Thur, Hvy, Jan 17)
High Chimes (IRE) 142[6] (3m 1f 110y, Chel, GS, Mar 12)
Hills Of Aran 147[1] (2m 7f, Stra, GF, Jun 14)
Himalayan Trail 145[1] (4m 1f 110y, Utto, GS, Mar 15)
Hobbs Hill 148 (3m, Asco, Gd, Mar 27)
Hold Em (IRE) 141[4] (3m, Kemp, Gd, Feb 21)
Holly Tree (IRE) 137[2] (2m 2f, Punc, Sft, May 27)
Homer Wells (IRE) 139[6] (3m, Gowr, Hvy, Jan 24)
Hoo La Baloo (FR) 150[3] (3m 5f 110y, Sand, Gd, Apr 26)
Hoopy (IRE) 139[3] (3m, Leop, Sft, Dec 27)
Hopkins (IRE) 137[1] (3m, Donc, GS, Feb 18)
Horner Woods (IRE) 158[2] (3m 110y, Chel, GS, Mar 11)
Howle Hill (IRE) 156[1] (2m 110y, Donc, Gd, Feb 2)
I'm So Lucky 147[2] (2m 2f 110y, Newb, GS, Dec 29)
I'msingingtheblues (IRE) 159[1] (2m 110y, Donc, GS, Jan 31)
Ice Tea (IRE) 144[1] (3m 1f, Weth, GS, Nov 15)

Idle Talk (IRE) 143 [2] (3m 2f, Carl, Sft, Nov 2)
Il Duce (IRE) 153 [2] (2m 5f, Chel, GS, Apr 16)
Imperial Commander (IRE) 169 [1] (2m 5f, Chel, GS, Mar 12)
In The High Grass (IRE) 137 [3] (2m 3f, Leop, Sft, Jan 27)
In The Loop (IRE) 137 [1] (3m 2f, Dowr, Sft, Mar 17)
Ingratitude (IRE) 141 [1] (2m 110y, Sedg, GF, Apr 7)
Iris De Balme (FR) 154 [1] (4m 110y, Ayr, Gd, Apr 19)
Irish Invader (IRE) 149 [1] (2m 2f, Thur, Sft, Feb 26)
Irish Raptor (IRE) 145 [1] (2m 5f 110y, Live, Gd, Apr 3)
Iron Man (FR) 144 [3] (3m, Chep, Gd, Oct 11)
Island Flyer (IRE) 138 [2] (3m 1f 110y, Winc, Sft, Nov 8)
Isn't That Lucky 144 [2] (2m 5f, Chel, GS, Mar 12)
Its A Dream (IRE) 144 [1] (3m 1f, Folk, GS, Dec 16)
Itsa Legend 136 [1] (2m 7f 110y, Taun, Sft, Dec 11)
J'y Vole (FR) 161 [1] (2m 4f, Punc, Hvy, Apr 29)
Jack The Giant (IRE) 164 [1] (2m 1f, Asco, Gd, Nov 22)
Jass 140 [1] (4m, Donc, GS, Jan 31)
Jaunty Flight 147 [1] (3m, Pert, Gd, Apr 22)
Jayo (FR) 148 [1] (2m, Naas, Sft, Jan 4)
Jazz Dance (IRE) 142 [1] (2m, Sout, GF, Sep 26)
Joe Lively (IRE) 165 [1] (3m 1f 110y, Chel, Hvy, Jan 24)
Joncol (IRE) 157 [3] (3m 1f, Punc, Sft, Apr 28)
Jubilant Note (IRE) 146 [2] (2m 1f 110y, Stra, Gd, Jul 12)
Just Amazing (IRE) 142 [2] (2m 5f 110y, Newt, GF, Aug 23)
Justified (IRE) 145 (2m, Nava, Sft, Nov 9)
Justpourit (IRE) 142 [3] (2m 4f, Punc, Yld, Apr 23)
Juveigneur (FR) 149 [4] (3m, Donc, Gd, Jan 26)
Kahuna (IRE) 141 [1] (2m 1f, Galw, Hvy, Jul 31)
Kalahari King (FR) 162 [2] (2m, Sand, Gd, Apr 25)
Kalca Mome (FR) 145 [5] (2m, Sand, Sft, Feb 2)
Kaldouas (FR) 141 [1] (2m 4f 110y, Worc, GF, Jun 18)
Kandjar D'allier (FR) 136 [1] (3m, Hayd, Gd, Nov 6)
Karanja 141 [1] (2m 7f 110y, Taun, Sft, Feb 7)
Kauto Star (FR) 185 [1] (3m 2f 110y, Chel, GS, Mar 13)
Keepitsecret (IRE) 138 [2] (2m 6f 110y, Mark, Gd, Jul 18)
Kelami (FR) 149 [2] (3m, Kemp, Gd, Feb 23)
Kenzo Iii (FR) 145 [1] (2m 5f, Winc, GS, Feb 16)
Kerryhead Windfarm (IRE) 145 [3] (2m 4f 120y, Kill, Sft, May 10)
Keys Pride (IRE) 140 [1] (2m 3f, List, Sft, Sep 13)
Kia Kaha 144 (2m 3f, Taun, Sft, Dec 11)
Kicking King (IRE) 142 [2] (2m 6f, Punc, Hvy, Oct 16)
Kicks For Free (IRE) 155 [2] (2m 5f, Chel, GS, Jan 1)
Kilbeggan Blade 142 [1] (3m 5f 110y, Sand, GS, Dec 6)
Kilcrea Asla (IRE) 137 [1] (3m, Ludl, Gd, Feb 26)
Kilcrea Castle (IRE) 146 [2] (2m 5f, Leop, Sft, Jan 11)
Killyglen (IRE) 153 [1] (3m 1f, Live, Gd, Apr 3)
King Barry (FR) 137 [3] (3m 4f, Kels, Gd, Mar 20)
King Harald (IRE) 140 [5] (3m 2f 110y, Chel, GS, Jan 1)
King Johns Castle (IRE) 157 [2] (4m 4f, Live, Gd, Apr 5)
King Louis (FR) 140 [1] (2m 2f 110y, Newb, Gd, Apr 12)
King Troy (IRE) 142 [4] (2m 6f 110y, Mark, Gd, Jul 18)
Kings Euro (IRE) 144 [2] (3m, Utto, GS, Mar 15)
Knight Legend (IRE) 155 [1] (2m 4f, Gowr, Gd, Oct 4)
Knowhere (IRE) 165 [1] (3m 1f 110y, Chel, GS, Jan 26)
Kornati Kid 150 [1] (3m 1f, Weth, Sft, Jan 31)
Kruguyrova (FR) 149 [2] (2m, Chel, GS, Mar 11)
L'ami (FR) 154 [2] (3m 7f, Chel, GS, Mar 10)
L'antartique (FR) 139 [4] (2m 1f, Newb, GS, Feb 9)
Lacdoudal (FR) 149 [3] (3m 5f 110y, Sand, Gd, Apr 25)
Laetitia (IRE) 136 [2] (2m 4f, Fair, Sft, Apr 15)
Lamanver Homerun 140 (2m 3f, Here, GS, Feb 23)
Laskari (FR) 143 [2] (3m, Kemp, Gd, Dec 27)
Le Beau Bai (FR) 138 [1] (3m 5f, Warw, Sft, Feb 20)
Le Burf (FR) 137 [1] (2m 4f 110y, Kemp, Gd, Feb 21)
Le Duc (FR) 136 [1] (3m 1f 110y, Chel, GS, Apr 16)
Le Volfoni (FR) 154 [3] (3m, Kemp, Gd, Feb 23)
Lead On (IRE) 144 [2] (2m 4f 110y, Kemp, Gd, Feb 23)
Leading Attraction (IRE) 149 [3] (3m 1f 110y, Winc, Sft, Nov 8)
Leading Contender (IRE) 141 [2] (3m 1f, Live, GS, Apr 4)
Leading Man (IRE) 136 [3] (4m, Donc, Gd, Feb 2)
Lennon (IRE) 154 [4] (2m, Live, Gd, Apr 3)
Lenrey 145 [2] (2m 1f, Leop, Yld, Mar 2)
Leslingtaylor (IRE) 145 [4] (2m, Live, Gd, Apr 2)
Light On The Broom (IRE) 142 [3] (2m 4f, Clon, Hvy, Nov 13)
Lightning Strike (GER) 145 [1] (2m 3f, Donc, Sft, Jan 24)
Limerick Boy (GER) 141 [1] (2m 4f 110y, Bang, Hvy, Feb 6)
Lochan Lacha (IRE) 137 [1] (2m 6f 100y, Fair, Gd, Apr 13)
Lodge Lane (IRE) 151 [1] (3m, Devo, Sft, Nov 21)
Lord Henry (IRE) 158 [2] (2m 1f, Asco, Gd, Nov 22)
Lord Jay Jay (IRE) 141 [1] (2m 1f 110y, Stra, Gd, May 23)
Lord Ryeford (IRE) 139 [5] (2m 4f 110y, Chel, Gd, Oct 18)
Lorient Express (FR) 140 [1] (2m, Sand, GS, Jan 31)
Love That Benny (USA) 137 [1] (3m, Pert, GF, Jul 29)
Lysander (GER) 139 [1] (2m 4f 110y, Bang, Sft, Mar 29)
Ma Yahab 137 [2] (3m 1f, Kels, Hvy, Apr 13)
Macmar (FR) 136 [2] (2m 7f 110y, Devo, GS, Mar 27)
Made In Taipan (IRE) 153 [3] (2m, Live, GS, Apr 4)
Madison Du Berlais (FR) 177 [1] (3m 1f, Live, Gd, Apr 2)
Magic Sky (FR) 142 [4] (2m, Sand, Sft, Feb 2)
Mahogany Blaze (FR) 156 [3] (2m, Sand, Gd, Apr 25)
Majestic Concorde (IRE) 144 [1] (2m 1f, Leop, Sft, Jan 11)
Maljimar (IRE) 151 [1] (2m 5f, Chel, GS, Jan 26)
Mansony (FR) 156 [1] (2m, Punc, Hvy, Feb 1)
Maralan (IRE) 147 [1] (2m, Naas, Sft, Feb 24)
Marcel (FR) 143 [1] (2m, Ayr, Gd, Apr 19)
Marodima (FR) 149 [3] (2m, Utto, Hvy, Feb 14)
Massini's Maguire (IRE) 154 [2] (2m 4f 110y, Sand, GS, Jan 31)
Master Medic (IRE) 145 [1] (2m 1f, Asco, GS, Dec 19)
Master Minded (FR) 186 [1] (2m, Chel, GS, Mar 13)
Mattock Ranger (IRE) 140 [2] (2m 5f, Leop, Yld, Mar 2)
Medicinal (IRE) 148 [2] (2m 4f, Font, Gd, Feb 22)
Merchent Paddy (IRE) 139 [1] (2m 5f, Leop, Sft, Jan 11)
Merigo (FR) 143 [1] (4m 1f, Newc, Hvy, Feb 21)
Mighty Matters (IRE) 140 [1] (2m 4f 110y, Sand, Gd, Mar 7)
Miko De Beauchene (FR) 161 [1] (3m 4f 110y, Hayd, GS, Feb 16)
Millenium Royal (FR) 141 [1] (3m 2f, Plum, Hvy, Feb 9)
Miss Mitch (IRE) 147 [1] (2m 5f 110y, Asco, GS, Jan 17)
Mister Gloss (IRE) 136 [1] (2m 4f 110y, Pert, GS, Sep 25)
Mister Mcgoldrick 162 [1] (2m 4f 110y, Chel, GS, Mar 13)
Mister Quasimodo 150 [1] (2m 4f 110y, Kemp, GS, Feb 8)
Mister Top Notch (IRE) 163 [5] (2m 5f, Leop, Sft, Jan 11)
Modicum (USA) 153 [3] (2m, Live, Gd, Apr 5)
Mon Mome (FR) 166 [1] (4m 4f, Live, GS, Apr 4)
Monet's Garden (IRE) 169 [2] (2m 5f 110y, Asco, Gd, Feb 16)
Money Trix (IRE) 155 [1] (2m 6f 110y, Kels, Sft, Feb 28)
Monkerhostin (FR) 160 [2] (3m, Asco, GS, Dec 20)
Montero (IRE) 139 [2] (2m 1f, Galw, Hvy, Aug 29)
Montgermont (FR) 140 [4] (2m 4f, Newc, Sft, Dec 20)
Moon Over Miami (GER) 151 [2] (2m 110y, Chel, GS, Mar 13)
Morgan Be 145 [2] (4m 1f, Newc, Hvy, Feb 21)

Moskova (IRE) 152 [1] (2m 4f, Fair, Sft, Apr 15)
Mossbank (IRE) 162 [2] (2m 4f 110y, Chel, GS, Mar 13)
Mount Sandel (IRE) 142 [1] (2m 6f, Font, Gd, Feb 22)
Mr Boo (IRE) 137 [3] (2m 5f 110y, Stra, Gd, May 23)
Mr Pointment (IRE) 140 [2] (3m, Newb, GS, Dec 29)
Mr Robert (IRE) 138 [5] (3m 1f 110y, Ffos, Gd, Aug 28)
Mr Strachan (IRE) 139 [3] (3m 1f, Ayr, Gd, Apr 19)
My Petra 150 [2] (2m 5f 110y, Asco, GS, Dec 20)
My Will (FR) 166 [5] (3m 2f 110y, Chel, GS, Mar 13)
Nacarat (FR) 170 [1] (3m, Kemp, Gd, Feb 21)
Nadover (FR) 143 [3] (3m 7f, Chel, Sft, Dec 12)
Naiad Du Misselot (FR) 144 [4] (2m 4f, Hayd, Sft, Jan 17)
Natal (FR) 156 [3] (2m 1f 110y, Devo, GS, Nov 4)
Naunton Brook 141 [2] (3m 1f 110y, Winc, GS, Feb 16)
Nenuphar Collonges (FR) 153 [4] (3m 1f, Punc, Hvy, May 2)
Neptune Collonges (FR) 178 [1] (3m, Leop, Sft, Feb 15)
Nevada Royale (FR) 141 [1] (3m, Devo, Hvy, Nov 11)
Nevertika (FR) 144 [1] (2m 3f, Donc, Gd, Jan 26)
New Alco (FR) 154 [2] (3m 110y, Chel, GS, Mar 11)
New Little Bric (FR) 151 [1] (2m 4f, Newb, Gd, Feb 28)
Newbay Prop (IRE) 136 [3] (3m 1f 110y, Chel, GS, Mar 12)
Newmill (IRE) 163 [4] (2m, Chel, GS, Mar 11)
Nice Try (IRE) 143 [1] (2m 4f 110y, Bang, GS, May 2)
Niche Market (IRE) 154 [1] (3m 5f, Fair, Gd, Apr 13)
Nickname (FR) 151 [1] (2m 1f, Gowr, Hvy, Jan 24)
Nine De Sivola (FR) 137 [3] (4m, Chel, GS, Mar 11)
Nine O (IRE) 136 [1] (2m 3f 120y, Lime, Sft, Dec 27)
No Full (FR) 138 [2] (2m 4f, Nava, Hvy, Mar 29)
Noland 166 [1] (2m 4f, Punc, Hvy, Dec 9)
Northern Alliance (IRE) 148 [4] (2m 5f, Chel, GS, Mar 12)
Nostringsattached (IRE) 140 [2] (3m 1f 110y, Ffos, Gd, Aug 28)
Notable D'estruval (FR) 140 [4] (3m, Leop, Sft, Dec 27)
Notre Pere (FR) 173 [1] (3m 1f, Punc, Hvy, Apr 29)
Nozic (FR) 165 [1] (3m 1f, Weth, Sft, Dec 26)
Nudge And Nurdle (IRE) 137 [1] (3m, Pert, Gd, Apr 23)
Nuvelli (IRE) 138 [1] (2m 4f, Nava, Hvy, Dec 6)
Oakfield Legend 137 [3] (3m 1f, Live, GS, Apr 4)
Oceanos Des Obeaux (FR) 141 [1] (2m 4f, Font, Gd, Feb 22)
Oedipe (FR) 154 [1] (3m 1f, Live, Gd, Apr 4)
Officier De Reserve (FR) 147 [4] (3m 5f 110y, Chep, Sft, Dec 27)
Oh Crick (FR) 151 [1] (2m, Live, Gd, Apr 2)
Okaido (FR) 138 (2m 5f, Chel, GS, Jan 1)
Old Benny 140 [4] (4m 110y, Ayr, Gd, Apr 19)
Ollie Magern 162 [2] (3m 1f, Weth, GF, Nov 1)
One Cool Cookie (IRE) 154 [3] (3m 1f, Fair, Sft, Feb 21)
One Sniff (IRE) 137 [1] (3m 110y, Bang, GS, Apr 19)
Oneway (IRE) 145 [3] (2m 4f, Newb, GS, Mar 1)
Oodachee 142 [2] (2m 5f 110y, Live, Gd, Apr 3)
Openide 140 [2] (3m 1f 110y, Chel, GS, Mar 13)
Opera Mundi (FR) 154 [3] (3m, Hayd, Sft, Jan 17)
Or Bleu (FR) 144 [1] (2m 110y, Chep, Hvy, Feb 12)
Or Jaune (FR) 138 [1] (2m 3f 110y, Devo, Gd, Mar 17)
Or Noir De Somoza (FR) 157 [4] (2m 1f, Asco, GS, Jan 17)
Oracle Des Mottes (FR) 139 [3] (2m 5f 110y, Asco, GS, Jan 17)
Original (FR) 150 [1] (2m, Kemp, Gd, Dec 27)
Ornais (FR) 157 [1] (3m 110y, Chel, Sft, Nov 14)
Osako D'airy (FR) 149 [1] (2m 3f 110y, Chep, Hvy, Feb 12)
Oscar Bay (IRE) 143 [1] (2m 4f, Stra, Gd, Mar 2)
Oscar India (IRE) 139 [1] (2m 3f, Naas, Sft, Nov 8)
Oscar Park (IRE) 137 [1] (2m 6f, Font, Gd, Feb 24)
Oscar Time (IRE) 142 (3m, Lime, Sft, Apr 5)
Oscatello (USA) 137 [2] (2m 7f 110y, Taun, Hvy, Feb 5)
Oslot (FR) 158 [4] (2m 3f, Asco, Gd, Nov 22)
Oulart 137 [1] (2m 4f, Kilb, Hvy, Aug 9)
Oumeyade (FR) 154 [1] (2m 1f 110y, Devo, GS, Nov 4)
Our Vic (IRE) 174 [1] (3m 1f, Live, Gd, Apr 3)
Out The Black (IRE) 140 [3] (4m 110y, Ayr, Gd, Apr 18)
Ouzbeck (FR) 157 (2m 4f 110y, Chel, Sft, Nov 15)
Over The Creek 140 [2] (4m, Chel, GS, Mar 13)
Pablo Du Charmil (FR) 157 [3] (2m, Kemp, Gd, Dec 27)
Paco Jack (IRE) 136 [1] (2m 6f, Galw, Hvy, Aug 30)
Palarshan (FR) 136 [5] (2m 5f 110y, Live, GS, Apr 4)
Palomar (USA) 138 [1] (2m, Catt, GS, Dec 28)
Panjo Bere (FR) 151 [1] (2m 1f, Asco, GS, Jan 17)
Parsons Legacy (IRE) 153 [1] (3m 110y, Chel, Gd, Oct 17)
Parsons Pistol (IRE) 149 [1] (3m, Naas, Hvy, Jan 17)
Pasco (SWI) 144 [1] (2m 110y, Hunt, GS, Feb 19)
Pass Me By 142 [5] (3m 7f, Chel, Sft, Dec 12)
Patman Du Charmil (FR) 141 [2] (2m 5f, Chel, GS, Jan 1)
Patsy Hall (IRE) 144 [4] (3m 110y, Chel, GS, Mar 11)
Pearl King (IRE) 142 [2] (2m, Worc, GF, May 22)
Pedros Brief (IRE) 136 [2] (2m 5f, Winc, GS, Feb 16)
Penzance 140 [3] (2m, Kemp, GS, Nov 12)
Pepsyrock (FR) 138 [1] (2m, Ayr, Gd, Apr 18)
Perce Rock 152 [1] (2m 1f, Fair, Gd, Apr 14)
Peter Pole (FR) 141 [1] (2m 4f 110y, Sout, Gd, Mar 24)
Petit Robin (FR) 166 [3] (2m, Chel, GS, Mar 11)
Phardessa 138 [1] (3m, Utto, Hvy, Feb 14)
Philson Run (IRE) 138 [5] (4m 110y, Ayr, Gd, Apr 19)
Piano Star 136 [1] (2m 6f, Kilb, Gd, Jul 17)
Ping Pong Sivola (FR) 143 [2] (2m 5f, Chel, GS, Mar 12)
Planet Of Sound 157 [3] (2m, Chel, GS, Mar 10)
Point Barrow (IRE) 144 [4] (3m, Gowr, Hvy, Jan 24)
Poker De Sivola (FR) 144 (3m 1f, Weth, Sft, Jan 31)
Pomme Tiepy (FR) 138 [5] (3m 5f, Fair, Gd, Apr 13)
Ponmeoath (IRE) 142 [3] (2m 4f, Thur, Hvy, Jan 29)
Pop (FR) 137 [1] (2m 3f, Here, GS, Feb 23)
Poquelin (FR) 141 [8] (2m 110y, Chel, GS, Mar 13)
Possol (FR) 160 [1] (3m, Pert, Gd, Apr 23)
Preacher Boy 142 [2] (3m, Newb, Sft, Mar 29)
Preists Leap (IRE) 158 [1] (3m, Gowr, Hvy, Jan 22)
Premier Dane (IRE) 137 (2m, Chel, Gd, Oct 18)
Present Glory (IRE) 142 [1] (3m, Hayd, Gd, Apr 11)
Presenting Copper (IRE) 145 [2] (2m 3f 110y, Chep, Sft, Dec 27)
Pressgang 144 [1] (2m 4f 110y, Kemp, Gd, Dec 26)
Principe Azzurro (FR) 138 [3] (3m 110y, Sand, GS, Jan 5)
Private Be 148 [3] (2m 4f 110y, Chel, Sft, Nov 15)
Psychomodo 137 [1] (2m, Carl, Hvy, Feb 16)
Pur De Sivola (FR) 146 (2m 4f 110y, Kemp, Gd, Feb 23)
Quatre Heures (FR) 136 [2] (2m 1f, Nava, Hvy, Jan 26)
Quickbeam (IRE) 142 [1] (2m 7f 110y, Taun, GS, Feb 26)
Racing Demon (IRE) 169 [3] (2m 5f 110y, Asco, Gd, Feb 16)
Rambling Minster 155 [1] (3m 4f, Hayd, Hvy, Feb 14)
Rare Bob (IRE) 159 [1] (3m 1f, Punc, Sft, Apr 28)
Rayshan (IRE) 141 [1] (2m 4f, Newc, GS, Feb 23)
Red Admiral (USA) 140 [1] (2m 4f 110y, Hunt, GF, Aug 31)
Regal Heights (IRE) 158 [1] (2m 5f 110y, Asco, Sft, Jan 19)
Reisk Superman (IRE) 141 [1] (2m 6f, Galw, GF, Jul 29)
Ring The Boss (IRE) 148 [1] (2m 4f 110y, Warw, Hvy, Jan 22)
Rinroe (IRE) 141 (2m 4f, Cork, Sft, Oct 19)

Robert The Brave 136[1] (2m 4f, Mark, Gd, Aug 15)
Rock Street (IRE) 136[2] (2m 1f, Fair, Gd, Apr 13)
Roll Along (IRE) 165[6] (3m 2f 110y, Chel, GS, Mar 13)
Roman Ark 149[2] (2m 1f, Kels, GS, Mar 1)
Ross River 136[3] (2m 6f, Kill, Gd, May 11)
Roulez Cool 151[2] (3m, Utto, GS, May 2)
Royal Auclair (FR) 145[3] (3m 2f 110y, Newb, GS, Mar 1)
Royal County Star (IRE) 150[2] (3m 5f, Fair, Yld, Mar 24)
Russian Around (IRE) 142[1] (3m, Utto, GS, May 2)
Russian Trigger 146[1] (4m 1f 110y, Utto, Sft, Mar 14)
Sa Suffit (FR) 143[1] (2m 110y, Hexh, Sft, Mar 12)
Salford City (IRE) 151[1] (2m, Pert, Gd, Apr 24)
Santa's Son (IRE) 157[1] (2m, Weth, Sft, Dec 27)
Schindlers Hunt (IRE) 167[2] (2m 4f, Live, Gd, Apr 3)
Scotsirish (IRE) 159[4] (2m 4f, Live, Gd, Apr 3)
Seymour Weld 144[1] (2m 4f, Mark, Gd, Aug 16)
Shardakhan (IRE) 140[1] (3m 2f 110y, Chep, Sft, Mar 24)
Sher Beau (IRE) 148[1] (2m 4f, Nava, Hvy, Mar 29)
Sherwoods Folly 141[5] (3m 5f 110y, Chep, Sft, Dec 27)
Shining Gale (IRE) 150[2] (3m 1f, Live, Gd, Apr 3)
Shouldhavehadthat (IRE) 138[1] (2m 6f 110y, Newb, GS, Nov 29)
Siegemaster (IRE) 145[3] (3m 1f, Live, Gd, Apr 3)
Silver Birch (IRE) 136[2] (4m 2f, Punc, Hvy, Apr 30)
Silverburn (IRE) 153[1] (2m 4f 110y, Sand, Sft, Feb 2)
Simon 153[4] (3m, Kemp, Gd, Feb 23)
Sir Bathwick (IRE) 136[2] (2m 4f 110y, Kemp, Gd, Nov 26)
Sir Frederick (IRE) 140[4] (2m 4f, Punc, Yld, Apr 23)
Sir Rembrandt (IRE) 138[7] (3m 2f 110y, Newb, GS, Mar 1)
Sizing Africa (IRE) 140[1] (2m 4f, Cork, Sft, Oct 19)
Sky's The Limit (FR) 145[3] (2m 4f, Dowr, Sft, Nov 1)
Slash And Burn (IRE) 140[2] (2m 5f 110y, Asco, Gd, Nov 21)
Slim Pickings (IRE) 147[5] (2m 5f, Leop, Yld, Mar 2)
Snoopy Loopy (IRE) 169[1] (3m, Hayd, GS, Nov 22)
Snowy Morning (IRE) 167[2] (3m 1f, Punc, Yld, Apr 23)
Something Wells (FR) 155[1] (2m 5f, Chel, GS, Mar 12)
Song Of Songs 136 (2m, Live, GS, Apr 4)
Sou'wester 144[1] (2m, Live, Gd, May 9)
Sound Accord (IRE) 140[3] (3m 110y, Warw, Gd, Mar 18)
Southern Vic (IRE) 157[3] (3m, Naas, Sft, Mar 14)
Southwestern (IRE) 140 (3m 1f, Punc, Hvy, May 2)
Spirit Of New York (IRE) 141[1] (2m 6f 110y, Mark, Gd, Jun 27)
Sporazene (IRE) 143[4] (2m 4f, Font, Gd, Feb 24)
Stan (NZ) 156[4] (2m 4f, Newb, Gd, Feb 28)
Standin Obligation (IRE) 149[2] (3m, Donc, Sft, Dec 13)
Star De Mohaison (FR) 169[2] (3m 1f 110y, Chel, GS, Dec 12)
Star Of Germany (IRE) 139[1] (2m 5f 110y, Newt, GF, Aug 22)
Starzaan (IRE) 154[1] (2m 5f, Winc, GS, Feb 16)
State Of Play 153[4] (4m 4f, Live, GS, Apr 4)
Stolen Moments (FR) 136[4] (3m, Chep, Hvy, Feb 12)
Straw Bear (USA) 141[5] (2m 5f, Chel, GS, Mar 12)
Strawberry (IRE) 138[3] (3m, Newb, Gd, Mar 21)
Striking Article (IRE) 136[1] (2m 110y, Hexh, Sft, Oct 11)
Surface To Air 149[1] (4m 110y, Utto, Gd, Jun 29)
Takeroc (FR) 160[3] (2m, Sand, GS, Dec 6)
Tamadot (IRE) 139[1] (2m 3f, Taun, Sft, Jan 27)
Tamarinbleu (FR) 170[1] (2m 1f, Asco, Sft, Jan 19)
Tana River (IRE) 142[1] (3m 3f 110y, Winc, GS, Oct 26)
Tarotino (FR) 152[1] (2m 4f 110y, Bang, Gd, May 1)
Tartak (FR) 159[1] (2m 4f, Live, Gd, Apr 2)
Tatenen (FR) 158[1] (2m, Chel, Sft, Nov 16)
Templer (IRE) 137 (2m 4f, Stra, Gd, Apr 19)
That's Rhythm (FR) 139[1] (3m 110y, Bang, Gd, Mar 21)
The Hairy Lemon 143[1] (2m 4f 110y, Kemp, Gd, Feb 23)
The Hollow Bottom 138[1] (2m 4f, Live, Sft, Oct 25)
The King Of Angels (IRE) 138[2] (3m 110y, Chel, Gd, Oct 17)
The Listener (IRE) 166[2] (2m 4f, Punc, Hvy, Dec 9)
The Market Man (NZ) 150[1] (2m 4f, Newb, GS, Nov 28)
The Package 142[2] (2m 4f, Newb, Gd, Feb 28)
The Sawyer (BEL) 140[2] (2m 4f, Punc, Hvy, Apr 29)
The Tother One (IRE) 141[1] (3m, Devo, GS, Oct 21)
The Vicar (IRE) 139[1] (2m 4f, Hayd, Hvy, Feb 14)
Theatre Dance (IRE) 137[4] (3m, Newb, Gd, Mar 21)
Themoonandsixpence (IRE) 139[1] (3m 1f, Wexf, Yld, Aug 28)
Three Mirrors 151[1] (2m 4f, Ayr, GS, Apr 18)
Thyne Again (IRE) 154[3] (2m 1f, Leop, Sft, Dec 27)
Tidal Bay (IRE) 171[2] (3m 1f, Weth, Sft, Dec 26)
Tiger Cry (IRE) 144[5] (2m 110y, Chel, GS, Mar 13)
Tikram 139[1] (2m 4f, Font, Gd, Feb 24)
Toby Jug 138[1] (3m 2f 110y, Newt, GF, Sep 1)
Too Forward (IRE) 145[4] (2m 5f, Chel, GS, Jan 1)
Top Of The Rock (IRE) 141[1] (2m 1f, Nava, Hvy, Nov 23)
Torduff King (IRE) 138[3] (3m, Leop, Sft, Jan 27)
Tot O'whiskey 140[3] (3m 1f 110y, Chel, GS, Dec 12)
Trafford Lad 156[1] (2m 4f, Fair, Sft, Nov 30)
Tramantano 141[3] (2m, Live, Gd, Apr 2)
Tranquil Sea (IRE) 146[2] (2m 5f, Punc, Hvy, May 1)
Tricky Trickster (IRE) 150[1] (4m, Chel, GS, Mar 11)
Trigger The Light 139[2] (3m 110y, Sand, Gd, Mar 7)
Trust Fund (IRE) 143[1] (2m 5f 110y, Live, Gd, Apr 2)
Tumbling Dice (IRE) 143[3] (2m, Cork, Hvy, Dec 14)
Turkish Surprise (FR) 142[3] (2m 4f, Hayd, Sft, Jan 17)
Turko (FR) 158[3] (2m 4f 110y, Chel, GS, Mar 13)
Turthen (FR) 138[2] (3m 2f 110y, Chel, GS, Mar 13)
Twist Magic (FR) 169[1] (2m, Sand, Gd, Apr 25)
Ungaro (FR) 155[2] (3m 2f, Donc, Gd, Mar 1)
Unowatimeen (IRE) 138[1] (2m 4f, Sedg, Hvy, Feb 5)
Valain (IRE) 137[6] (2m, Live, Gd, Apr 2)
Verasi 138[1] (3m 110y, Warw, Hvy, Jan 12)
Vic Venturi (IRE) 157[2] (3m, Leop, Sft, Dec 27)
Villon (IRE) 140[2] (2m, Ayr, Hvy, Feb 9)
Vintage Treasure (IRE) 140[7] (2m 110y, Chel, GS, Mar 14)
Vodka Bleu (FR) 147[5] (2m 5f 110y, Asco, Gd, Feb 16)
Voy Por Ustedes (FR) 178[1] (2m 4f, Live, Gd, Apr 4)
Wanango (GER) 153[1] (2m, Utto, GS, Feb 16)
War Of Attrition (IRE) 160[3] (2m 4f, Punc, Hvy, Dec 9)
War Of The World (IRE) 138[1] (2m 7f, Stra, GF, Sep 5)
Warpath (IRE) 137[1] (2m, Worc, GF, May 22)
Washington Lad (IRE) 140[3] (2m 6f, Galw, Sft, Jul 29)
Watch My Back 138[2] (2m 4f 110y, Sout, Gd, May 10)
Watson Lake (IRE) 158[2] (2m 1f, Leop, Sft, Dec 27)
Wee Robbie 143[3] (2m 4f 110y, Sand, Sft, Feb 2)
Well Chief (GER) 165[2] (2m, Chel, GS, Mar 11)
West End Rocker (IRE) 141[2] (3m 110y, Warw, Gd, Mar 18)
What A Friend 158[1] (3m 1f 110y, Chel, GS, Dec 12)
Wheresben (IRE) 152[1] (3m, Leop, Sft, Dec 27)
Whyso Mayo (IRE) 139[3] (3m 1f, Punc, Hvy, May 2)
Wichita Lineman (IRE) 156[1] (3m 110y, Chel, GS, Mar 10)
Will Be Done (IRE) 154[2] (3m 1f, Weth, Sft, Jan 31)
William Butler (IRE) 146[3] (2m 6f 110y, Mark, Sft, Jul 19)
Wishwillow Lord (IRE) 140[4] (2m, Punc, Gd, Apr 24)
Without A Doubt 137[2] (3m 110y, Sand, Gd, Mar 8)
Yes Sir (IRE) 151[1] (2m 4f 110y, Weth, GF, Oct 31)

RACING POST RATINGS TOP 600 HURDLERS

Aachen 142 [1] (2m, Towc, Hvy, Feb 22)
Academy Sir Harry (IRE) 138 [1] (2m, Nava, Sft, Nov 9)
Acambo (GER) 140 [1] (2m 110y, Hexh, Gd, Jun 21)
Accordello (IRE) 133 [3] (3m, Hayd, GS, Feb 16)
According To Dick (IRE) 146 [3] (3m 110y, Live, Gd, Apr 3)
According To Pete 144 [1] (3m, Hayd, GS, Nov 22)
Adamant Approach (IRE) 138 [9] (3m, Leop, Hvy, Jan 13)
Afsoun (FR) 160 [2] (2m 110y, Hayd, Gd, Jan 17)
Aigle D'or 150 [2] (2m 110y, Chel, Sft, Nov 16)
Ainama (IRE) 148 [3] (2m 4f, Live, GS, Apr 4)
Aitmatov (GER) 158 [6] (3m, Chel, GS, Mar 13)
Al Eile (IRE) 166 [1] (2m 4f, Live, Gd, Apr 5)
Alderburn 134 [3] (3m, Hayd, GS, Nov 22)
Aldhaher Beebers (IRE) 138 [1] (3m, List, Fm, Jun 2)
Alexander Severus (IRE) 132 [4] (2m 110y, Chel, GS, Mar 11)
Alexander Taipan (IRE) 140 [5] (2m 5f, Nava, Sft, Feb 17)
Alfie Flits 141 [6] (2m 110y, Live, Gd, Apr 3)
Alice Bradys Call (USA) 134 [3] (2m, Fair, Gd, Apr 12)
Alph 148 [4] (2m 3f 110y, Asco, Gd, Nov 22)
Alpha Ridge (IRE) 154 [1] (3m, Gowr, Hvy, Jan 22)
Alpine Eagle (IRE) 133 [7] (2m, Leop, Yld, Jan 11)
Alsadaa (USA) 141 [1] (2m, Sand, GF, Apr 25)
Amazing King (IRE) 134 [3] (2m, Muss, Gd, Feb 1)
Amber Brook (IRE) 142 [1] (2m 6f, Winc, Sft, Nov 8)
Ambobo (USA) 133 [5] (2m 4f, Punc, Sft, Feb 18)
American Trilogy (IRE) 151 [2] (2m 110y, Live, Gd, Apr 3)
Andytown (IRE) 149 [1] (2m 4f 110y, Chel, GS, Mar 13)
Annie's Answer (IRE) 135 [7] (2m 4f 110y, Chel, GS, Mar 14)
Any Given Day (IRE) 141 [2] (2m 3f 110y, Mark, Gd, Aug 15)
Apartman (CZE) 132 [1] (2m, Ayr, Gd, Apr 18)
Apt Approach (IRE) 132 [2] (2m 4f, Ball, Sft, May 24)
Arcalis 144 [7] (2m 1f, Chel, GS, Mar 13)
Argento Luna 134 [1] (2m 5f, Newb, Gd, Mar 21)
Art Professor (IRE) 132 [1] (2m, Asco, Gd, Nov 21)
Ashkazar (FR) 157 [1] (2m, Winc, Sft, Feb 14)
Asian Royale (IRE) 135 [1] (3m 110y, Ayr, GS, Apr 18)
Astarador (FR) 138 [1] (2m 1f, Muss, GS, Feb 3)
Aura About You (IRE) 138 [3] (2m 4f, Chel, GS, Mar 10)
Auroras Encore (IRE) 137 [1] (2m 4f, Live, Gd, Apr 3)
Australia Day (IRE) 137 [1] (2m, Worc, Gd, Sep 6)
Awesome George 134 [1] (2m 3f 110y, Mark, Gd, Apr 25)
Backbord (GER) 137 [1] (2m 3f 110y, Asco, Gd, Feb 16)
Baddam 133 [1] (3m, Worc, GF, May 20)
Badgerlaw (IRE) 132 [3] (3m, Leop, Yld, Jan 11)
Baffin Island (IRE) 142 [1] (2m 2f, Thur, Sft, Jan 13)
Bahrain Storm (IRE) 157 [1] (2m, Galw, Yld, Jul 30)
Baily View (IRE) 139 [2] (3m, Fair, Gd, Apr 13)
Bakbenscher 136 [2] (2m 4f, Sand, Gd, Mar 7)
Balakan (IRE) 134 [1] (2m, List, Fm, Jun 2)
Ballycullen Boy (IRE) 134 [2] (2m 4f, Thur, Yld, Mar 6)
Ballydub (IRE) 149 [2] (2m 6f, Sand, Sft, Jan 31)
Ballyfitz 149 [2] (3m, Chel, Gd, Apr 18)
Baltiman (IRE) 132 [2] (2m, Punc, Yld, Feb 20)
Barker (IRE) 138 [1] (2m, Leop, Hvy, Jan 13)
Baron De'l (IRE) 135 [4] (2m, Leop, Sft, Dec 27)
Battlecry 139 [1] (3m 110y, Donc, Gd, Jan 26)
Beau Michael 148 [4] (2m 110y, Weth, Sft, Dec 6)
Bedlam Boy (IRE) 137 [3] (2m 4f, Live, Gd, Apr 2)
Belcantista (FR) 135 [2] (2m, Asco, GS, Dec 20)
Beneath The Radar (IRE) 135 [1] (2m, Ball, Sft, Apr 22)
Benetwood (IRE) 138 [1] (2m 3f, Newt, Gd, Jul 19)
Bensalem (IRE) 151 [2] (2m 4f 110y, Chel, Hvy, Jan 24)
Bergo (GER) 133 [2] (2m, Asco, Gd, Nov 21)
Bernabeu (USA) 132 [2] (2m 4f, Wexf, Yld, Aug 28)
Berties Dream (IRE) 137 [1] (2m 4f, Galw, Hvy, Aug 30)
Beshabar (IRE) 134 [1] (2m 4f, Sand, Gd, Mar 8)
Best Prospect (IRE) 132 [1] (2m, Newc, Hvy, Feb 21)
Big Buck's (FR) 176 [1] (3m 110y, Live, Gd, Apr 2)
Big Eared Fran (IRE) 139 [1] (2m 4f, Sand, Gd, Mar 7)
Big Fella Thanks 138 [2] (3m 110y, Ayr, GS, Apr 18)
Big Zeb (IRE) 148 [1] (2m, Fair, Gd, Apr 13)
Binocular (FR) 172 [1] (2m, Asco, GS, Dec 20)
Bit Of A Devil (IRE) 140 [4] (3m, Fair, Gd, Apr 12)
Black Apalachi (IRE) 137 [5] (3m, Punc, Sft, Feb 1)
Blaeberry 133 [3] (3m 110y, Kemp, Gd, Nov 26)
Blazing Bailey 163 [1] (3m 110y, Live, Gd, Apr 3)
Blue Bajan (IRE) 158 [4] (2m, Ayr, Gd, Apr 18)
Blythe Knight (IRE) 157 [2] (2m, Winc, GS, Feb 16)
Bob Lingo (IRE) 135 [1] (2m, Punc, Hvy, Oct 29)
Border Castle 151 [1] (2m, Ayr, Gd, Apr 19)
Borrowaddy (IRE) 133 [1] (3m, Kilb, Sft, Apr 25)
Bouggler 142 [1] (2m 4f, Live, GS, Apr 4)
Boulavogue (IRE) 133 [2] (2m 4f, Punc, Gd, Apr 24)
Brave Inca (IRE) 163 [2] (2m 4f, Fair, Sft, Nov 30)
Brave Right (IRE) 137 [1] (2m 4f, Punc, Yld, Apr 26)
Breedsbreeze (IRE) 143 [1] (2m 110y, Sand, Sft, Jan 5)
Browns Baily (IRE) 133 [1] (2m 6f, Thur, Sft, Jan 13)
Buachaill On Eirne (IRE) 133 [3] (2m 4f, Punc, Sft, Feb 18)
Buena Vista (IRE) 143 [3] (3m, Hayd, Gd, May 10)
Bullhill Flyer (IRE) 132 [3] (2m 2f, Cork, Yld, Aug 24)
Bureaucrat 133 [1] (2m 3f, Newt, GF, May 8)
Burton Port (IRE) 132 [2] (2m 4f, Hayd, Gd, Apr 11)
Bywell Beau (IRE) 135 [1] (2m 110y, Kels, Hvy, Jan 11)
Caim Hill (IRE) 136 [2] (2m 4f, Fair, Gd, Apr 14)
Calgary Bay (IRE) 133 [2] (2m 110y, Newb, GS, Apr 12)
Call Me Max 132 [3] (2m 3f, Cork, Yld, Oct 19)
Callherwhatulike (IRE) 135 [1] (2m 4f, Cork, Hvy, Apr 24)
Candy Girl (IRE) 135 [2] (2m 2f, Fair, Hvy, Dec 13)
Cape Tribulation 155 [1] (3m 110y, Donc, Sft, Jan 24)
Captain Americo (IRE) 134 [1] (3m 110y, Kemp, Gd, Feb 28)
Captain Cee Bee (IRE) 159 [1] (2m 110y, Chel, GS, Mar 11)
Caracciola (GER) 137 [4] (2m, Sand, Gd, Apr 26)
Carole's Legacy 135 [4] (2m 5f, Newb, Gd, Mar 21)
Carrickboy (IRE) 134 [1] (2m 1f 110y, Mark, Sft, Feb 16)
Carruthers 150 [1] (3m, Bang, Sft, Feb 8)
Carthalawn (IRE) 135 [4] (2m, Fair, Gd, Apr 14)
Catch Me (GER) 166 [1] (2m 5f, Nava, Hvy, Feb 16)
Cedrus Libani (IRE) 136 [1] (2m 110y, Hayd, GF, Nov 6)
Celestial Halo (IRE) 167 [2] (2m 110y, Chel, GS, Mar 10)
Chantaco (USA) 133 [1] (2m, Winc, Sft, Mar 30)
Chariot Charger (IRE) 134 [2] (2m 3f 110y, Asco, Hvy, Feb 14)
Charity Lane (IRE) 140 [2] (2m 6f, Winc, Sft, Feb 14)
Charlie Crab 133 [3] (2m 4f, Muss, Gd, Dec 29)
Chasing Cars (IRE) 144 [2] (2m 4f, Fair, Sft, Mar 23)
Chelsea Harbour (IRE) 148 [1] (3m, Clon, Hvy, Nov 13)
Chief Dan George (IRE) 151 [4] (3m, Chel, GS, Jan 26)
Chief Yeoman 139 [1] (2m 6f, Sand, Sft, Jan 31)
China Rock (IRE) 150 [4] (2m 5f, Chel, GS, Mar 11)

Chomba Womba (IRE) 151 [3] (2m, Asco, GS, Dec 20)
Clan Tara (IRE) 140 [2] (3m, Fair, Hvy, Jan 23)
Clopf (IRE) 155 [3] (2m, Fair, Sft, Nov 29)
Cockleshell Road (IRE) 132 [1] (2m 4f, Fair, Sft, Jan 1)
Cockney Trucker (IRE) 133 [3] (2m 1f, Chel, GS, Mar 13)
Coe (IRE) 133 [2] (3m 110y, Donc, Gd, Jan 26)
College Daisy (IRE) 135 [1] (2m 3f, Kilb, Sft, Aug 21)
Comhla Ri Coig 147 [2] (3m 110y, Live, Gd, Apr 3)
Companero (IRE) 148 [1] (3m, Hexh, Hvy, Nov 19)
Conflictofinterest 132 [3] (2m, Kemp, GS, Feb 21)
Conna Castle (IRE) 134 [3] (2m 2f, Cork, Sft, Aug 23)
Connak (IRE) 132 [1] (3m, Chep, Sft, Mar 8)
Convincing 135 [7] (2m 4f, Fair, Sft, Nov 30)
Coolcashin (IRE) 152 [1] (2m 4f, Fair, Gd, Apr 13)
Cooldine (IRE) 151 [1] (2m 4f, Thur, Yld, Mar 6)
Copper Bleu (IRE) 152 [2] (2m 4f, Live, GS, Apr 4)
Cork All Star (IRE) 146 [2] (2m, Dowr, Sft, Oct 31)
Corskeagh Royale (IRE) 134 [2] (2m 4f, Punc, Hvy, Nov 16)
Corum (IRE) 136 [1] (2m 1f, Newt, Sft, Aug 4)
County Zen (FR) 139 [3] (2m 110y, Newb, GS, Feb 9)
Cousin Vinny (IRE) 154 (2m 2f, Leop, Sft, Feb 15)
Crack Away Jack 166 [4] (2m 110y, Chel, GS, Mar 10)
Crescent Island (IRE) 136 [2] (2m 5f 110y, Chel, Gd, Apr 18)
Cryptic 140 [1] (2m 6f, Winc, GS, Jan 31)
Cuan Na Grai (IRE) 138 [2] (2m, Tipp, Sft, Jul 19)
Culcabock (IRE) 138 [1] (2m 110y, Live, GS, Apr 4)
Cybergenic (FR) 133 [3] (2m 4f 110y, Hayd, Gd, Mar 21)
Dan Dare (USA) 134 [1] (2m, Fair, Hvy, Nov 12)
Dancing Tornado (IRE) 140 [3] (2m 3f 110y, Asco, Hvy, Feb 14)
Danehill Willy (IRE) 133 [2] (2m 1f 110y, Mark, Gd, Jul 18)
Dani California 138 [1] (2m, Tram, Gd, Aug 14)
Dansimar 141 [2] (2m 5f, Kemp, GS, Feb 21)
Dariak (FR) 147 [1] (2m 1f, Tral, Sft, Sep 30)
Dave's Dream (IRE) 144 [1] (2m 110y, Sand, Gd, Mar 7)
De Valira (IRE) 144 [4] (2m, Gowr, Sft, Feb 16)
Deal Done (FR) 139 [2] (2m 4f, Punc, Sft, Feb 18)
Deal Maker (FR) 132 [3] (2m 4f, Thur, Yld, Mar 6)
Decoy Daddy (IRE) 134 [4] (2m 1f, Kill, Gd, May 11)
Dee Ee Williams (IRE) 146 [2] (2m, Asco, GS, Dec 19)
Deep Purple 140 [2] (2m 110y, Sand, Sft, Jan 5)
Definitive Edge 134 [1] (2m 4f, Galw, Hvy, Aug 29)
Definity (IRE) 147 [2] (3m, Chel, GS, Apr 17)
Desert Quest (IRE) 140 [3] (2m, Sand, Gd, Apr 26)
Deutschland (USA) 139 [2] (2m, Galw, Yld, Jul 30)
Diamond Harry 154 [3] (2m 5f, Chel, GS, Mar 11)
Doctor David 138 [1] (2m, Hayd, GS, Mar 22)
Dolphin Bay (IRE) 138 [2] (2m, Punc, Hvy, Nov 16)
Don't Push It (IRE) 144 [2] (3m, Chel, GS, Jan 1)
Dooneys Gate (IRE) 134 [4] (2m, Cork, Hvy, Dec 14)
Door Boy (IRE) 135 [5] (2m, Asco, GS, Dec 19)
Dragon Eye (IRE) 136 [3] (2m 5f, Chel, Sft, Nov 16)
Dreamy Gent (IRE) 141 [4] (2m, Hayd, Gd, May 10)
Drumconvis (IRE) 133 [1] (3m, Fair, Sft, Mar 22)
Dual Gales (IRE) 132 [3] (2m 1f, Kill, Gd, Jul 16)
Duc De Regniere (FR) 159 [2] (3m 1f, Asco, GS, Dec 20)
Dundrum (IRE) 135 [2] (2m, Fair, Gd, Apr 12)
Eagle's Pass (IRE) 147 [3] (2m 4f, Bell, Yld, Jul 4)
Earth Magic (IRE) 146 [1] (3m, Gowr, Hvy, Jan 24)
Earth Planet (IRE) 136 [4] (2m 3f 110y, Sand, Gd, Apr 26)
Ebadiyan (IRE) 143 (2m 1f, Chel, GS, Mar 13)
Ebaziyan (IRE) 156 [3] (2m, Punc, Gd, Apr 25)
Edgbriar (FR) 134 [1] (2m 3f 110y, Donc, Sft, Jan 23)
El Dancer (GER) 143 [1] (2m 110y, Live, Gd, Apr 3)
Eleazar (GER) 134 [1] (2m 5f, Kemp, GS, Feb 21)
Ellerslie Tom 137 [2] (2m, Hayd, Gd, May 9)
Elusive Dream 155 [1] (2m 4f, Live, Gd, Apr 3)
Emotional Moment (IRE) 139 [4] (2m 7f, Nava, Hvy, Dec 6)
Endless Power (IRE) 137 [3] (2m 4f, Ayr, Sft, Jan 10)
Enlightenment (IRE) 132 [2] (2m 110y, Stra, Gd, Jul 30)
Ernst Blofeld (IRE) 134 [3] (2m 4f 110y, Chel, Hvy, Jan 24)
Essex (IRE) 154 [4] (2m 4f, Punc, Sft, May 2)
European Dream (IRE) 134 [2] (2m 1f 110y, Mark, Sft, Feb 16)
Faasel (IRE) 151 [2] (3m 110y, Live, Gd, Apr 3)
Fair Along (GER) 164 [3] (3m, Chel, Hvy, Jan 24)
Faltering Fullback 140 [2] (2m 4f, Punc, Sft, May 2)
Farmer Brown (IRE) 152 [8] (2m 110y, Chel, GS, Mar 11)
Farringdon 141 [2] (2m 1f, Gowr, Hvy, Jan 22)
Fen Game (IRE) 133 [2] (2m, Leop, Yld, Dec 28)
Fingers 139 [1] (2m 4f, Bell, Yld, Jul 4)
Finns Cross (IRE) 135 [2] (2m 1f, Bell, Gd, Aug 28)
First Point (GER) 140 [1] (2m 3f, Newt, GF, Jun 16)
Fisher Bridge (IRE) 140 [1] (2m, Fair, Gd, Apr 14)
Five Dream (FR) 148 [3] (2m 110y, Sand, Sft, Dec 6)
Fiveforthree (IRE) 168 [1] (3m, Punc, Hvy, Apr 30)
Fixed Fee (IRE) 139 [1] (2m, Cork, Gd, Mar 22)
Flight Leader (IRE) 147 [8] (3m 110y, Live, Gd, Apr 3)
Footy Facts (IRE) 147 [3] (2m 5f, Nava, Sft, Feb 17)
Foreman (GER) 140 [5] (3m, Chel, Gd, Apr 18)
Forest Pennant (IRE) 144 [2] (3m, Chep, Gd, Oct 25)
Forpadydeplasterer (IRE) 143 [4] (2m 4f 110y, Chel, GS, Mar 14)
Forty Five (IRE) 133 [1] (2m 4f, Fake, GS, Feb 27)
Fosters Cross (IRE) 150 (2m, Galw, Yld, Jul 30)
Franchoek (IRE) 153 [3] (2m 4f 110y, Chel, GS, Jan 1)
Fredensborg (NZ) 136 [2] (2m 110y, Sand, Gd, Mar 8)
Freds Benefit (IRE) 136 [2] (2m 4f, Punc, Hvy, Jan 12)
French Opera 138 [5] (2m 4f, Live, Gd, Apr 2)
French Saulaie (FR) 142 [3] (2m 1f, Chel, GS, Mar 14)
Fresh Winter 138 [1] (3m, Bang, Hvy, Mar 29)
From Dawn To Dusk 140 [1] (2m 4f 110y, Chel, Gd, Apr 15)
Gansey (IRE) 133 [2] (2m 5f 110y, Ayr, Gd, Apr 19)
Gaspara (FR) 143 [3] (2m 4f 110y, Chel, GS, Jan 1)
Gauvain (GER) 134 [5] (2m 4f 110y, Chel, GS, Jan 26)
Gay Sloane (IRE) 132 [1] (2m 3f, Lime, Gd, Jun 13)
General Striker 134 [2] (2m 6f, Thur, Hvy, Oct 23)
Giles Cross (IRE) 134 [1] (3m, Chep, Hvy, Dec 6)
Give It Time 142 [3] (2m 3f, Naas, Hvy, Jan 17)
Go Native (IRE) 152 [1] (2m 110y, Chel, GS, Mar 10)
Golan Way 143 [4] (2m, Asco, GS, Dec 19)
Gold Gun (USA) 132 [3] (2m 3f 110y, Asco, Sft, Jan 19)
Golden Empire (FR) 138 [1] (2m 4f, Nava, Sft, Mar 1)
Gone To Lunch (IRE) 151 [2] (3m 110y, Live, Gd, Apr 4)
Good Fella (IRE) 132 [1] (2m 6f, Fair, Yld, Mar 24)
Got Attitude (IRE) 132 [1] (3m, Punc, Yld, Apr 23)
Grand Opera (IRE) 134 [1] (2m 1f, Kill, Sft, Aug 21)
Grand Schlem (FR) 136 [3] (2m 110y, Chel, GS, Mar 11)
Grand Theatre (IRE) 134 [1] (3m 110y, Ayr, Gd, Apr 17)
Green Mile 134 [2] (3m, Hayd, Gd, May 9)
Greenbridge (IRE) 144 [1] (2m, Kemp, GS, Mar 26)
Gringo 135 [2] (2m, Sand, GF, Apr 25)
Group Captain 146 [2] (2m 3f 110y, Asco, GS, Jan 17)

Gullible Gordon (IRE) 138 [1] (3m 110y, Taun, Sft, Dec 11)
Gunner Jack 132 [2] (3m, Newc, Gd, Mar 14)
Gusda (IRE) 139 [2] (3m, Leop, Sft, Dec 27)
Handfull Of Euros (IRE) 132 [5] (2m 1f, Kill, Sft, May 10)
Hangover (IRE) 133 [1] (2m 4f, Gowr, Sft, Feb 14)
Harchibald (FR) 160 [1] (2m, Kemp, Gd, Dec 26)
Hardy Eustace (IRE) 159 [1] (2m, Punc, Hvy, Nov 16)
Harmony Brig (IRE) 133 [1] (2m 4f, Ayr, Sft, Jan 10)
Harper Valley (IRE) 140 [3] (2m, Ayr, Gd, Apr 18)
Head Of The Posse (IRE) 142 [1] (2m 4f, Punc, Sft, Feb 18)
Healys Bar (IRE) 137 [3] (2m 4f, Lime, Hvy, May 17)
Heathcliff (IRE) 133 [4] (3m 1f, Hayd, Sft, Feb 14)
Heathcote 133 [2] (2m 110y, Chep, Sft, Mar 24)
Heavenly Blues (GER) 141 [3] (2m, Tipp, Hvy, Oct 5)
Hebridean (IRE) 134 [1] (2m, Kemp, GS, Feb 21)
Helium (FR) 134 [1] (2m 110y, Sand, Sft, Dec 5)
Hell's Bay (FR) 138 [1] (2m 4f, Chep, Gd, Oct 25)
Hennessy (IRE) 141 [2] (3m, Chel, GS, Jan 1)
Hidden Agent (IRE) 133 [1] (3m, Punc, Gd, Apr 24)
Hide The Evidence (IRE) 139 [8] (2m 110y, Live, Gd, Apr 5)
Hills Of Aran 152 [1] (2m 4f, Font, Gd, Mar 27)
Hold Em (IRE) 132 [1] (2m 4f 110y, Hunt, Gd, Feb 21)
Home Hunter (IRE) 132 [2] (3m, Punc, Yld, Apr 23)
Hora 148 [2] (2m 5f 110y, Chel, Gd, Apr 16)
Horner Woods (IRE) 141 [1] (2m 4f, Fair, Yld, Apr 8)
How's Business 141 [1] (2m 4f 110y, Utto, Gd, May 2)
Hurricane Fly (IRE) 158 [1] (2m, Punc, Sft, Apr 28)
I Have Dreamed (IRE) 132 [1] (2m 1f, Here, GS, Feb 23)
I'm So Lucky 142 [2] (2m, Hayd, Gd, May 10)
I'msingingtheblues (IRE) 137 [7] (2m 1f, Chel, GS, Mar 14)
Ignotus 133 [1] (2m 2f, Kels, GS, Mar 1)
Imperial Hills (IRE) 133 [4] (2m, Punc, Sft, Apr 28)
Inchidaly Rock (IRE) 147 [2] (3m 110y, Live, Gd, Apr 3)
Indian Groom (IRE) 133 [5] (2m 110y, Chel, GS, Mar 11)
Indian Pace (IRE) 134 [1] (2m, Galw, Gd, Jul 31)
Indian Spring (IRE) 136 [4] (2m, Fair, Gd, Apr 13)
Inglis Drever 174 [1] (3m, Chel, GS, Mar 13)
Ireland's Call (IRE) 140 [3] (2m, Tram, Gd, Aug 14)
Is It Me (USA) 135 [2] (2m 1f, Bang, Gd, Aug 15)
Issaquah (IRE) 135 [2] (2m 110y, Live, GS, Apr 4)
Itsa Legend 132 [4] (3m 110y, Newb, GS, Feb 9)
Izita Star 132 [3] (2m 1f, Bang, Gd, Sep 11)
Jaunty Flight 147 [1] (2m 5f, Newb, Sft, Mar 29)
Jayo (FR) 143 [1] (2m 3f, Cork, Yld, Mar 23)
Jazz Messenger (FR) 156 [2] (2m, Gowr, Sft, Feb 14)
Jered (IRE) 163 [1] (2m, Dowr, Sft, Oct 31)
Jessies Dream (IRE) 142 [1] (2m 4f, Punc, Hvy, Apr 30)
Jimmy Ber (IRE) 132 [6] (2m, Fair, Gd, Apr 13)
Joe Jo Star 137 [1] (2m, Hayd, Gd, May 9)
Jubilant Note (IRE) 142 [3] (2m 3f, Lime, Gd, Jun 13)
Judge Roy Bean (IRE) 139 [2] (2m 2f, Fair, Sft, Nov 29)
Jumbo Rio (IRE) 147 [1] (2m, Punc, Sft, May 2)
Junior 143 [1] (2m 4f, Sand, Sft, Dec 5)
Kahuna (IRE) 143 [1] (2m, Slig, Hvy, Aug 6)
Kalahari King (FR) 147 [4] (2m 110y, Chel, GS, Mar 11)
Kalderon (GER) 149 [4] (2m 4f, Live, Gd, Apr 5)
Kangaroo Court (IRE) 138 [2] (2m 3f 110y, Asco, GS, Jan 17)
Karabak (FR) 156 [2] (2m 5f, Chel, GS, Mar 11)
Kasbah Bliss (FR) 173 [2] (3m, Chel, GS, Mar 13)
Katchit (IRE) 167 [1] (2m 110y, Chel, GS, Mar 11)
Katies Tuitor 150 [1] (2m 1f 110y, Mark, Gd, Sep 27)
Kawagino (IRE) 152 [2] (2m 5f, Kemp, Sft, Jan 12)
Kayf Aramis 139 [2] (3m, Chel, Gd, Apr 16)
Kazal (FR) 167 [3] (3m, Chel, GS, Mar 13)
Kempes (IRE) 146 [2] (2m, Punc, Sft, Apr 28)
Kennel Bridge 136 [1] (2m 4f, Punc, Sft, Dec 31)
Khachaturian (IRE) 133 [1] (2m 4f, Bang, Gd, Oct 11)
Khyber Kim 147 [2] (2m 110y, Newb, GS, Nov 29)
Kicks For Free (IRE) 150 [6] (3m 110y, Live, Gd, Apr 3)
Kilbeggan Blade 136 [1] (3m, Towc, Sft, Jan 18)
Kimberlite King (IRE) 138 [3] (2m, Naas, Sft, Feb 22)
King's Revenge 134 [3] (2m 110y, Chel, Sft, Nov 16)
Kirbybroguelantern (IRE) 140 [1] (2m 4f, Naas, Hvy, Oct 25)
Knockara Beau (IRE) 148 [5] (2m 5f, Chel, GS, Mar 11)
Krackatara 132 (2m 3f, Devo, GS, Mar 27)
La Vecchia Scuola (IRE) 137 [1] (2m, Ayr, Gd, Apr 19)
Labelthou (FR) 134 [8] (2m 4f 110y, Chel, GS, Mar 14)
Laertes 136 [2] (2m 6f 110y, Utto, Gd, Mar 15)
Lake Legend 133 [2] (2m 4f 110y, Leic, Sft, Nov 30)
Larkwing (IRE) 144 [2] (2m, Tipp, Hvy, Oct 5)
Leading Run (IRE) 133 [4] (2m 4f, Cork, Gd, Mar 22)
Lease Lend 133 (2m 4f, Hayd, GS, Mar 22)
Leg Spinner (IRE) 133 [4] (3m, Galw, Gd, Aug 3)
Leo's Lucky Star (USA) 141 [3] (2m 110y, Chel, Gd, Oct 17)
Leslingtaylor (IRE) 132 [5] (2m 1f 110y, Mark, Gd, Sep 27)
Lethal Weapon (IRE) 134 [1] (2m, Leop, Sft, Dec 26)
Liberate 142 [1] (3m, Hayd, Gd, May 10)
Lightning Strike (GER) 141 [6] (2m 4f 110y, Chel, GS, Mar 14)
Line Ball (IRE) 142 [2] (2m 4f, Nava, Hvy, Dec 20)
Liskennett (IRE) 135 [2] (3m, Chel, GS, Mar 14)
Little Josh (IRE) 132 [1] (2m 4f, Chep, Hvy, Feb 12)
Lodge Lane (IRE) 150 [1] (2m 3f, Devo, Sft, Jan 1)
Lough Derg (FR) 161 [2] (2m 3f 110y, Asco, Hvy, Feb 14)
Lounaos (FR) 147 [4] (2m, Leop, Yld, Jan 27)
Lucky At Last (IRE) 137 [2] (2m 4f, Bell, Yld, Jul 4)
Lucky Wish 134 [3] (2m, Galw, Yld, Jul 30)
Lurgan (IRE) 133 [1] (2m 6f, Thur, Hvy, Jan 29)
Lyceum (GER) 148 [4] (2m 1f, Tral, Sft, Sep 30)
Lyes Green 135 [3] (2m 5f, Kemp, Sft, Jan 12)
Mad Max (IRE) 144 [1] (2m 3f, Newb, Sft, Jan 14)
Made In Taipan (IRE) 151 [2] (2m 4f, Naas, Hvy, Oct 25)
Mahonia (IRE) 138 [2] (2m 1f, Chel, GS, Dec 12)
Majestic Concorde (IRE) 139 [6] (2m, Galw, Gd, Jul 31)
Mamlook (IRE) 137 [4] (3m 110y, Live, Gd, Apr 3)
Marodima (FR) 140 [1] (2m, Worc, Gd, May 11)
Massasoit (IRE) 151 [1] (2m 4f, Live, Sft, Oct 26)
Master Of Arts (USA) 133 [1] (2m 110y, Donc, GS, Jan 31)
Medermit (FR) 151 [2] (2m 110y, Chel, GS, Mar 10)
Megans Joy (IRE) 141 [1] (2m, Tipp, Hvy, Oct 5)
Mendo 133 [4] (2m 4f 110y, Chel, GS, Mar 14)
Merrydown (IRE) 142 [6] (3m 110y, Live, Gd, Apr 3)
Micheal Flips (IRE) 145 [1] (2m, Kemp, Gd, Dec 26)
Michel Le Bon (FR) 140 [1] (3m 110y, Newb, Gd, Mar 20)
Mick The Man (IRE) 139 [3] (2m 4f, Punc, Sft, Feb 18)
Middleton Dene (IRE) 141 [4] (2m 5f, Kemp, GS, Nov 12)
Midnight Chase 136 [2] (2m 4f 110y, Chel, GS, Mar 13)
Midnight Sail 138 [6] (3m, Chel, GS, Mar 13)
Mighty Man (FR) 166 [2] (3m 110y, Live, Gd, Apr 2)
Mikael D'haguenet (FR) 158 [1] (2m 4f, Punc, Hvy, May 1)
Miko De Beauchene (FR) 140 [2] (3m, Chel, GS, Mar 13)

Millenium Royal (FR) 146 [5] (3m, Chel, GS, Jan 26)
Mirage Dore (FR) 145 [2] (2m 5f, Chel, GS, Mar 11)
Missis Potts 137 [6] (2m 110y, Newb, GS, Feb 9)
Mister Gloss (IRE) 136 [1] (2m 6f, Sand, Sft, Dec 6)
Mister Hight (FR) 146 [5] (2m, Punc, Gd, Apr 22)
Mister Mcgoldrick 133 [5] (2m 4f 110y, Sout, GS, Feb 17)
Mister Top Notch (IRE) 151 [1] (2m, Fair, Yld, Mar 24)
Mobaasher (USA) 161 [3] (3m 1f, Asco, GS, Dec 20)
Mon Michel (IRE) 135 [3] (2m 110y, Sand, Sft, Jan 5)
Montana Slim (IRE) 143 [1] (2m 4f, Punc, Sft, Apr 29)
Moore's Law (USA) 134 [4] (2m 3f, Cork, Yld, Mar 23)
Moscow Catch (IRE) 134 (3m 110y, Live, Gd, Apr 3)
Mourad (IRE) 150 [3] (2m 1f, Chel, GS, Mar 13)
Mourne Rambler (IRE) 144 [1] (2m 6f, Fair, Gd, Apr 14)
Mr Bennett (IRE) 133 [3] (3m, Chep, Hvy, Dec 6)
Mr Gardner (IRE) 150 [1] (2m 5f, Newb, Gd, Mar 20)
Mr Thriller (FR) 142 [6] (2m 110y, Chel, GS, Mar 11)
Mr Warbucks (IRE) 137 [3] (2m 4f, Tipp, Yld, Jun 18)
Muirhead (IRE) 163 [5] (2m 110y, Chel, GS, Mar 10)
Mutual Friend (USA) 140 [1] (2m, Sout, Gd, May 10)
My Way De Solzen (FR) 162 [5] (3m, Chel, GS, Mar 13)
Naiad Du Misselot (FR) 136 [1] (2m 4f 110y, Chel, GS, Mar 14)
Nakai (FR) 141 [2] (2m 5f, Kemp, GS, Nov 12)
Nenuphar Collonges (FR) 147 [4] (3m 110y, Live, Gd, Apr 4)
Newmill (IRE) 142 [4] (2m, Gowr, Sft, Feb 14)
Nicanor (FR) 142 [4] (2m 4f, Fair, Gd, Apr 13)
Ninetieth Minute (IRE) 150 [1] (2m 5f, Chel, GS, Mar 11)
No One Tells Me 136 [2] (2m, Cork, Yld, Aug 22)
No Refuge (IRE) 153 [3] (3m 1f, Weth, GF, Nov 1)
Noble Alan (GER) 142 [1] (2m, Ayr, Gd, Apr 18)
Noble Prince (GER) 138 [1] (2m 4f, Punc, Hvy, May 19)
Northern Alliance (IRE) 137 [4] (2m, Galw, Yld, Jul 30)
Numide (FR) 141 [4] (2m, Asco, GS, Dec 20)
Nycteos (FR) 139 [1] (2m 5f, Kemp, Sft, Jan 12)
Oceana Gold 138 [4] (2m 1f, Bang, Gd, Aug 15)
Ogee 148 [3] (3m, Hayd, Gd, May 9)
Oligarch Society (IRE) 136 [1] (2m, Lime, Hvy, Mar 15)
On Raglan Road (IRE) 148 [2] (2m 4f, Live, Sft, Oct 26)
On The Way Out (IRE) 141 [9] (2m, Leop, Yld, Jan 11)
One Gulp 147 [1] (3m 110y, Kemp, Gd, Nov 26)
Onnix (FR) 140 [2] (2m 5f, Kemp, Gd, Dec 26)
Osako D'airy (FR) 139 [3] (2m 110y, Sand, Sft, Feb 2)
Osana (FR) 166 [2] (2m 110y, Chel, GS, Mar 11)
Oscar Dan Dan (IRE) 142 [7] (2m 4f, Punc, Hvy, May 1)
Oscar Looby (IRE) 135 [1] (2m, Gowr, Yld, Mar 21)
Oscar Rebel (IRE) 142 [7] (2m 6f, Fair, Gd, Apr 14)
Our Bob (IRE) 133 [4] (2m 2f, Leop, Sft, Feb 10)
Over Sixty 136 [4] (2m 4f, Chel, GS, Mar 10)
Overclear 134 [3] (2m 1f, Devo, GS, Feb 10)
Overserved 147 [2] (2m 4f 110y, Utto, GS, May 3)
P'tit Fute (FR) 153 [1] (3m, Leop, Yld, Jan 11)
Pandorama (IRE) 157 [1] (2m 4f, Nava, Hvy, Nov 23)
Pasco (SWI) 133 [1] (2m 110y, Newb, GS, Feb 9)
Pause And Clause (IRE) 143 [3] (2m 5f, Chel, GS, Mar 11)
Peacock (FR) 135 [2] (2m 3f 110y, Asco, Gd, Feb 16)
Pearl King (IRE) 142 [5] (2m, Hayd, Gd, May 10)
Penn Da Benn (FR) 138 [1] (2m 6f, Winc, Sft, Feb 14)
Pennek (FR) 139 [3] (3m, Chel, GS, Mar 12)
Penzance 141 [6] (2m, Sand, Gd, Apr 26)
Peplum (FR) 133 [3] (2m 4f, Punc, Gd, Apr 24)
Perce Rock 150 [1] (2m 3f, Lime, Sft, Dec 27)
Persian City (IRE) 135 [4] (2m 4f, Lime, Sft, Apr 5)
Personal Column 135 [7] (2m 1f, Chel, GS, Mar 14)
Pesoto (FR) 136 (2m 3f, Naas, Sft, Nov 8)
Pettifour (IRE) 159 [2] (3m, Punc, Hvy, Apr 30)
Pierrot Lunaire (USA) 155 [2] (2m 4f, Font, Gd, Feb 22)
Pigeon Island 146 [1] (2m, Kemp, Gd, Feb 23)
Planet Of Sound 134 [2] (2m, Hayd, GS, Mar 22)
Poquelin (FR) 143 [1] (2m, Sand, Gd, Apr 26)
Powerstation (IRE) 157 [3] (3m, Chel, GS, Mar 12)
Premier Dane (IRE) 142 [3] (2m 3f 110y, Donc, Gd, Feb 2)
Premier Victory (IRE) 145 [1] (2m 4f, Ball, Sft, May 24)
Presenting Copper (IRE) 138 [1] (2m 1f, Chel, Hvy, Jan 24)
Pride Of Dulcote (FR) 153 [2] (3m, Chel, GS, Mar 13)
Prince Taime (FR) 142 [2] (2m 4f 110y, Utto, Gd, May 2)
Procas De Thaix (FR) 134 [4] (2m 110y, Newb, Gd, Feb 28)
Prudent Honour (IRE) 140 [2] (2m 3f, Naas, Sft, Mar 14)
Psycho (IRE) 149 [2] (2m, Fair, Gd, Apr 13)
Punchestowns (FR) 172 [2] (3m, Chel, GS, Mar 12)
Punjabi 167 [2] (2m, Punc, Hvy, May 1)
Quartino 136 [1] (2m, List, Sft, Sep 18)
Quartz De Thaix (FR) 134 [1] (2m 1f, Bang, Hvy, Feb 6)
Quevega (FR) 159 [3] (2m, Punc, Hvy, May 1)
Quickbeam (IRE) 136 [1] (2m 6f 110y, Stra, Sft, Apr 20)
Quinmaster (USA) 136 [5] (2m, Punc, Gd, Apr 22)
Quiscover Fontaine (FR) 142 [1] (2m, Lime, Hvy, Jan 28)
Qulinton (FR) 137 [1] (2m 4f, Chep, Gd, Apr 4)
Quwetwo 134 [1] (2m 110y, Donc, Sft, Jan 23)
Raise Your Heart (IRE) 149 [1] (2m 2f, Cork, Sft, Aug 23)
Rare Bob (IRE) 135 [3] (3m, Fair, Sft, Mar 22)
Raslan 142 [1] (2m 6f, Newt, GF, Aug 23)
Rathmore Castle (IRE) 140 (2m 4f, Cork, Yld, Jul 11)
Razor Royale (IRE) 136 [7] (2m 4f 110y, Chel, GS, Mar 14)
Realt Dubh (IRE) 134 [7] (2m 5f, Chel, GS, Mar 11)
Red Moloney (USA) 146 [6] (2m 110y, Chel, GS, Mar 10)
Reel Charmer 133 [2] (3m 110y, Ayr, Gd, Apr 17)
Refinement (IRE) 149 [2] (3m, Punc, Gd, Apr 24)
Reve De Sivola (FR) 144 [6] (2m 1f, Chel, GS, Mar 13)
Ring The Boss (IRE) 148 [2] (2m 4f, Punc, Yld, Apr 26)
Ringaroses 142 [2] (2m 3f 110y, Donc, Gd, Feb 2)
Rippling Ring (SAF) 146 [5] (2m 110y, Chel, GS, Mar 11)
River Canon (FR) 135 [3] (2m 4f, Lime, Sft, Apr 5)
River Liane (FR) 150 [3] (2m, Leop, Hvy, Jan 25)
Riverside Theatre 145 [3] (2m, Punc, Sft, Apr 28)
Roberto Goldback (IRE) 146 [5] (2m 4f, Punc, Hvy, May 1)
Rocco's Hall (IRE) 146 [2] (3m, Punc, Hvy, Apr 30)
Royal Paradise (FR) 138 [4] (2m 6f, Leop, Hvy, Jan 25)
Royal Rationale (IRE) 136 [1] (2m 3f, Newt, Gd, May 18)
Safari Run (IRE) 134 [2] (2m 1f, Sedg, GS, Apr 29)
Salford City (IRE) 143 [2] (2m, Punc, Gd, Apr 22)
Sam Adams (IRE) 139 [2] (3m, Punc, Hvy, Apr 29)
Sanglote (FR) 133 [2] (2m, List, Sft, Sep 18)
Santia 137 (2m 6f, Newt, GF, Aug 23)
Sarteano (FR) 133 [1] (2m, Fair, Gd, Apr 12)
Saticon 135 [3] (2m 110y, Chel, GS, Mar 11)
Scavenger 140 (2m 6f, Thur, Hvy, Jan 17)
Schelm (GER) 134 [8] (2m, Galw, Gd, Jul 31)
Schindler's Gold (IRE) 133 [2] (2m 6f, Nava, Yld, Sep 27)
Scriptwriter (IRE) 134 [5] (2m 3f 110y, Asco, GS, Jan 17)
Secret Tune 140 [2] (2m, Ayr, Gd, Apr 18)

See U Bob (IRE) 134[1] (2m 1f, Kill, Sft, May 10)
Sentry Duty (FR) 153[1] (2m, Asco, GS, Dec 20)
Serabad (FR) 147[1] (2m 4f, Live, Sft, Nov 23)
Serpentaria 143[1] (2m 4f, Cork, Gd, Mar 22)
Sesenta (IRE) 143[1] (2m 4f, Punc, Sft, May 2)
Shakervilz (FR) 153[1] (2m 4f, Nava, Hvy, Dec 14)
Shalone 143[1] (2m 5f, Kemp, GS, Nov 12)
Shatabdi (IRE) 136[3] (2m 3f 110y, Sand, Gd, Apr 26)
Shirley Casper (IRE) 139[2] (2m 2f, Punc, Sft, May 2)
Shoreacres (IRE) 138[7] (2m 110y, Chel, GS, Mar 10)
Show Blessed (IRE) 134[1] (2m 3f, Naas, Sft, Aug 3)
Siegemaster (IRE) 140[4] (3m, Chel, GS, Mar 14)
Silk Drum (IRE) 134[1] (2m 110y, Donc, Sft, Jan 23)
Silk Hall (UAE) 136[5] (2m 110y, Live, Gd, Apr 3)
Silver Jaro (FR) 140[1] (2m 1f, Chel, GS, Mar 14)
Silverhand (IRE) 139[5] (2m, Punc, Sft, Apr 28)
Sir Overbury 135[2] (3m, Leop, Hvy, Jan 13)
Sizing Europe (IRE) 168[1] (2m, Leop, Yld, Jan 27)
Ski Sunday 143[2] (2m 110y, Live, Gd, Apr 2)
Sky Hall (IRE) 139[1] (2m 3f, Naas, Sft, Oct 12)
Snap Tie (IRE) 158[7] (2m 110y, Chel, GS, Mar 10)
Solstice Knight (IRE) 134[4] (2m 4f, Punc, Hvy, Apr 30)
Solwhit (FR) 167[1] (2m, Punc, Hvy, May 1)
Somersby (IRE) 147[3] (2m 110y, Chel, GS, Mar 10)
Son Of Flicka 134[2] (2m 110y, Hayd, GS, Jan 17)
Son Of Oscar (IRE) 137[1] (2m 4f, Cork, Gd, May 2)
Songe (FR) 154[1] (2m 110y, Hayd, Gd, Jan 17)
Sonnyanjoe (IRE) 138[7] (3m, Chel, GS, Jan 26)
Souffleur 147[2] (3m, Hayd, GS, Nov 22)
Sound Accord (IRE) 134[2] (3m, Hayd, GS, Feb 16)
Splurge (IRE) 137[2] (2m, Wexf, Yld, Mar 17)
Sporazene (IRE) 152[1] (2m 1f, Bang, GF, Aug 16)
Sports Line (IRE) 139[1] (2m, Naas, Sft, Mar 14)
Squadron 141[4] (2m 110y, Chel, Sft, Nov 16)
Stage Manager (IRE) 137[1] (2m, Galw, Gd, Jul 28)
Star De Mohaison (FR) 134[3] (3m, Chel, GS, Jan 1)
Star Of Angels 138[4] (2m 5f, Chel, GS, Mar 11)
Starluck (IRE) 147[4] (2m 1f, Chel, GS, Mar 13)
Starting Point 134[1] (2m 110y, Kels, Hvy, Jan 11)
Straw Bear (USA) 156[2] (2m 110y, Sand, Sft, Feb 2)
Streets Of Gold (IRE) 138[5] (3m, Cork, Gd, May 15)
Sublimity (FR) 165[1] (2m, Leop, Yld, Dec 29)
Sullumo (GER) 140[3] (3m 1f 110y, Chel, Sft, Nov 15)
Sunnyhillboy (IRE) 144[1] (2m 4f, Live, Gd, Apr 2)
Superior Wisdom (IRE) 139[2] (3m 110y, Live, Gd, Apr 5)
Sweet Kiln (IRE) 140[2] (3m, Gowr, Hvy, Jan 24)
Sweetheart 140[2] (3m, Asco, GS, Jan 17)
Synchronised (IRE) 133[1] (3m 1f, Hayd, Sft, Feb 14)
Take The Breeze (FR) 136[1] (2m, Utto, Hvy, Feb 14)
Takeroc (FR) 149[2] (2m, Ayr, Gd, Apr 19)
Tarablaze 141[1] (3m 1f, Hayd, Sft, Feb 14)
Taravada 138[2] (2m 3f, Cork, Sft, Apr 12)
Tasheba 135[3] (2m 3f 110y, Sand, GF, Apr 25)
Tataniano (FR) 148[1] (2m 1f, Chel, Gd, Apr 16)
Tawaagg 134[1] (2m, Galw, Sft, Jul 29)
Tazbar (IRE) 155[1] (3m, Chel, GS, Apr 17)
Temoin 144[6] (2m 6f, Sand, Sft, Feb 2)
Ten Fires (GER) 133[2] (2m 2f, Fair, Hvy, Oct 11)
Tharawaat (IRE) 140 (2m, Punc, Sft, May 2)
The Bishop Looney (IRE) 136[2] (2m 4f, Thur, Sft, Feb 26)
The God Of Love (USA) 134[6] (2m, Gowr, GF, Jun 21)
The Jazz Musician (IRE) 139[1] (2m 110y, Chep, Sft, Mar 24)
The Last Hurrah (IRE) 134[4] (2m, Leop, Yld, Mar 2)
The Midnight Club (IRE) 150[3] (3m, Chel, GS, Mar 13)
The Nightingale (FR) 142[1] (2m 3f 110y, Taun, GS, Nov 27)
The Package 139[2] (2m 110y, Sand, Gd, Feb 15)
The Polomoche (IRE) 148[1] (2m 5f 110y, Ayr, Gd, Apr 18)
The Tother One (IRE) 149[3] (3m 110y, Live, Gd, Apr 4)
Theatre Belle 134[2] (2m 4f, Ayr, Sft, Jan 10)
Theatre Girl 141[2] (2m 110y, Donc, Gd, Jan 26)
Themoonandsixpence (IRE) 135[1] (2m 6f, Kill, Yld, Jul 15)
Thetwincamdrift (IRE) 137[2] (3m 1f, Hayd, Sft, Feb 14)
Tighten Your Belt (IRE) 133[2] (3m 1f, Weth, Sft, Jan 31)
Tilabay (IRE) 139[1] (2m, List, Sft, Sep 14)
Time Electric (IRE) 137[5] (2m, Galw, Yld, Jul 30)
Time For Rupert (IRE) 148[1] (3m 110y, Live, Gd, Apr 3)
Time To Sell (IRE) 136[2] (2m 2f, Cork, Hvy, Jan 5)
Tisfreetdream (IRE) 134[1] (2m 6f 110y, Utto, Gd, Mar 28)
Torphichen 134[1] (2m 110y, Sand, Sft, Feb 13)
Toshi (USA) 133 (2m 1f, Bang, Gd, Sep 11)
Tot Of The Knar 136[4] (3m, Chel, GS, Jan 1)
Trafford Lad 146[2] (2m 4f, Naas, Sft, Jan 6)
Tranquil Sea (IRE) 146[1] (2m 4f, Punc, Gd, Apr 25)
Trenchant 144[4] (2m 4f, Live, GS, Apr 4)
Trompette (USA) 137 (2m 110y, Sand, Sft, Jan 5)
Trouble At Bay (IRE) 143[6] (2m 4f, Live, Gd, Apr 3)
Truckers Delight (IRE) 136[1] (2m, Punc, Sft, Apr 28)
Turpin Green (IRE) 141[7] (3m, Chel, Hvy, Jan 24)
Uimhiraceathair (IRE) 135[2] (2m 4f, Punc, Hvy, May 19)
United (GER) 151[3] (2m 4f, Live, GS, Apr 4)
Ursis (FR) 140[1] (2m 6f, Mark, Gd, Sep 28)
Valain (IRE) 140[1] (2m, Ffos, Gd, Aug 28)
Vale Of Avocia (IRE) 135[1] (2m 4f, List, Hvy, Sep 16)
Venalmar 148[2] (2m 4f 110y, Chel, GS, Mar 14)
Very Cool 134[2] (3m, Hayd, Gd, May 10)
Vic Venturi (IRE) 133[4] (2m 4f, Punc, Sft, Feb 18)
Victram (IRE) 133[4] (2m 110y, Sand, Gd, Mar 8)
Viking Rebel (IRE) 136[3] (3m 110y, Pert, GS, Apr 24)
Viper 148[1] (2m 4f, Muss, GF, Dec 8)
Vital Plot (USA) 138 (2m, Leop, Yld, Jan 11)
Voler La Vedette (IRE) 135[1] (2m 2f, Punc, Sft, May 2)
Walkon (FR) 152[1] (2m 110y, Live, Gd, Apr 2)
Warne's Way (IRE) 140[2] (2m 3f 110y, Asco, Sft, Jan 19)
Watchurhouse (IRE) 133[1] (2m 4f, Tram, Sft, Dec 31)
Weapon's Amnesty (IRE) 154[1] (3m, Chel, GS, Mar 13)
Wellforth (IRE) 135[1] (3m, Bell, Hvy, Aug 27)
Wendel (GER) 144[1] (2m 3f 110y, Asco, Hvy, Feb 14)
Western Charmer (IRE) 140[8] (2m 4f, Punc, Hvy, May 1)
Whatuthink (IRE) 155[2] (3m, Gowr, Hvy, Jan 22)
Wheresben (IRE) 138[4] (3m, Leop, Hvy, Jan 13)
Whinstone Boy (IRE) 136[1] (2m 3f, Lime, Hvy, Jan 28)
Whispered Promises (USA) 148[3] (2m 1f, Chel, GS, Jan 26)
Whiteoak (IRE) 153[2] (2m, Winc, Sft, Feb 14)
Wichita Lineman (IRE) 155[2] (2m 4f 110y, Chel, GS, Jan 1)
Wild Cane Ridge (IRE) 148[1] (2m 4f, Ayr, Hvy, Jan 2)
Wingman (IRE) 137[1] (2m 110y, Newb, GS, Feb 9)
Won In The Dark (IRE) 161[2] (2m, Leop, Yld, Dec 29)
Woodbine Willie (IRE) 140[6] (2m 4f, Punc, Sft, Feb 18)
Woolcombe Folly (IRE) 143[1] (2m 110y, Stra, Gd, May 24)
Working Title (IRE) 135[3] (2m 3f 110y, Asco, GS, Jan 17)
Your Amount (IRE) 133[1] (2m 4f, Live, Gd, May 9)
Zaynar (FR) 154[1] (2m 1f, Chel, GS, Mar 13)

TOPSPEED TEN TO FOLLOW Dave Edwards

Cape Tribulation (Malcolm Jefferson)

Cape Tribulation owes his place in this list to a wide-margin success over an extended three miles at Doncaster in January when a time figure of 150 was exceptional for a novice. On soft ground he annihilated the opposition and looks a performer brimming with potential. Not disgraced when fading into fifth in the Albert Bartlett won by Weapon's Amnesty at the Festival in March, Cape Tribulation was a shade disappointing when favourite but well beaten at Aintree behind Bouggler. A subsequent lack-lustre effort on the Flat means he has questions to answer but with ease in the ground he may deliver a rousing response. ■

Chapoturgeon (Paul Nicholls)

On the Thursday of the Cheltenham Festival there were three chases run over 2m 5f and while direct time comparisons can mislead this is less likely at the Festival where in the main contests are truly run. Of the three, the best time was recorded by Chapoturgeon in the Jewson Novices Handicap – including some smart splits – and after applying the Topspeed modus operandi he emerged just 4lb 'inferior' to Imperial Commander who prevailed in the Ryanair. All this was no mean feat for a novice and although he was a beaten favourite in two subsequent starts it could be that he is best when fresh. ■

Cockney Trucker (Phillip Hobbs)

Cockney Trucker did not enjoy the rewards his efforts deserved last season with just one win, at Newbury in November, but that could change in the months ahead. Decent ground is a pre-requisite and although that was in short supply last winter he still performed with credit. He had shown fair form in bumpers and reached the frame on his hurdling bow at Cheltenham in October prior to his Prestbury Park win the following month. For one so inexperienced he ran a blinder to finish third in the County Hurdle there in March which represented a personal best on the clock. He is likely to be upped in trip this season which should play to his strengths. ■

Killyglen (Howard Johnson)

A progressive hurdler in Ireland, Killyglen made a successful chasing debut at Carlisle in October and then joined his current handler for whom he won at Ayr in January with the minimum of fuss. Proven on testing ground, he ran below expectations at Cheltenham when pulled up. They were always going a stride too quick for him in the RSA Chase where he made a couple of mistakes but he showed his true colours at Liverpool three weeks later registering a clear-cut victory in the Mildmay. Relatively lightly-raced, he seems to handle any ground and could be a candidate for the Hennessy. ■

Master Of Arts (David Pipe)

A prolific winner on the Flat for Sir Mark Prescott, Master Of Arts was purchased for a sizeable 310,000 guineas and made a successful hurdling debut at Doncaster in January comfortably accounting for smart yardstick Copper Bleu. Pitched into the Triumph Hurdle despite his relative inexperience, he jumped indifferently and never threatened. It later transpired that he had suffered an injury during the race and his season was curtailed. Restored to fitness, he will be keen to make up for lost time and could take high rank among the two-mile hurdlers. ■

Micheal Flips (Andrew Turnell)

Micheal Flips cost current connections £200,000 after winning a point-to-point over three miles in Ireland and then showed his versatility with a silky success over an extended two miles on his hurdling debut at Stratford. At Kempton on Boxing Day he recorded a faster time than Christmas Hurdle winner Archibald when lifting a valuable novice over course and distance, dipping over threes seconds inside standard. He appeared to be left flat-footed when tenth in the Supreme Novices but then finished leaden legged when upped in trip at Aintree. Hopefully he will strengthen up and prove competitive in some major contests this season. ■

Somersby (Henrietta Knight)

Highly regarded by his trainer, Somersby has shown plenty already but the best is hopefully still to come. Although running green he convincingly landed a Kempton novice hurdle in November and was then a shade disappointing when a well-beaten third behind Karabak at Ascot. Timewise he produced an outstanding effort in Cheltenham's Supreme Novices Hurdle, finishing a close third behind Go Native and Medermit. Outpaced, he made up ground, hand-over-fist, in the closing stages and the time of the race was only fractionally slower than the Champion run over trip and track later in the day. ■

The Polomoche (Nicky Henderson)

The Polomoche shrugged off the anchor of top-weight at Stratford with ease on his seasonal return in October and after the handicapper had his say finished a respectable fifth behind stable-mate Sentry Duty in a hot Ascot handicap a week later. He did not run again until the Coral Cup in March and was surprisingly made favourite and never looked likely to land a telling blow. Pulled up on a recovery mission at Aintree, he was fitted with a cross-noseband at Ayr later in the month when he made all under top-weight. He is likely to be novice chasing this term and has the attributes necessary to more than pay his way. ■

Tricky Trickster (Paul Nicholls)

Fore some reason long-distances races tend to be slowly or at best moderately-run affairs, which surely defies the purpose, but the four-mile National Hunt Chase at last season's Cheltenham Festival bucked the trend as it turned into a war of attrition and Tricky Trickster emerged a clear cut winner. A Topspeed 142 was thoroughly deserved. Tricky Trickster in the main jumped well and powered clear on the run in to win handsomely. Firm ground prevented his participation in the Scottish National at Ayr and he subsequently changed hands for £320,000 and is now with Paul Nicholls. He has only had six starts under rules but will still be entered for the Gold Cup. He may also target the Grand National, one of the few top races missing from the Champion trainer's CV. ■

Wessex King (Henry Daly)

Patience is a virtue and Wessex King is the embodiment of this trainer who could reap dividends from this promising sort. Progressive last season, Wessex King broke the ice at Taunton in November and then chased home Teenage Idol at Wetherby the following month. He ran a race full of promise at Kempton in February beating all but King Brex and was then put away for the season. Effective at two miles, he should stay further and if switched to fences could be placed to advantage by his shrewd handler. ■

TOPSPEED TOP 20 CHASERS

Master Minded (FR) 185 [1] (2m, Chel, GS, Mar 13)
Voy Por Ustedes (FR) 181 [1] (2m 4f, Live, Gd, Apr 4)
Denman (IRE) 178 [1] (3m 2f 110y, Chel, GS, Mar 14)
Tamarinbleu (FR) 174 [1] (2m 1f, Asco, Sft, Jan 19)
Kauto Star (FR) 173 [2] (3m 2f 110y, Chel, GS, Mar 14)
Neptune Collonges (FR) 173 [1] (3m 1f, Punc, Yld, Apr 23)
Notre Pere (FR) 172 [1] (3m 1f, Punc, Hvy, Apr 29)
Twist Magic (FR) 169 [1] (2m, Sand, Gd, Apr 25)
Tidal Bay (IRE) 168 [1] (2m, Chel, GS, Mar 11)
Snowy Morning (IRE) 167 [2] (3m 1f, Punc, Yld, Apr 23)
Halcon Genelardais (FR) 166 [4] (3m 2f 110y, Chel, GS, Mar 14)
Noland 165 [1] (2m 4f, Punc, Hvy, Dec 9)
The Listener (IRE) 164 [2] (2m 4f, Punc, Hvy, Dec 9)
Andreas (FR) 161 [1] (2m, Sand, Gd, Apr 26)
Ashley Brook (IRE) 161 [1] (2m 1f 110y, Devo, GS, Nov 4)
Jack The Giant (IRE) 161 [1] (2m 1f, Asco, Gd, Nov 22)
Snoopy Loopy (IRE) 161 [2] (2m 4f 110y, Hunt, GS, Dec 11)
Barbers Shop 160 [2] (2m 4f 110y, Chel, Sft, Nov 15)
Exotic Dancer (FR) 160 [3] (3m 2f 110y, Chel, GS, Mar 13)
Imperial Commander (IRE) 160 [1] (2m 4f 110y, Chel, Sft, Nov 15)

TOPSPEED TO 20 HURDLERS

Inglis Drever 175 [1] (3m, Chel, GS, Mar 13)
Kasbah Bliss (FR) 174 [2] (3m, Chel, GS, Mar 13)
Kazal (FR) 168 [3] (3m, Chel, GS, Mar 13)
Solwhit (FR) 167 [1] (2m, Punc, Hvy, May 1)
Punjabi 166 [2] (2m, Punc, Hvy, May 1)
Blazing Bailey 163 [4] (3m, Chel, GS, Mar 13)
My Way De Solzen (FR) 162 [5] (3m, Chel, GS, Mar 13)
Sizing Europe (IRE) 162 [4] (2m, Punc, Hvy, May 1)
Catch Me (GER) 161 [1] (2m 5f, Nava, Hvy, Feb 16)
Fiveforthree (IRE) 161 [1] (3m, Punc, Hvy, Apr 30)
Sublimity (FR) 160 [1] (2m, Leop, Yld, Dec 29)
Aitmatov (GER) 159 [6] (3m, Chel, GS, Mar 13)
Captain Cee Bee (IRE) 159 [1] (2m 110y, Chel, GS, Mar 11)
Binocular (FR) 158 [1] (2m 110y, Live, Gd, Apr 3)
Quevega (FR) 158 [3] (2m, Punc, Hvy, May 1)
Ashkazar (FR) 157 [1] (2m, Winc, Sft, Feb 14)
Katchit (IRE) 157 [2] (2m, Kemp, Gd, Oct 19)
Brave Inca (IRE) 156 [1] (2m, Leop, Hvy, Jan 25)
Osana (FR) 156 [2] (2m 110y, Chel, GS, Mar 11)
Snap Tie (IRE) 156 [1] (2m, Kemp, Gd, Oct 19)

▲ **Denman**

CHELTENHAM PREVIEW Colin Boag

Last season Paul Nicholls came within a whisker of landing all four Championship races at the Cheltenham Festival. What a yankee the Gold Cup, Champion Hurdle, Champion Chase and World Hurdle would make, and why not add in the Ryanair to turn it into a Canadian?

It's a brave person who'd bet against Paul Nicholls winning the Gold Cup, as with **Kauto Star** and Denman he seems to have things pretty well covered. The Irish are sure to latch on to Cooldine and Notre Pere, their young pretenders, but I just can't see them threatening the Nicholls pair. As to which of the British runners will win? It's hard to call and to some extent it will be ground dependent: if it came up soft that would threaten Kauto Star's prospects, but would be right up Denman's street. I'm a Kauto man and he'll do for me. The main thing for racing is that they both get to post safely and at the top of their game.

The Champion Hurdle is a much more open affair, with Hurricane Fly made favourite on the basis of his outstanding novice form. The problem for me is that he needs to find more than a stone of improvement to be in Champion Hurdle class, and in a vintage year he'd need to find even more than that – the bookies believe that he will, but I think there's a bit of the 'talking horse' about him. The other Irish challenger, Solwhit, looks a more realistic contender to me, but I still believe that this race will be won by a home challenger. The two for me are **Binocular** and Celestial Halo. The latter loves Cheltenham, while some believe that the Henderson runner doesn't. I think that view is based on sketchy data, and my money's on Nicky Henderson getting Binocular to prove himself a Champion next March.

The Champion Chase looks to be a certainty for **Master Minded** if Paul Nicholls gets him to post safe and sound. The only worry is that last year at Cheltenham the horse didn't seem to be quite at his imperious best, although that was still plenty good enough. Paul clearly has a plan to address this and I just can't see Master Minded being beaten.

The World Hurdle also looks to be at Paul's mercy as **Big Buck's** looks to be the one to beat. Of the ones that he beat last year, I just can't see any logical reason why they should overturn the form, and the danger, if there is one, will probably come from some of those being stepped up in trip. It might be stretching Katchit to think that he'll stay three miles, but Alan King has another possible in Karabak. He'll stay, but can he bridge the gap in class to get close to Big Buck's?

The Ryanair has rapidly become the fifth Championship race of the Festival, and it has an altogether more open feel to it. Last season's renewal saw the second favourite, Imperial Commander, see off the market leader, **Voy Por Ustedes**, and these two seem likely to be prominent in the market next-time around. I strongly fancy Voy Por Ustedes to turn the tables if they meet again, as he made a most uncharacteristic jumping error four from home and did wonderfully well to get back into the race at all. If you want an outsider at a big price, consider **JackThe Giant** and hope for good ground.

Just thinking about the Cheltenham Festival whets the appetite for the best week's racing anywhere in the world. It would be wonderful if we have found a winner or two – or even more – but whatever happens, try to get to Prestbury Park for March, or if you can't, then make sure you're by your television with your betting boots on! ■

▲ **Kauto Star**

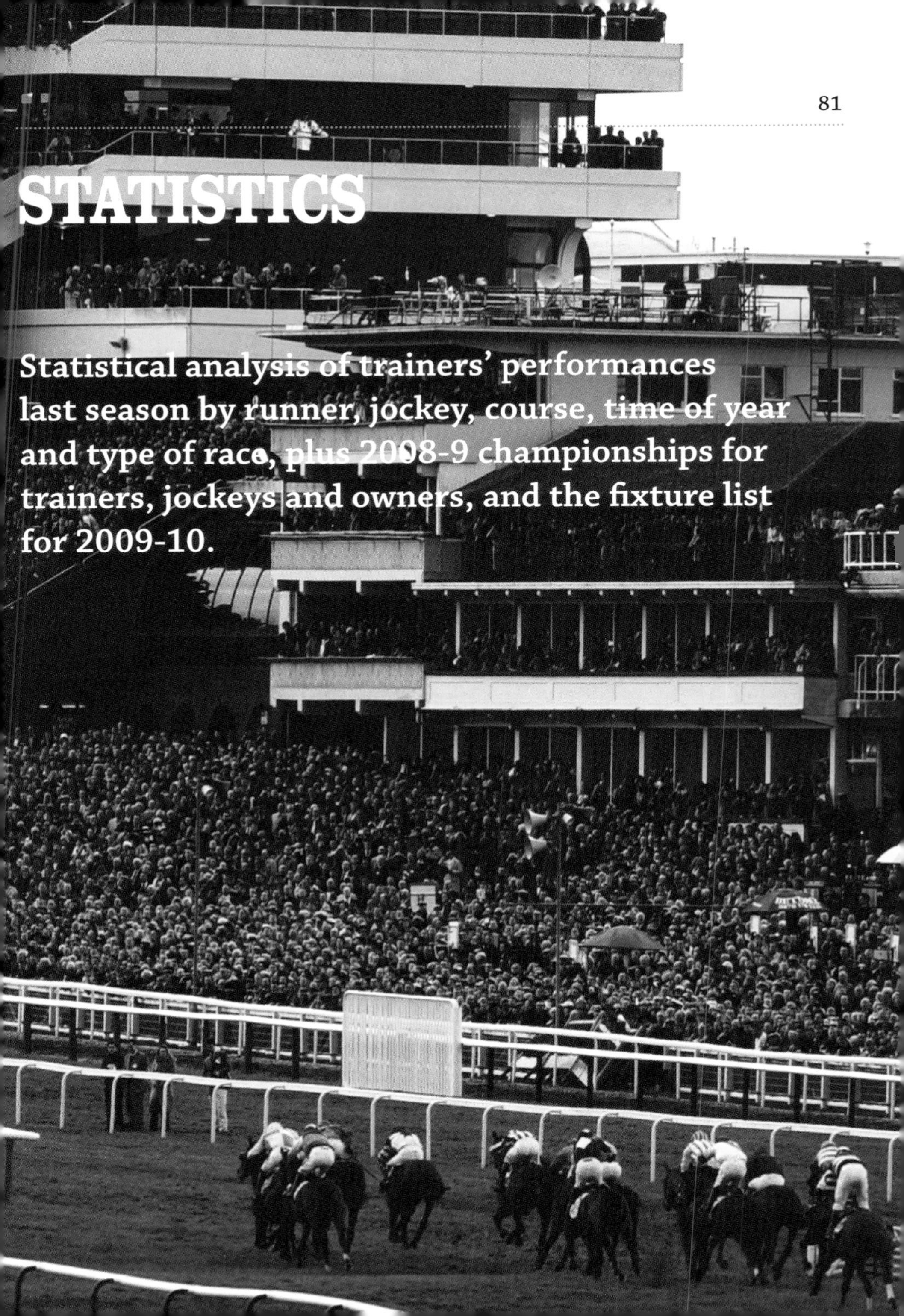

STATISTICS

Statistical analysis of trainers' performances last season by runner, jockey, course, time of year and type of race, plus 2008-9 championships for trainers, jockeys and owners, and the fixture list for 2009-10.

PETER BOWEN

LITTLE NEWCASTLE, PEMBROKES

	No. of Hrs	Races Run	1st	2nd	3rd	Unpl	Per cent	£1 Level Stake
NH Flat	*13*	*19*	*2*	*0*	*2*	*15*	*10.5*	*-8.00*
Hurdles	*58*	*189*	*22*	*19*	*17*	*131*	*11.6*	*-35.26*
Chases	*40*	*184*	*20*	*19*	*23*	*122*	*10.9*	*-40.32*
Totals	**88**	**392**	**44**	**38**	**42**	**268**	**11.2**	**-83.58**
07-08	*88*	*432*	*42*	*35*	*44*	*311*	*9.7*	*-128.76*
06-07	*71*	*355*	*72*	*44*	*49*	*190*	*20.3*	*+29.96*

BY MONTH

NH Flat	W-R	Per cent	£1 Level Stake
May	0-3	0.0	-3.00
June	1-3	33.3	+5.00
July	0-0	0.0	0.00
August	1-2	50.0	+1.00
September	0-2	0.0	-2.00
October	0-1	0.0	-1.00
November	0-1	0.0	-1.00
December	0-4	0.0	-4.00
January	0-3	0.0	-3.00
February	0-0	0.0	0.00
March	0-0	0.0	0.00
April	0-0	0.0	0.00

Hurdles	W-R	Per cent	£1 Level Stake
May	8-29	27.6	+10.99
June	2-16	12.5	+3.50
July	4-19	21.1	+20.50
August	3-21	14.3	-8.25
September	1-14	7.1	-9.00
October	0-15	0.0	-15.00
November	1-18	5.6	-12.50
December	1-16	6.3	-14.50
January	0-10	0.0	-10.00
February	2-8	25.0	+22.00
March	0-15	0.0	-15.00
April	0-8	0.0	-8.00

Chases	W-R	Per cent	£1 Level Stake
May	3-13	23.1	+0.43
June	0-20	0.0	-20.00
July	1-14	7.1	+3.00
August	4-13	30.8	+6.75
September	2-17	11.8	+4.00
October	1-20	5.0	-16.75
November	1-19	5.3	+15.00
December	2-20	10.0	-13.38
January	1-13	7.7	-9.75
February	1-4	25.0	+1.00
March	3-15	20.0	+0.38
April	1-16	6.3	-11.00

Totals	W-R	Per cent	£1 Level Stake
May	11-45	24.4	+8.42
June	3-39	7.7	-11.50
July	5-33	15.2	+23.50
August	8-36	22.2	-0.50
September	3-33	9.1	-7.00
October	1-36	2.8	-32.75
November	2-38	5.3	+1.50
December	3-40	7.5	-31.88
January	1-26	3.8	-22.75
February	3-12	25.0	+23.00
March	3-30	10.0	-14.62
April	1-24	4.2	-19.00

DISTANCE

Hurdles	W-R	Per cent	£1 Level Stake
2m-2m3f	4-48	8.3	-10.00
2m4f-2m7f	14-90	15.6	-11.51
3m+	4-51	7.8	-13.75

Chases	W-R	Per cent	£1 Level Stake
2m-2m3f	2-17	11.8	-9.75
2m4f-2m7f	9-76	11.8	-18.50
3m+	9-91	9.9	-12.07

RACE CLASS

	W-R	Per cent	£1 Level Stake
Class 1	5-43	11.6	+30.25
Class 2	4-25	16.0	+9.50
Class 3	6-87	6.9	-55.63
Class 4	21-166	12.7	-54.83
Class 5	4-50	8.0	-13.25
Class 6	4-21	19.0	+0.38

FIRST TIME OUT

	W-R	Per cent	£1 Level Stake
Bumpers	1-13	7.7	-10.00
Hurdles	8-49	16.3	+12.00
Chases	4-26	15.4	-13.32
Totals	13-88	14.8	-11.32

JOCKEYS

	W-R	Per cent	£1 Level Stake
T J O'Brien	13-95	13.7	-15.89
S E Durack	11-102	10.8	-9.44
Donal Devereux	7-45	15.6	-6.50
Bernie Wharfe	6-55	10.9	-14.75
P J Brennan	2-7	28.6	+15.50
Richard Johnson	2-15	13.3	+1.00
A P McCoy	1-16	6.3	-12.25
Jamie Moore	1-16	6.3	-12.25
O Dayman	1-28	3.6	-16.00

COURSE RECORD

	Total W-R	Non-Hndcps Hurdles	Non-Hndcps Chases	Hndcps Hurdles	Hndcps Chases	NH Flat	Per cent	£1 Level Stake
Nton Abbot	7-31	1-9	1-3	1-9	2-7	2-3	22.6	+3.13
Cartmel	5-13	3-3	1-1	1-6	0-3	0-0	38.5	+0.86
Uttoxeter	4-25	0-7	0-1	4-10	0-6	0-1	16.0	+14.00
Folkestone	3-6	0-0	1-2	1-3	1-1	0-0	50.0	+13.38
Sedgefield	3-9	2-3	0-2	0-0	1-4	0-0	33.3	+2.50
Mrket Rsn	3-16	0-1	0-0	1-5	2-10	0-0	18.8	+16.50
Kelso	2-7	0-2	1-1	1-4	0-0	0-0	28.6	-3.57
Plumpton	2-12	0-2	0-0	1-2	1-8	0-0	16.7	+8.00
Aintree	2-18	0-0	0-4	2-6	0-8	0-0	11.1	-6.00
Haydock	1-3	0-0	1-1	0-2	0-0	0-0	33.3	+31.00
Newcastle	1-4	0-0	0-0	0-1	1-3	0-0	25.0	+1.00
Warwick	1-4	0-0	1-1	0-2	0-1	0-0	25.0	-1.13
Catterick	1-5	0-1	1-1	0-1	0-1	0-1	20.0	-1.50
Ascot	1-6	0-2	0-0	1-2	0-2	0-0	16.7	+11.00
Wetherby	1-6	0-1	0-1	0-1	1-2	0-1	16.7	-2.75
Fakenham	1-7	0-1	0-1	0-1	1-4	0-0	14.3	+2.00
Exeter	1-12	0-3	1-3	0-2	0-4	0-0	8.3	-4.50
Cheltenham	1-13	0-1	1-5	0-4	0-3	0-0	7.7	-9.75
Huntingdon	1-13	0-1	0-2	1-5	0-5	0-0	7.7	-9.25
Stratford	1-14	0-2	0-3	1-4	0-4	0-1	7.1	-1.00
Southwell	1-16	0-4	1-4	0-3	0-4	0-1	6.3	-3.00
Bangor	1-18	0-3	0-4	1-8	0-3	0-0	5.6	-10.50

HENRY DALY

STANTON LACY, SHROPSHIRE

	No. of Hrs	Races Run	1st	2nd	3rd	Unpl	Per cent	£1 Level Stake
NH Flat	*17*	*24*	*2*	*1*	*1*	*20*	*8.3*	*-17.00*
Hurdles	*41*	*131*	*14*	*18*	*20*	*79*	*10.7*	*+1.96*
Chases	*33*	*127*	*15*	*12*	*23*	*77*	*11.8*	*-41.17*
Totals	**73**	**282**	**31**	**31**	**44**	**176**	**11.0**	**-56.21**
07-08	*72*	*235*	*27*	*32*	*39*	*137*	*11.5*	*-54.63*
06-07	*68*	*252*	*37*	*39*	*32*	*144*	*14.7*	*-12.49*

BY MONTH

NH Flat	W-R	Per cent	£1 Level Stake
May	2-4	50.0	+3.00
June	0-0	0.0	0.00
July	0-0	0.0	0.00
August	0-0	0.0	0.00
September	0-0	0.0	0.00
October	0-1	0.0	-1.00
November	0-6	0.0	-6.00
December	0-2	0.0	-2.00
January	0-2	0.0	-2.00
February	0-5	0.0	-5.00
March	0-2	0.0	-2.00
April	0-2	0.0	-2.00

Hurdles	W-R	Per cent	£1 Level Stake
May	2-10	20.0	+8.75
June	0-5	0.0	-5.00
July	1-2	50.0	+1.75
August	0-0	0.0	0.00
September	0-1	0.0	-1.00
October	0-18	0.0	-18.00
November	4-20	20.0	+26.50
December	0-14	0.0	-14.00
January	1-15	6.7	-3.00
February	2-11	18.2	+27.33
March	3-19	15.8	-11.38
April	1-16	6.3	-10.00

Chases	W-R	Per cent	£1 Level Stake
May	0-4	0.0	-4.00
June	1-3	33.3	+6.00
July	0-0	0.0	0.00
August	0-0	0.0	0.00
September	1-2	50.0	+3.00
October	0-8	0.0	-8.00
November	4-29	13.8	-10.26
December	2-19	10.5	-9.00
January	2-11	18.2	+9.50
February	2-18	11.1	-9.17
March	2-20	10.0	-9.00
April	1-13	7.7	-10.25

Totals	W-R	Per cent	£1 Level Stake
May	4-18	22.2	+7.75
June	1-8	12.5	+1.00
July	1-2	50.0	+1.75
August	0-0	0.0	0.00
September	1-3	33.3	+2.00
October	0-27	0.0	-27.00
November	8-55	14.5	+10.24
December	2-35	5.7	-25.00
January	3-28	10.7	+4.50
February	4-34	11.8	+13.16
March	5-41	12.2	-22.38
April	2-31	6.5	-22.25

DISTANCE

Hurdles	W-R	Per cent	£1 Level Stake
2m-2m3f	10-74	13.5	+33.33
2m4f-2m7f	3-39	7.7	-17.88
3m+	1-18	5.6	-13.50

Chases	W-R	Per cent	£1 Level Stake
2m-2m3f	6-30	20.0	-0.59
2m4f-2m7f	3-36	8.3	-21.67
3m+	6-61	9.8	-18.92

RACE CLASS

	W-R	Per cent	£1 Level Stake
Class 1	0-21	0.0	-21.00
Class 2	3-27	11.1	-9.75
Class 3	6-85	7.1	-53.17
Class 4	17-120	14.2	+37.12
Class 5	4-23	17.4	-7.92
Class 6	1-6	16.7	-1.50

FIRST TIME OUT

	W-R	Per cent	£1 Level Stake
Bumpers	2-17	11.8	-10.00
Hurdles	3-30	10.0	+0.75
Chases	3-26	11.5	-12.67
Totals	8-73	11.0	-21.92

JOCKEYS

	W-R	Per cent	£1 Level Stake
Richard Johnson	14-98	14.3	-30.42
Andrew Tinkler	8-69	11.6	+11.50
Mark Bradburne	6-65	9.2	-4.13
Robert Thornton	1-1	100.0	+3.33
P J Brennan	1-2	50.0	+2.50
Mr O Greenall	1-7	14.3	+1.00

COURSE RECORD

	Total W-R	Non-Hndcps Hurdles	Non-Hndcps Chases	Hndcps Hurdles	Hndcps Chases	NH Flat	Per cent	£1 Level Stake
Hereford	5-14	1-3	1-3	0-1	2-5	1-2	35.7	+6.24
Ludlow	5-24	1-9	0-3	2-5	1-5	1-2	20.8	+8.83
Huntingdon	3-14	2-4	1-2	0-2	0-6	0-0	21.4	-2.00
Bangor	3-20	2-8	0-0	0-3	1-5	0-4	15.0	+22.75
Taunton	2-9	2-4	0-2	0-2	0-1	0-0	22.2	+14.00
Warwick	2-9	0-1	0-1	0-0	2-4	0-3	22.2	+8.00
Ascot	2-10	1-1	0-2	0-1	1-4	0-2	20.0	+0.50
Doncaster	2-14	0-4	2-2	0-2	0-4	0-2	14.3	-4.67
Uttoxeter	2-15	1-6	0-1	0-3	1-4	0-1	13.3	+9.00
Perth	1-3	0-0	1-2	0-0	0-1	0-0	33.3	-0.25
Fakenham	1-5	0-2	0-2	0-0	1-1	0-0	20.0	+2.50
Aintree	1-7	1-2	0-0	0-2	0-3	0-0	14.3	+6.00
Haydock	1-11	0-0	0-2	0-4	1-4	0-1	9.1	-2.50
Towcester	1-25	1-12	0-3	0-3	0-5	0-2	4.0	-22.63

TOM GEORGE

SLAD, GLOUCS

	No. of Hrs	Races Run	1st	2nd	3rd	Unpl	Per cent	£1 Level Stake
NH Flat	*13*	*17*	*0*	*4*	*1*	*12*	*0.0*	*-17.00*
Hurdles	*38*	*100*	*17*	*11*	*2*	*70*	*17.0*	*-33.25*
Chases	*25*	*110*	*20*	*26*	*14*	*50*	*18.2*	*-13.01*
Totals	**61**	**227**	**37**	**41**	**17**	**132**	**16.3**	**-63.26**
07-08	*61*	*237*	*32*	*25*	*23*	*157*	*13.5*	*-10.90*
06-07	*57*	*222*	*30*	*16*	*25*	*151*	*13.5*	*-48.11*

BY MONTH

NH Flat	W-R	Per cent	£1 Level Stake
May	0-1	0.0	-1.00
June	0-2	0.0	-2.00
July	0-0	0.0	0.00
August	0-1	0.0	-1.00
September	0-0	0.0	0.00
October	0-3	0.0	-3.00
November	0-4	0.0	-4.00
December	0-1	0.0	-1.00
January	0-2	0.0	-2.00
February	0-0	0.0	0.00
March	0-0	0.0	0.00
April	0-3	0.0	-3.00

Hurdles	W-R	Per cent	£1 Level Stake
May	1-8	12.5	-3.00
June	1-6	16.7	-3.80
July	1-3	33.3	0.00
August	1-2	50.0	-0.20
September	1-4	25.0	-1.00
October	2-5	40.0	-0.43
November	3-15	20.0	-6.16
December	1-5	20.0	-0.50
January	1-12	8.3	-9.00
February	1-15	6.7	-8.50
March	3-15	20.0	+6.33
April	1-10	10.0	-7.00

Chases	W-R	Per cent	£1 Level Stake
May	2-12	16.7	+3.00
June	3-6	50.0	+3.12
July	1-5	20.0	-2.00
August	1-8	12.5	-4.75
September	0-2	0.0	-2.00
October	1-7	14.3	-2.50
November	3-18	16.7	-4.88
December	1-13	7.7	-6.00
January	1-10	10.0	-6.25
February	5-9	55.6	+20.00
March	1-11	9.1	-8.25
April	1-9	11.1	-2.50

Totals	W-R	Per cent	£1 Level Stake
May	3-21	14.3	-1.00
June	4-14	28.6	-2.68
July	2-8	25.0	-2.00
August	2-11	18.2	-5.95
September	1-6	16.7	-3.00
October	3-15	20.0	-5.93
November	6-37	16.2	-15.04
December	2-19	10.5	-7.50
January	2-24	8.3	-17.25
February	6-24	25.0	+11.50
March	4-26	15.4	-1.92
April	2-22	9.1	-12.50

DISTANCE

Hurdles	W-R	Per cent	£1 Level Stake
2m-2m3f	9-58	15.5	-15.25
2m4f-2m7f	5-26	19.2	-11.07
3m+	3-16	18.8	-6.93

Chases	W-R	Per cent	£1 Level Stake
2m-2m3f	7-32	21.9	+0.25
2m4f-2m7f	9-44	20.5	-9.76
3m+	4-34	11.8	-3.50

RACE CLASS

	W-R	Per cent	£1 Level Stake
Class 1	2-20	10.0	-2.50
Class 2	3-20	15.0	-4.75
Class 3	7-41	17.1	-1.67
Class 4	20-93	21.5	-19.84
Class 5	5-46	10.9	-27.51
Class 6	0-7	0.0	-7.00

FIRST TIME OUT

	W-R	Per cent	£1 Level Stake
Bumpers	0-13	0.0	-13.00
Hurdles	6-27	22.2	+1.69
Chases	2-21	9.5	-15.89
Totals	8-61	13.1	-27.20

JOCKEYS

	W-R	Per cent	£1 Level Stake
P J Brennan	19-104	18.3	-34.67
A P McCoy	6-18	33.3	+16.08
Denis O'Regan	3-13	23.1	+2.50
Sam Thomas	2-20	10.0	-11.00
A Coleman	1-1	100.0	+11.00
Dominic Elsworth	1-1	100.0	+3.50
Charlie Huxley	1-2	50.0	+3.00
R P Flint	1-3	33.3	+1.00
Richard Johnson	1-7	14.3	-1.00
Andrew Thornton	1-8	12.5	-5.25
Felix De Giles	1-12	8.3	-10.43

COURSE RECORD

	Total W-R	Non-Hndcps Hurdles	Non-Hndcps Chases	Hndcps Hurdles	Hndcps Chases	NH Flat	Per cent	£1 Level Stake
Nton Abbot	4-15	1-5	1-2	0-0	2-7	0-1	26.7	-3.59
Lingfield	3-6	1-1	0-1	0-0	2-4	0-0	50.0	+0.99
Towcester	3-10	2-4	0-2	1-1	0-2	0-1	30.0	-0.43
Newbury	3-17	0-6	0-1	2-2	1-7	0-1	17.6	-2.67
Kempton	2-5	0-0	1-1	0-1	1-3	0-0	40.0	+10.50
Mrket Rsn	2-5	1-1	0-0	0-1	1-3	0-0	40.0	+1.00
Huntingdon	2-6	1-2	1-2	0-1	0-0	0-1	33.3	+3.00
Chepstow	2-10	2-6	0-1	0-0	0-2	0-1	20.0	-1.50
Wincanton	2-11	1-3	0-0	1-2	0-6	0-0	18.2	+6.00
Plumpton	1-2	0-1	0-0	0-0	1-1	0-0	50.0	+4.00
Doncaster	1-3	0-1	0-0	0-0	1-2	0-0	33.3	+0.75
Kelso	1-3	0-0	0-0	0-0	1-1	0-2	33.3	+1.50
Sandown	1-3	0-0	0-0	0-1	1-2	0-0	33.3	+4.00
Fontwell	1-5	0-0	0-0	0-1	1-4	0-0	20.0	-1.75
Ludlow	1-6	0-2	0-1	0-1	1-1	0-1	16.7	+0.50
Sedgefield	1-6	0-1	0-1	0-2	1-2	0-0	16.7	-2.50
Stratford	1-8	0-2	0-0	0-0	1-6	0-0	12.5	+3.00
Uttoxeter	1-8	0-1	0-0	1-3	0-4	0-0	12.5	-5.00
Aintree	1-9	0-3	1-2	0-1	0-2	0-1	11.1	-2.50
Taunton	1-9	0-4	0-0	0-3	1-2	0-0	11.1	-5.50
Worcester	1-9	0-1	0-2	1-3	0-1	0-2	11.1	-6.80
Hereford	1-10	0-4	0-0	1-3	0-3	0-0	10.0	-8.27
Southwell	1-10	1-8	0-0	0-1	0-1	0-0	10.0	-7.00

NICK GIFFORD

FINDON, W SUSSEX

	No. of Hrs	Races Run	1st	2nd	3rd	Unpl	Per cent	£1 Level Stake
NH Flat	*9*	*19*	*4*	*4*	*4*	*7*	*21.1*	*-4.50*
Hurdles	*31*	*92*	*9*	*11*	*15*	*57*	*9.8*	*-40.08*
Chases	*13*	*59*	*12*	*6*	*11*	*30*	*20.3*	*+23.16*
Totals	**45**	**170**	**25**	**21**	**30**	**94**	**14.7**	**-21.42**
07-08	*44*	*141*	*18*	*13*	*15*	*95*	*12.8*	*-34.54*
06-07	*38*	*118*	*14*	*14*	*14*	*76*	*11.9*	*-38.97*

BY MONTH

NH Flat	W-R	Per cent	£1 Level Stake
May	0-1	0.0	-1.00
June	0-0	0.0	0.00
July	0-0	0.0	0.00
August	0-0	0.0	0.00
September	0-0	0.0	0.00
October	0-0	0.0	0.00
November	0-3	0.0	-3.00
December	1-5	20.0	-2.25
January	0-1	0.0	-1.00
February	3-5	60.0	+6.75
March	0-3	0.0	-3.00
April	0-1	0.0	-1.00

Hurdles	W-R	Per cent	£1 Level Stake
May	0-3	0.0	-3.00
June	0-2	0.0	-2.00
July	0-0	0.0	0.00
August	0-0	0.0	0.00
September	0-2	0.0	-2.00
October	2-6	33.3	+10.00
November	3-12	25.0	+1.00
December	1-19	5.3	-17.33
January	1-12	8.3	-8.25
February	2-22	9.1	-4.50
March	0-10	0.0	-10.00
April	0-4	0.0	-4.00

Chases	W-R	Per cent	£1 Level Stake
May	2-5	40.0	+5.50
June	0-4	0.0	-4.00
July	0-1	0.0	-1.00
August	1-1	100.0	+7.00
September	1-2	50.0	+9.00
October	1-6	16.7	-2.25
November	2-9	22.2	+9.00
December	1-7	14.3	0.00
January	0-7	0.0	-7.00
February	0-3	0.0	-3.00
March	2-8	25.0	+6.00
April	2-6	33.3	+3.91

Totals	W-R	Per cent	£1 Level Stake
May	2-9	22.2	+1.50
June	0-6	0.0	-6.00
July	0-1	0.0	-1.00
August	1-1	100.0	+7.00
September	1-4	25.0	+7.00
October	3-12	25.0	+7.75
November	5-24	20.8	+7.00
December	3-31	9.7	-19.58
January	1-20	5.0	-16.25
February	5-30	16.7	-0.75
March	2-21	9.5	-7.00
April	2-11	18.2	-1.09

DISTANCE

Hurdles	W-R	Per cent	£1 Level Stake
2m-2m3f	6-58	10.3	-28.08
2m4f-2m7f	3-30	10.0	-8.00
3m+	0-4	0.0	-4.00

Chases	W-R	Per cent	£1 Level Stake
2m-2m3f	3-21	14.3	+8.00
2m4f-2m7f	6-25	24.0	+12.25
3m+	3-13	23.1	+2.91

RACE CLASS

	W-R	Per cent	£1 Level Stake
Class 1	0-14	0.0	-14.00
Class 2	1-7	14.3	-2.50
Class 3	6-45	13.3	-5.67
Class 4	10-74	13.5	-14.75
Class 5	6-22	27.3	+16.75
Class 6	2-8	25.0	-1.25

FIRST TIME OUT

	W-R	Per cent	£1 Level Stake
Bumpers	1-9	11.1	-6.00
Hurdles	4-25	16.0	-0.50
Chases	1-11	9.1	-6.00
Totals	6-45	13.3	-12.50

JOCKEYS

	W-R	Per cent	£1 Level Stake
Liam Treadwell	14-79	17.7	+2.08
Jay Pemberton	7-52	13.5	-9.75
Mr D H Dunsdon	3-12	25.0	+2.25
Mark Bradburne	1-4	25.0	+7.00

COURSE RECORD

	Total W-R	Non-Hndcps Hurdles	Non-Hndcps Chases	Hndcps Hurdles	Hndcps Chases	NH Flat	Per cent	£1 Level Stake
Fontwell	8-34	1-13	1-3	0-4	4-10	2-4	23.5	+11.50
Towcester	4-16	1-6	1-4	0-1	0-3	2-2	25.0	+6.50
Plumpton	3-20	2-7	0-0	0-5	1-6	0-2	15.0	-5.00
Sandown	2-15	1-6	0-0	1-4	0-3	0-2	13.3	-1.33
Chepstow	1-1	0-0	1-1	0-0	0-0	0-0	100.0	+0.91
Lingfield	1-3	0-1	1-2	0-0	0-0	0-0	33.3	+6.00
Warwick	1-3	1-2	0-0	0-1	0-0	0-0	33.3	+0.50
Cheltenham	1-6	1-2	0-1	0-1	0-1	0-1	16.7	+5.00
Folkestone	1-9	0-3	0-1	0-0	1-4	0-1	11.1	-2.00
Ascot	1-13	1-5	0-1	0-3	0-3	0-1	7.7	-8.50
Huntingdon	1-13	0-4	0-1	0-2	1-4	0-2	7.7	-6.00
Kempton	1-13	0-4	0-0	0-4	1-3	0-2	7.7	-5.00

HOWARD JOHNSON

BILLY ROW, CO DURHAM

	No. of Hrs	Races Run	1st	2nd	3rd	Unpl	Per cent	£1 Level Stake
NH Flat	*23*	*36*	*4*	*2*	*5*	*24*	*11.1*	*-17.63*
Hurdles	*96*	*275*	*51*	*33*	*26*	*165*	*18.5*	*-59.48*
Chases	*57*	*184*	*28*	*26*	*19*	*111*	*15.2*	*-69.19*
Totals	**153**	**495**	**83**	**61**	**50**	**300**	**16.8**	**-146.30**
07-08	*129*	*414*	*64*	*36*	*50*	*264*	*15.5*	*-69.99*
06-07	*127*	*399*	*55*	*49*	*47*	*248*	*13.8*	*-175.43*

BY MONTH

NH Flat	W-R	Per cent	£1 Level Stake	Hurdles	W-R	Per cent	£1 Level Stake
May	0-0	0.0	0.00	May	1-14	7.1	-7.00
June	0-0	0.0	0.00	June	0-1	0.0	-1.00
July	0-0	0.0	0.00	July	0-0	0.0	0.00
August	0-0	0.0	0.00	August	0-0	0.0	0.00
September	0-1	0.0	-1.00	September	2-14	14.3	+3.88
October	0-3	0.0	-3.00	October	8-32	25.0	+8.09
November	1-4	25.0	0.00	November	11-46	23.9	+1.75
December	1-4	25.0	-1.13	December	11-36	30.6	-3.18
January	0-3	0.0	-3.00	January	6-34	17.6	-9.43
February	0-6	0.0	-6.00	February	2-25	8.0	-22.50
March	1-6	16.7	-2.50	March	5-39	12.8	-11.06
April	1-9	11.1	-1.00	April	5-34	14.7	-19.03

Chases	W-R	Per cent	£1 Level Stake	Totals	W-R	Per cent	£1 Level Stake
May	0-6	0.0	-6.00	May	1-20	5.0	-13.00
June	0-0	0.0	0.00	June	0-1	0.0	-1.00
July	0-0	0.0	0.00	July	0-0	0.0	0.00
August	0-0	0.0	0.00	August	0-0	0.0	0.00
September	1-6	16.7	-2.75	September	3-21	14.3	+0.13
October	4-24	16.7	-10.11	October	12-59	20.3	-5.02
November	6-30	20.0	-9.98	November	18-80	22.5	-8.23
December	6-28	21.4	+4.75	December	18-68	26.5	+0.44
January	2-21	9.5	-14.56	January	8-58	13.8	-26.99
February	0-13	0.0	-13.00	February	2-44	4.5	-41.50
March	6-34	17.6	-13.65	March	12-79	15.2	-27.21
April	3-22	13.6	-3.90	April	9-65	13.8	-23.93

DISTANCE

Hurdles	W-R	Per cent	£1 Level Stake	Chases	W-R	Per cent	£1 Level Stake
2m-2m3f	37-151	24.5	+19.38	2m-2m3f	7-58	12.1	-29.06
2m4f-2m7f	12-88	13.6	-48.98	2m4f-2m7f	12-73	16.4	-23.86
3m+	2-36	5.6	-29.88	3m+	9-53	17.0	-16.27

RACE CLASS

	W-R	Per cent	£1 Level Stake
Class 1	1-59	1.7	-51.00
Class 2	4-41	9.8	-9.64
Class 3	14-97	14.4	-48.41
Class 4	42-210	20.0	-49.43
Class 5	20-62	32.3	+27.31
Class 6	2-26	7.7	-15.13

FIRST TIME OUT

	W-R	Per cent	£1 Level Stake
Bumpers	1-23	4.3	-15.00
Hurdles	19-84	22.6	+19.17
Chases	10-46	21.7	-7.47
Totals	30-153	19.6	-3.30

JOCKEYS

	W-R	Per cent	£1 Level Stake
Denis O'Regan	69-351	19.7	-57.21
A P McCoy	3-11	27.3	+1.50
C I Gillies	3-21	14.3	-9.53
J P O'Farrell	3-49	6.1	-34.50
Timmy Murphy	2-14	14.3	-10.44
Mr D J Oakden	1-2	50.0	+0.88
Peter Buchanan	1-5	20.0	+1.00
Dougie Costello	1-5	20.0	-1.00

COURSE RECORD

	Total W-R	Non-Hndcps Hurdles	Non-Hndcps Chases	Hndcps Hurdles	Hndcps Chases	NH Flat	Per cent	£1 Level Stake
Musselbgh	16-47	11-19	0-4	0-12	2-6	3-6	34.0	+4.31
Hexham	13-40	8-19	2-5	2-5	0-5	1-6	32.5	+29.45
Wetherby	13-70	6-32	2-9	2-12	3-13	0-4	18.6	-0.71
Carlisle	7-33	0-0	4-15	0-0	3-18	0-0	21.2	-11.45
Kelso	7-36	5-19	0-1	1-8	1-5	0-3	19.4	-13.98
Sedgefield	6-43	3-16	3-9	0-8	0-9	0-1	14.0	-27.39
Ayr	5-17	3-6	2-3	0-4	0-2	0-2	29.4	-4.08
Newcastle	4-32	2-16	1-3	0-3	1-6	0-4	12.5	-14.00
Doncaster	3-19	3-7	0-5	0-3	0-3	0-1	15.8	-1.40
Catterick	3-22	1-4	1-6	0-5	1-5	0-2	13.6	-10.93
Mrket Rsn	2-9	2-4	0-1	0-2	0-1	0-1	22.2	+12.50
Huntingdon	2-13	1-5	1-1	0-3	0-4	0-0	15.4	-5.50
Perth	1-24	1-10	0-2	0-6	0-4	0-2	4.2	-21.13
Aintree	1-26	0-9	1-5	0-3	0-8	0-1	3.8	-18.00

HENRIETTA KNIGHT

WEST LOCKINGE, OXON

	No. of Hrs	Races Run	1st	2nd	3rd	Unpl	Per cent	£1 Level Stake
NH Flat	*16*	*29*	*3*	*1*	*0*	*25*	*10.3*	*+6.00*
Hurdles	*34*	*99*	*4*	*8*	*9*	*78*	*4.0*	*-26.13*
Chases	*20*	*78*	*8*	*17*	*7*	*46*	*10.3*	*-40.13*
Totals	**57**	**206**	**15**	**26**	**16**	**149**	**7.3**	**-60.26**
07-08	*71*	*224*	*21*	*27*	*13*	*163*	*9.4*	*-90.57*
06-07	*79*	*270*	*33*	*33*	*27*	*177*	*12.2*	*-100.19*

BY MONTH

NH Flat	W-R	Per cent	£1 Level Stake
May	0-2	0.0	-2.00
June	0-0	0.0	0.00
July	0-0	0.0	0.00
August	0-0	0.0	0.00
September	0-0	0.0	0.00
October	0-1	0.0	-1.00
November	1-8	12.5	-3.00
December	1-6	16.7	+20.00
January	1-2	50.0	+2.00
February	0-3	0.0	-3.00
March	0-1	0.0	-1.00
April	0-6	0.0	-6.00

Hurdles	W-R	Per cent	£1 Level Stake
May	1-7	14.3	+34.00
June	0-5	0.0	-5.00
July	0-0	0.0	0.00
August	0-0	0.0	0.00
September	0-1	0.0	-1.00
October	0-4	0.0	-4.00
November	1-20	5.0	-16.50
December	1-16	6.3	+10.00
January	0-12	0.0	-12.00
February	1-9	11.1	-6.63
March	0-15	0.0	-15.00
April	0-10	0.0	-10.00

Chases	W-R	Per cent	£1 Level Stake
May	2-3	66.7	+5.63
June	0-5	0.0	-5.00
July	0-2	0.0	-2.00
August	0-0	0.0	0.00
September	0-0	0.0	0.00
October	0-10	0.0	-10.00
November	0-14	0.0	-14.00
December	0-11	0.0	-11.00
January	2-11	18.2	-0.75
February	2-7	28.6	+3.50
March	2-8	25.0	+0.50
April	0-7	0.0	-7.00

Totals	W-R	Per cent	£1 Level Stake
May	3-12	25.0	+37.63
June	0-10	0.0	-10.00
July	0-2	0.0	-2.00
August	0-0	0.0	0.00
September	0-1	0.0	-1.00
October	0-15	0.0	-15.00
November	2-42	4.8	-33.50
December	2-33	6.1	+19.00
January	3-25	12.0	-10.75
February	3-19	15.8	-6.13
March	2-24	8.3	-15.50
April	0-23	0.0	-23.00

DISTANCE

Hurdles	W-R	Per cent	£1 Level Stake
2m-2m3f	3-52	5.8	+18.50
2m4f-2m7f	0-37	0.0	-37.00
3m+	1-10	10.0	-7.63

Chases	W-R	Per cent	£1 Level Stake
2m-2m3f	4-24	16.7	-3.00
2m4f-2m7f	4-41	9.8	-24.13
3m+	0-13	0.0	-13.00

RACE CLASS

	W-R	Per cent	£1 Level Stake
Class 1	1-15	6.7	-11.25
Class 2	1-14	7.1	-7.00
Class 3	2-59	3.4	-50.00
Class 4	9-94	9.6	+25.63
Class 5	2-17	11.8	-10.63
Class 6	0-7	0.0	-7.00

FIRST TIME OUT

	W-R	Per cent	£1 Level Stake
Bumpers	2-16	12.5	-7.00
Hurdles	2-28	7.1	+39.00
Chases	1-13	7.7	-9.88
Totals	5-57	8.8	+22.12

JOCKEYS

	W-R	Per cent	£1 Level Stake
Sam Thomas	4-45	8.9	-3.50
A P McCoy	3-17	17.6	-7.38
Dominic Elsworth	3-27	11.1	+9.50
Paul Moloney	2-22	9.1	+22.13
Jason Maguire	1-2	50.0	+1.00
Denis O'Regan	1-11	9.1	-5.50
G Lee	1-15	6.7	-9.50

COURSE RECORD

	Total W-R	Non-Hndcps Hurdles	Non-Hndcps Chases	Hndcps Hurdles	Hndcps Chases	NH Flat	Per cent	£1 Level Stake
Ludlow	3-18	0-6	0-3	0-1	0-2	3-6	16.7	+17.00
Southwell	2-7	1-2	0-0	0-2	1-2	0-1	28.6	+0.88
Huntingdon	2-13	0-3	1-4	0-2	1-4	0-0	15.4	-6.88
Haydock	1-4	0-0	0-0	0-0	1-4	0-0	25.0	+3.00
Hereford	1-7	0-2	1-2	0-1	0-0	0-2	14.3	-3.50
Cheltenham	1-13	0-2	1-2	0-5	0-3	0-1	7.7	-9.25
Fontwell	1-14	1-10	0-0	0-3	0-1	0-0	7.1	+12.00
Towcester	1-14	1-5	0-1	0-2	0-3	0-3	7.1	+27.00
Kempton	1-15	1-1	0-2	0-5	0-5	0-2	6.7	-11.50
Ascot	1-16	0-7	1-3	0-2	0-3	0-1	6.3	-10.50

EMMA LAVELLE

WILDHERN, HANTS

	No. of Hrs	Races Run	1st	2nd	3rd	Unpl	Per cent	£1 Level Stake
NH Flat	*16*	*24*	*3*	*2*	*2*	*17*	*12.5*	*-10.50*
Hurdles	*38*	*110*	*15*	*17*	*12*	*66*	*13.6*	*-22.66*
Chases	*22*	*60*	*11*	*3*	*2*	*44*	*18.3*	*+30.41*
Totals	**62**	**194**	**29**	**22**	**16**	**127**	**14.9**	**-2.75**
07-08	*57*	*185*	*20*	*16*	*19*	*130*	*10.8*	*-85.10*
06-07	*55*	*184*	*28*	*22*	*20*	*114*	*15.2*	*+8.89*

BY MONTH

NH Flat	W-R	Per cent	£1 Level Stake
May	0-1	0.0	-1.00
June	0-0	0.0	0.00
July	0-0	0.0	0.00
August	0-0	0.0	0.00
September	0-1	0.0	-1.00
October	0-0	0.0	0.00
November	2-5	40.0	+4.50
December	0-3	0.0	-3.00
January	0-3	0.0	-3.00
February	0-3	0.0	-3.00
March	1-4	25.0	0.00
April	0-4	0.0	-4.00

Hurdles	W-R	Per cent	£1 Level Stake
May	0-9	0.0	-9.00
June	0-4	0.0	-4.00
July	0-0	0.0	0.00
August	0-5	0.0	-5.00
September	0-0	0.0	0.00
October	2-15	13.3	-8.00
November	1-12	8.3	+5.00
December	4-18	22.2	+5.10
January	2-13	15.4	-7.25
February	2-10	20.0	-1.25
March	2-13	15.4	-8.59
April	2-11	18.2	+10.33

Chases	W-R	Per cent	£1 Level Stake
May	1-9	11.1	-0.50
June	1-3	33.3	+10.00
July	0-3	0.0	-3.00
August	0-5	0.0	-5.00
September	0-0	0.0	0.00
October	4-4	100.0	+33.00
November	1-10	10.0	-1.50
December	1-9	11.1	-1.50
January	0-2	0.0	-2.00
February	0-0	0.0	0.00
March	2-7	28.6	+7.00
April	1-8	12.5	-6.09

Totals	W-R	Per cent	£1 Level Stake
May	1-19	5.3	-10.50
June	1-7	14.3	+6.00
July	0-3	0.0	-3.00
August	0-10	0.0	-10.00
September	0-1	0.0	-1.00
October	6-19	31.6	+25.00
November	4-27	14.8	+8.00
December	5-30	16.7	+0.60
January	2-18	11.1	-12.25
February	2-13	15.4	-4.25
March	5-24	20.8	-1.59
April	3-23	13.0	+0.24

DISTANCE

Hurdles	W-R	Per cent	£1 Level Stake
2m-2m3f	9-66	13.6	-17.24
2m4f-2m7f	6-33	18.2	+5.58
3m+	0-11	0.0	-11.00

Chases	W-R	Per cent	£1 Level Stake
2m-2m3f	2-13	15.4	+3.00
2m4f-2m7f	6-34	17.6	+22.50
3m+	3-13	23.1	+4.91

RACE CLASS

	W-R	Per cent	£1 Level Stake
Class 1	1-19	5.3	-2.00
Class 2	5-14	35.7	+17.25
Class 3	7-57	12.3	-25.24
Class 4	12-73	16.4	+18.74
Class 5	2-15	13.3	-5.00
Class 6	2-16	12.5	-6.50

FIRST TIME OUT

	W-R	Per cent	£1 Level Stake
Bumpers	2-16	12.5	-7.00
Hurdles	5-29	17.2	+7.50
Chases	4-17	23.5	+17.50
Totals	11-62	17.7	+18.00

JOCKEYS

	W-R	Per cent	£1 Level Stake
Jack Doyle	19-137	13.9	-11.91
Noel Fehily	4-6	66.7	+26.91
Tom Siddall	3-15	20.0	+2.75
Paul Moloney	1-3	33.3	+5.50
A P McCoy	1-7	14.3	-4.50
Timmy Murphy	1-7	14.3	-2.50

COURSE RECORD

	Total W-R	Non-Hndcps Hurdles	Non-Hndcps Chases	Hndcps Hurdles	Hndcps Chases	NH Flat	Per cent	£1 Level Stake
Kempton	5-17	3-6	0-0	0-2	2-5	0-4	29.4	+7.16
Chepstow	4-13	1-5	0-0	1-3	1-2	1-3	30.8	+5.33
Exeter	3-13	1-6	0-0	1-3	1-3	0-1	23.1	+18.50
Huntingdon	3-15	1-5	0-2	0-1	2-7	0-0	20.0	+7.00
Wincanton	2-6	0-1	0-0	0-2	1-1	1-2	33.3	+9.00
Taunton	2-7	2-4	0-2	0-0	0-1	0-0	28.6	-2.40
Folkestone	2-8	1-3	0-3	0-0	0-0	1-2	25.0	+3.00
Doncaster	1-2	1-2	0-0	0-0	0-0	0-0	50.0	+7.00
Lingfield	1-2	1-2	0-0	0-0	0-0	0-0	50.0	-0.09
Aintree	1-3	1-2	0-0	0-0	0-1	0-0	33.3	+14.00
Ludlow	1-4	0-0	1-1	0-0	0-3	0-0	25.0	+6.00
Leicester	1-5	0-1	0-0	0-0	1-4	0-0	20.0	+2.50
Sandown	1-9	1-1	0-0	0-3	0-3	0-2	11.1	-5.75
Ascot	1-11	0-5	0-1	0-3	1-1	0-1	9.1	-8.00
Stratford	1-13	0-2	0-0	0-5	1-6	0-0	7.7	0.00

DONALD McCAIN

CHOLMONDELEY, CHESHIRE

	No. of Hrs	Races Run	1st	2nd	3rd	Unpl	Per cent	£1 Level Stake
NH Flat	*36*	*50*	*4*	*10*	*5*	*31*	*8.0*	*-23.50*
Hurdles	*77*	*289*	*33*	*43*	*35*	*178*	*11.4*	*-90.91*
Chases	*39*	*144*	*25*	*20*	*15*	*84*	*17.4*	*+18.29*
Totals	**115**	**483**	**62**	**73**	**55**	**293**	**12.8**	**-96.12**
07-08	*98*	*434*	*58*	*66*	*47*	*263*	*13.4*	*-112.94*
06-07	*87*	*364*	*40*	*49*	*46*	*229*	*11.0*	*-119.29*

BY MONTH

NH Flat	W-R	Per cent	£1 Level Stake
May	0-6	0.0	-6.00
June	0-0	0.0	0.00
July	0-0	0.0	0.00
August	0-0	0.0	0.00
September	0-3	0.0	-3.00
October	0-8	0.0	-8.00
November	1-8	12.5	-4.50
December	0-3	0.0	-3.00
January	0-2	0.0	-2.00
February	0-3	0.0	-3.00
March	1-6	16.7	-3.00
April	2-11	18.2	+9.00

Hurdles	W-R	Per cent	£1 Level Stake
May	4-29	13.8	+14.00
June	0-15	0.0	-15.00
July	0-12	0.0	-12.00
August	0-12	0.0	-12.00
September	0-12	0.0	-12.00
October	2-21	9.5	-12.90
November	0-32	0.0	-32.00
December	8-33	24.2	+44.00
January	7-22	31.8	+0.46
February	2-34	5.9	-29.95
March	6-37	16.2	-8.02
April	4-30	13.3	-15.50

Chases	W-R	Per cent	£1 Level Stake
May	2-10	20.0	+0.50
June	0-4	0.0	-4.00
July	1-9	11.1	-5.50
August	0-4	0.0	-4.00
September	1-1	100.0	+10.00
October	1-15	6.7	-5.00
November	6-30	20.0	+22.50
December	6-20	30.0	+17.75
January	3-10	30.0	+3.13
February	3-18	16.7	-7.08
March	2-13	15.4	0.00
April	0-10	0.0	-10.00

Totals	W-R	Per cent	£1 Level Stake
May	6-45	13.3	+8.50
June	0-19	0.0	-19.00
July	1-21	4.8	-17.50
August	0-16	0.0	-16.00
September	1-16	6.3	-5.00
October	3-44	6.8	-25.90
November	7-70	10.0	-14.00
December	14-56	25.0	+58.75
January	10-34	29.4	+1.59
February	5-55	9.1	-40.03
March	9-56	16.1	-11.02
April	6-51	11.8	-16.50

DISTANCE

Hurdles	W-R	Per cent	£1 Level Stake
2m-2m3f	15-144	10.4	-33.63
2m4f-2m7f	13-106	12.3	-37.33
3m+	5-39	12.8	-19.95

Chases	W-R	Per cent	£1 Level Stake
2m-2m3f	3-28	10.7	-9.13
2m4f-2m7f	11-47	23.4	+19.17
3m+	11-69	15.9	+8.25

RACE CLASS

	W-R	Per cent	£1 Level Stake
Class 1	2-26	7.7	-15.25
Class 2	0-38	0.0	-38.00
Class 3	12-92	13.0	-13.72
Class 4	39-230	17.0	+15.23
Class 5	5-67	7.5	-40.88
Class 6	4-30	13.3	-3.50

FIRST TIME OUT

	W-R	Per cent	£1 Level Stake
Bumpers	2-36	5.6	-27.50
Hurdles	6-54	11.1	+19.00
Chases	1-25	4.0	-19.50
Totals	9-115	7.8	-28.00

JOCKEYS

	W-R	Per cent	£1 Level Stake
Jason Maguire	42-269	15.6	-37.62
P J Benson	7-77	9.1	-7.50
Brian Harding	3-13	23.1	+7.75
G Lee	3-23	13.0	-1.00
A P McCoy	2-11	18.2	+2.50
A P Lane	2-29	6.9	-20.00
R P McLernon	1-1	100.0	+14.00
Mr T W C Edwards	1-1	100.0	+1.25
Timmy Murphy	1-5	20.0	-1.50

COURSE RECORD

	Total W-R	Non-Hndcps Hurdles	Non-Hndcps Chases	Hndcps Hurdles	Hndcps Chases	NH Flat	Per cent	£1 Level Stake
Bangor	13-68	7-34	0-4	2-11	3-13	1-6	19.1	-4.35
Wetherby	7-33	3-10	2-3	0-10	2-6	0-4	21.2	-0.50
Ayr	6-16	2-5	1-4	1-3	2-3	0-1	37.5	+8.19
Haydock	6-23	3-7	2-3	0-6	1-6	0-1	26.1	+23.00
Uttoxeter	5-52	3-21	0-2	1-13	0-7	1-9	9.6	-36.13
Mrket Rsn	3-12	0-2	1-2	0-3	1-1	1-4	25.0	+11.00
Sedgefield	3-17	3-7	0-2	0-5	0-1	0-2	17.6	-0.67
Exeter	2-4	0-2	0-0	0-0	1-1	1-1	50.0	+16.50
Catterick	2-15	1-2	0-1	0-7	1-3	0-2	13.3	+13.00
Kelso	2-18	1-7	0-2	0-4	1-4	0-1	11.1	+4.00
Hexham	2-24	1-12	0-0	0-5	1-2	0-5	8.3	-12.09
Aintree	2-30	0-11	0-0	2-8	0-7	0-4	6.7	+1.00
Leicester	1-3	1-1	0-1	0-1	0-0	0-0	33.3	+12.00
Sandown	1-5	0-0	1-2	0-3	0-0	0-0	20.0	-2.75
Wincanton	1-5	0-1	1-1	0-3	0-0	0-0	20.0	-1.50
Perth	1-6	0-2	0-0	0-2	1-2	0-0	16.7	+5.00
Cartmel	1-11	0-5	1-2	0-2	0-2	0-0	9.1	-6.00
Hereford	1-12	1-7	0-0	0-4	0-1	0-0	8.3	-7.00
Newcastle	1-12	1-6	0-0	0-1	0-4	0-1	8.3	-7.00
Towcester	1-12	0-3	1-2	0-2	0-3	0-2	8.3	-10.33
Southwell	1-13	0-4	1-2	0-2	0-5	0-0	7.7	-9.50

GARY MOORE

LOWER BEEDING, W SUSSEX

	No. of Hrs	Races Run	1st	2nd	3rd	Unpl	Per cent	£1 Level Stake
NH Flat	10	18	3	3	2	10	16.7	-7.83
Hurdles	95	288	28	32	28	199	9.7	-102.48
Chases	34	106	16	7	12	71	15.1	-9.03
Totals	**117**	**412**	**47**	**42**	**42**	**280**	**11.4**	**-119.34**
07-08	99	395	60	55	54	224	15.2	-63.73
06-07	107	408	44	51	67	246	10.8	-65.82

BY MONTH

NH Flat	W-R	Per cent	£1 Level Stake
May	0-2	0.0	-2.00
June	0-2	0.0	-2.00
July	0-0	0.0	0.00
August	1-1	100.0	+3.50
September	0-0	0.0	0.00
October	1-1	100.0	+0.67
November	0-1	0.0	-1.00
December	0-1	0.0	-1.00
January	0-1	0.0	-1.00
February	1-6	16.7	-2.00
March	0-1	0.0	-1.00
April	0-2	0.0	-2.00

Hurdles	W-R	Per cent	£1 Level Stake
May	3-22	13.6	-10.92
June	0-7	0.0	-7.00
July	1-7	14.3	+14.00
August	1-6	16.7	+1.00
September	3-17	17.6	-4.39
October	0-14	0.0	-14.00
November	3-44	6.8	-32.80
December	5-32	15.6	-5.25
January	0-15	0.0	-15.00
February	4-39	10.3	+2.00
March	5-53	9.4	-15.38
April	3-32	9.4	-14.75

Chases	W-R	Per cent	£1 Level Stake
May	0-12	0.0	-12.00
June	1-4	25.0	-2.17
July	0-3	0.0	-3.00
August	0-0	0.0	0.00
September	0-0	0.0	0.00
October	0-4	0.0	-4.00
November	2-15	13.3	-9.95
December	1-14	7.1	-10.75
January	5-12	41.7	+32.00
February	5-13	38.5	+0.58
March	2-18	11.1	+11.25
April	0-11	0.0	-11.00

Totals	W-R	Per cent	£1 Level Stake
May	3-36	8.3	-24.92
June	1-13	7.7	-11.17
July	1-10	10.0	+11.00
August	2-7	28.6	+4.50
September	3-17	17.6	-4.39
October	1-19	5.3	-17.33
November	5-60	8.3	-43.75
December	6-47	12.8	-17.00
January	5-28	17.9	+16.00
February	10-58	17.2	+0.58
March	7-72	9.7	-5.13
April	3-45	6.7	-27.75

DISTANCE

Hurdles	W-R	Per cent	£1 Level Stake
2m-2m3f	24-239	10.0	-75.73
2m4f-2m7f	4-46	8.7	-23.75
3m+	0-3	0.0	-3.00

Chases	W-R	Per cent	£1 Level Stake
2m-2m3f	11-52	21.2	-1.58
2m4f-2m7f	3-41	7.3	-8.70
3m+	2-13	15.4	+1.25

RACE CLASS

	W-R	Per cent	£1 Level Stake
Class 1	2-29	6.9	-6.00
Class 2	4-33	12.1	+14.83
Class 3	12-109	11.0	-62.20
Class 4	18-174	10.3	-67.27
Class 5	10-56	17.9	+10.63
Class 6	1-11	9.1	-9.33

FIRST TIME OUT

	W-R	Per cent	£1 Level Stake
Bumpers	1-10	10.0	-5.50
Hurdles	6-84	7.1	-57.55
Chases	1-23	4.3	-21.17
Totals	8-117	6.8	-84.22

JOCKEYS

	W-R	Per cent	£1 Level Stake
Jamie Moore	35-258	13.6	-74.97
Philip Hide	9-91	9.9	-13.88
Andrew Glassonbury	2-18	11.1	-0.50
C Wallis	1-9	11.1	+6.00

COURSE RECORD

	Total W-R	Non-Hndcps Hurdles	Non-Hndcps Chases	Hndcps Hurdles	Hndcps Chases	NH Flat	Per cent	£1 Level Stake
Fontwell	16-78	10-31	3-8	1-21	1-11	1-7	20.5	-11.80
Plumpton	7-46	3-23	2-4	1-10	1-8	0-1	15.2	-19.32
Kempton	5-35	1-12	2-4	0-10	2-8	0-1	14.3	+3.08
Exeter	3-11	1-2	1-3	1-6	0-0	0-0	27.3	+3.50
Folkestone	3-19	1-9	1-3	0-5	1-2	0-0	15.8	-7.80
Worcester	2-3	1-1	0-0	0-0	0-1	1-1	66.7	+22.50
Wincanton	2-9	0-1	0-0	2-6	0-2	0-0	22.2	+4.50
Ascot	2-12	0-1	1-2	0-7	0-1	1-1	16.7	+9.00
Lingfield	2-12	0-1	0-1	1-5	1-5	0-0	16.7	+20.00
Hereford	1-4	0-2	0-0	1-2	0-0	0-0	25.0	+8.00
Stratford	1-14	1-3	0-0	0-8	0-3	0-0	7.1	-8.50
Cheltenham	1-15	0-4	0-1	1-8	0-2	0-0	6.7	-9.00
Huntingdon	1-18	0-2	0-3	1-9	0-3	0-1	5.6	-12.50
Sandown	1-28	0-9	0-2	1-12	0-4	0-1	3.6	-13.00

FERDY MURPHY

WEST WITTON, N YORKS

	No. of Hrs	Races Run	1st	2nd	3rd	Unpl	Per cent	£1 Level Stake
NH Flat	*12*	*18*	*1*	*1*	*0*	*16*	*5.6*	*-14.50*
Hurdles	*55*	*174*	*18*	*26*	*12*	*118*	*10.3*	*-80.25*
Chases	*60*	*236*	*26*	*30*	*23*	*156*	*11.0*	*-78.24*
Totals	**101**	**428**	**45**	**57**	**35**	**290**	**10.5**	**-172.99**
07-08	*108*	*412*	*45*	*46*	*47*	*274*	*10.9*	*-150.40*
06-07	*104*	*443*	*62*	*64*	*38*	*278*	*14.0*	*-55.17*

BY MONTH

NH Flat	W-R	Per cent	£1 Level Stake
May	0-1	0.0	-1.00
June	0-0	0.0	0.00
July	0-1	0.0	-1.00
August	0-0	0.0	0.00
September	0-1	0.0	-1.00
October	0-3	0.0	-3.00
November	0-2	0.0	-2.00
December	0-3	0.0	-3.00
January	0-1	0.0	-1.00
February	0-0	0.0	0.00
March	1-3	33.3	+0.50
April	0-3	0.0	-3.00

Hurdles	W-R	Per cent	£1 Level Stake
May	3-18	16.7	+2.50
June	1-2	50.0	0.00
July	0-2	0.0	-2.00
August	0-1	0.0	-1.00
September	0-1	0.0	-1.00
October	0-14	0.0	-14.00
November	1-28	3.6	-18.00
December	4-28	14.3	-11.42
January	2-19	10.5	-9.17
February	0-17	0.0	-17.00
March	3-22	13.6	-11.42
April	4-22	18.2	+2.25

Chases	W-R	Per cent	£1 Level Stake
May	2-8	25.0	-1.38
June	0-5	0.0	-5.00
July	1-3	33.3	+9.00
August	1-1	100.0	+5.50
September	0-1	0.0	-1.00
October	1-15	6.7	-12.75
November	4-52	7.7	-25.88
December	6-44	13.6	+3.50
January	1-27	3.7	-17.00
February	4-22	18.2	-2.32
March	2-35	5.7	-28.17
April	4-23	17.4	-2.75

Totals	W-R	Per cent	£1 Level Stake
May	5-27	18.5	+0.12
June	1-7	14.3	-5.00
July	1-6	16.7	+6.00
August	1-2	50.0	+4.50
September	0-3	0.0	-3.00
October	1-32	3.1	-29.75
November	5-82	6.1	-45.88
December	10-75	13.3	-10.92
January	3-47	6.4	-27.17
February	4-39	10.3	-19.32
March	6-60	10.0	-39.09
April	8-48	16.7	-3.50

DISTANCE

Hurdles	W-R	Per cent	£1 Level Stake
2m-2m3f	4-76	5.3	-64.67
2m4f-2m7f	9-62	14.5	-13.08
3m+	5-36	13.9	-2.50

Chases	W-R	Per cent	£1 Level Stake
2m-2m3f	10-74	13.5	-26.63
2m4f-2m7f	7-72	9.7	-33.12
3m+	9-90	10.0	-18.50

RACE CLASS

	W-R	Per cent	£1 Level Stake
Class 1	1-22	4.5	-18.75
Class 2	2-41	4.9	-29.63
Class 3	13-104	12.5	-11.24
Class 4	21-192	10.9	-81.29
Class 5	8-62	12.9	-25.08
Class 6	0-7	0.0	-7.00

FIRST TIME OUT

	W-R	Per cent	£1 Level Stake
Bumpers	1-12	8.3	-8.50
Hurdles	3-42	7.1	-13.50
Chases	3-47	6.4	-32.75
Totals	7-101	6.9	-54.75

JOCKEYS

	W-R	Per cent	£1 Level Stake
G Lee	35-286	12.2	-107.49
Keith Mercer	4-47	8.5	-25.75
Richard McGrath	2-4	50.0	+14.50
Ewan Whillans	2-18	11.1	-2.00
Tom Siddall	1-2	50.0	+15.00
Michael O'Connell	1-35	2.9	-31.25

COURSE RECORD

	Total W-R	Non-Hndcps Hurdles	Non-Hndcps Chases	Hndcps Hurdles	Hndcps Chases	NH Flat	Per cent	£1 Level Stake
Musselbgh	9-42	1-16	1-3	3-8	4-14	0-1	21.4	+5.38
Sedgefield	5-44	1-10	0-10	3-10	1-13	0-1	11.4	-19.42
Perth	4-18	1-5	1-1	2-6	0-6	0-0	22.2	+5.13
Mrket Rsn	3-12	0-2	0-2	0-1	3-7	0-0	25.0	+15.00
Kelso	3-25	2-9	1-2	0-5	0-9	0-0	12.0	-7.75
Catterick	3-26	2-6	0-5	0-3	1-9	0-3	11.5	-9.67
Cartmel	2-3	0-1	0-0	1-1	1-1	0-0	66.7	+14.50
Leicester	2-7	0-2	2-3	0-0	0-2	0-0	28.6	-0.88
Hexham	2-16	1-5	0-1	0-3	1-6	0-1	12.5	-4.25
Uttoxeter	2-16	0-7	1-1	0-3	1-3	0-2	12.5	-4.13
Haydock	2-18	0-2	1-4	0-2	0-7	1-3	11.1	-10.17
Carlisle	2-23	0-0	0-7	0-0	2-16	0-0	8.7	-17.50
Stratford	1-3	0-0	0-0	0-2	1-1	0-0	33.3	+2.50
Towcester	1-7	0-1	0-0	0-2	1-3	0-1	14.3	-3.00
Wetherby	1-10	0-0	1-2	0-3	0-5	0-0	10.0	-4.50
Huntingdon	1-14	0-3	0-1	0-3	1-7	0-0	7.1	-2.00
Ayr	1-19	0-1	0-3	1-5	0-10	0-0	5.3	-10.50
Aintree	1-24	0-4	1-3	0-7	0-8	0-2	4.2	-20.75

BRENDAN POWELL

UPPER LAMBOURN, BERKS

	No. of Hrs	Races Run	1st	2nd	3rd	Unpl	Per cent	£1 Level Stake
NH Flat	*22*	*39*	*1*	*2*	*5*	*31*	*2.6*	*-5.00*
Hurdles	*71*	*236*	*14*	*18*	*18*	*186*	*5.9*	*-113.90*
Chases	*42*	*133*	*7*	*11*	*12*	*103*	*5.3*	*-89.79*
Totals	**95**	**408**	**22**	**31**	**35**	**320**	**5.4**	**-208.69**
07-08	*118*	*490*	*53*	*43*	*50*	*344*	*10.8*	*-162.34*
06-07	*89*	*352*	*48*	*35*	*40*	*229*	*13.6*	*-87.75*

BY MONTH

NH Flat	W-R	Per cent	£1 Level Stake	**Hurdles**	W-R	Per cent	£1 Level Stake
May	0-4	0.0	-4.00	May	0-14	0.0	-14.00
June	0-2	0.0	-2.00	June	2-20	10.0	+6.00
July	0-0	0.0	0.00	July	1-9	11.1	-5.75
August	1-2	50.0	+32.00	August	1-11	9.1	-6.50
September	0-1	0.0	-1.00	September	1-15	6.7	-2.00
October	0-5	0.0	-5.00	October	2-23	8.7	-10.25
November	0-2	0.0	-2.00	November	4-35	11.4	+2.60
December	0-6	0.0	-6.00	December	3-33	9.1	-8.00
January	0-3	0.0	-3.00	January	0-22	0.0	-22.00
February	0-3	0.0	-3.00	February	0-15	0.0	-15.00
March	0-7	0.0	-7.00	March	0-17	0.0	-17.00
April	0-4	0.0	-4.00	April	0-22	0.0	-22.00

Chases	W-R	Per cent	£1 Level Stake	**Totals**	W-R	Per cent	£1 Level Stake
May	2-16	12.5	-2.67	May	2-34	5.9	-20.67
June	0-7	0.0	-7.00	June	2-29	6.9	-3.00
July	0-2	0.0	-2.00	July	1-11	9.1	-7.75
August	0-3	0.0	-3.00	August	2-16	12.5	+22.50
September	0-1	0.0	-1.00	September	1-17	5.9	-4.00
October	0-9	0.0	-9.00	October	2-37	5.4	-24.25
November	2-20	10.0	-8.38	November	6-57	10.5	-7.78
December	1-18	5.6	-5.00	December	4-57	7.0	-19.00
January	0-20	0.0	-20.00	January	0-45	0.0	-45.00
February	1-13	7.7	-10.25	February	1-31	3.2	-28.25
March	0-10	0.0	-10.00	March	0-34	0.0	-34.00
April	1-14	7.1	-11.50	April	1-40	2.5	-37.50

DISTANCE

Hurdles	W-R	Per cent	£1 Level Stake	**Chases**	W-R	Per cent	£1 Level Stake
2m-2m3f	8-137	5.8	-70.75	2m-2m3f	5-40	12.5	-18.79
2m4f-2m7f	4-80	5.0	-48.15	2m4f-2m7f	0-48	0.0	-48.00
3m+	2-19	10.5	+5.00	3m+	2-45	4.4	-23.00

RACE CLASS

	W-R	Per cent	£1 Level Stake
Class 1	0-6	0.0	-6.00
Class 2	0-20	0.0	-20.00
Class 3	7-90	7.8	-14.50
Class 4	7-201	3.5	-170.44
Class 5	7-73	9.6	-13.75
Class 6	1-18	5.6	+16.00

FIRST TIME OUT

	W-R	Per cent	£1 Level Stake
Bumpers	1-22	4.5	+12.00
Hurdles	6-52	11.5	+16.00
Chases	2-21	9.5	-7.67
Totals	9-95	9.5	+20.33

JOCKEYS

	W-R	Per cent	£1 Level Stake
Wilson Renwick	8-141	5.7	-91.63
A P McCoy	5-37	13.5	+3.18
S P Jones	3-49	6.1	-28.25
James Davies	2-56	3.6	-38.00
Mr Jeremiah McGrath	1-2	50.0	+32.00
Brian Toomey	1-3	33.3	+10.00
T J O'Brien	1-7	14.3	+2.00
J A McCarthy	1-21	4.8	-6.00

COURSE RECORD

	Total W-R	Non-Hndcps Hurdles	Non-Hndcps Chases	Hndcps Hurdles	Hndcps Chases	NH Flat	Per cent	£1 Level Stake
Exeter	3-23	2-8	1-2	0-10	0-2	0-1	13.0	+5.50
Fontwell	3-65	2-26	0-6	1-17	0-13	0-3	4.6	-30.00
Leicester	2-5	0-1	1-2	1-1	0-1	0-0	40.0	+12.63
Ascot	2-10	0-5	1-2	1-2	0-1	0-0	20.0	+10.00
Worcester	2-14	1-6	0-1	1-4	0-1	0-2	14.3	+2.25
Nton Abbot	2-15	1-7	0-2	0-3	0-1	1-2	13.3	+23.50
Huntingdon	2-30	1-9	1-4	0-3	0-8	0-6	6.7	-22.17
Carlisle	1-3	0-0	1-2	0-0	0-1	0-0	33.3	-0.25
Doncaster	1-10	1-5	0-2	0-0	0-3	0-0	10.0	-5.00
Plumpton	1-10	1-3	0-0	0-2	0-4	0-1	10.0	-7.90
Southwell	1-16	0-6	0-0	1-5	0-2	0-3	6.3	-12.25
Hereford	1-17	0-5	1-2	0-4	0-4	0-2	5.9	-4.00
Towcester	1-24	0-10	0-0	0-4	1-6	0-4	4.2	-15.00

OLIVER SHERWOOD

UPPER LAMBOURN, BERKS

	No. of Hrs	Races Run	1st	2nd	3rd	Unpl	Per cent	£1 Level Stake
NH Flat	*12*	*19*	*1*	*5*	*4*	*9*	*5.3*	*-9.00*
Hurdles	*36*	*125*	*11*	*14*	*15*	*85*	*8.8*	*-54.59*
Chases	*15*	*63*	*12*	*6*	*11*	*34*	*19.0*	*-2.17*
Totals	**51**	**207**	**24**	**25**	**30**	**128**	**11.6**	**-65.76**
07-08	*47*	*170*	*27*	*21*	*21*	*101*	*15.9*	*+3.17*
06-07	*45*	*143*	*20*	*23*	*19*	*81*	*14.0*	*-48.85*

BY MONTH

NH Flat	W-R	Per cent	£1 Level Stake
May	0-2	0.0	-2.00
June	0-0	0.0	0.00
July	0-2	0.0	-2.00
August	0-0	0.0	0.00
September	0-0	0.0	0.00
October	0-0	0.0	0.00
November	1-2	50.0	+8.00
December	0-3	0.0	-3.00
January	0-1	0.0	-1.00
February	0-2	0.0	-2.00
March	0-2	0.0	-2.00
April	0-5	0.0	-5.00

Hurdles	W-R	Per cent	£1 Level Stake
May	1-12	8.3	-7.00
June	0-5	0.0	-5.00
July	0-4	0.0	-4.00
August	0-2	0.0	-2.00
September	0-1	0.0	-1.00
October	3-14	21.4	+7.38
November	0-20	0.0	-20.00
December	4-13	30.8	+19.61
January	0-9	0.0	-9.00
February	1-19	5.3	-16.25
March	1-14	7.1	-9.67
April	1-12	8.3	-7.67

Chases	W-R	Per cent	£1 Level Stake
May	0-2	0.0	-2.00
June	0-1	0.0	-1.00
July	0-1	0.0	-1.00
August	0-3	0.0	-3.00
September	0-0	0.0	0.00
October	1-6	16.7	-4.67
November	1-10	10.0	-7.25
December	1-9	11.1	-5.00
January	1-8	12.5	-5.63
February	3-7	42.9	+11.67
March	4-10	40.0	+17.70
April	1-6	16.7	-2.00

Totals	W-R	Per cent	£1 Level Stake
May	1-16	6.3	-11.00
June	0-6	0.0	-6.00
July	0-7	0.0	-7.00
August	0-5	0.0	-5.00
September	0-1	0.0	-1.00
October	4-20	20.0	+2.71
November	2-32	6.3	-19.25
December	5-25	20.0	+11.61
January	1-18	5.6	-15.63
February	4-28	14.3	-6.58
March	5-26	19.2	+6.03
April	2-23	8.7	-14.67

DISTANCE

Hurdles	W-R	Per cent	£1 Level Stake
2m-2m3f	5-58	8.6	-26.50
2m4f-2m7f	5-49	10.2	-12.72

Chases	W-R	Per cent	£1 Level Stake
2m-2m3f	2-5	40.0	+2.75
2m4f-2m7f	3-13	23.1	+3.04

RACE CLASS

	W-R	Per cent	£1 Level Stake
Class 1	1-9	11.1	-4.67
Class 2	3-16	18.8	+9.00
Class 3	4-43	9.3	-29.80
Class 4	14-105	13.3	-20.64
Class 5	1-20	5.0	-15.67
Class 6	1-14	7.1	-4.00

FIRST TIME OUT

	W-R	Per cent	£1 Level Stake
Bumpers	1-12	8.3	-2.00
Hurdles	2-31	6.5	-22.25
Chases	1-8	12.5	-5.63
Totals	4-51	7.8	-29.88

JOCKEYS

	W-R	Per cent	£1 Level Stake
Dominic Elsworth	12-111	10.8	-46.59
S P Jones	5-48	10.4	-3.33
Mr O Greenall	3-4	75.0	+3.58
R P Flint	1-1	100.0	+1.75
Noel Fehily	1-1	100.0	+11.00
Wayne Hutchinson	1-3	33.3	+2.50
A P McCoy	1-11	9.1	-6.67

COURSE RECORD

	Total W-R	Non-Hndcps Hurdles	Non-Hndcps Chases	Hndcps Hurdles	Hndcps Chases	NH Flat	Per cent	£1 Level Stake
Hereford	5-13	1-4	1-1	2-3	0-2	1-3	38.5	+28.62
Newbury	3-8	0-2	1-1	1-4	1-1	0-0	37.5	+7.71
Fontwell	3-17	0-6	2-2	1-6	0-1	0-2	17.6	+11.67
Southwell	2-6	1-3	1-1	0-1	0-0	0-1	33.3	-2.04
Towcester	2-13	0-2	0-0	0-4	2-6	0-1	15.4	-2.50
Folkestone	1-4	1-3	0-0	0-0	0-1	0-0	25.0	+1.00
Doncaster	1-5	1-2	0-0	0-2	0-1	0-0	20.0	-2.25
Perth	1-5	0-0	1-2	0-2	0-1	0-0	20.0	-1.00
Warwick	1-5	0-3	0-0	0-0	1-2	0-0	20.0	+7.00
Carlisle	1-6	0-0	1-2	0-0	0-4	0-0	16.7	-4.80
Chepstow	1-6	0-1	0-1	0-0	1-3	0-1	16.7	-3.25
Mrket Rsn	1-6	1-2	0-0	0-2	0-1	0-1	16.7	-1.00
Exeter	1-9	0-1	0-0	1-5	0-3	0-0	11.1	-4.67
Huntingdon	1-15	1-6	0-2	0-5	0-2	0-0	6.7	-11.25

SUE SMITH

HIGH ELDWICK, W YORKS

	No. of Hrs	Races Run	1st	2nd	3rd	Unpl	Per cent	£1 Level Stake
NH Flat	16	23	6	1	0	16	26.1	+39.75
Hurdles	55	152	15	12	17	108	9.9	-19.63
Chases	57	258	27	34	34	163	10.5	-53.04
Totals	**91**	**433**	**48**	**47**	**51**	**287**	**11.1**	**-32.92**
07-08	*85*	*451*	*49*	*53*	*55*	*294*	*10.9*	*+54.11*
06-07	*96*	*439*	*51*	*50*	*54*	*284*	*11.6*	*-96.31*

BY MONTH

NH Flat	W-R	Per cent	£1 Level Stake
May	0-0	0.0	0.00
June	1-2	50.0	+24.00
July	0-2	0.0	-2.00
August	0-0	0.0	0.00
September	0-0	0.0	0.00
October	2-4	50.0	+8.25
November	1-1	100.0	+7.00
December	1-5	20.0	+4.00
January	0-3	0.0	-3.00
February	0-3	0.0	-3.00
March	1-1	100.0	+6.50
April	0-2	0.0	-2.00

Hurdles	W-R	Per cent	£1 Level Stake
May	2-13	15.4	-3.00
June	0-4	0.0	-4.00
July	0-3	0.0	-3.00
August	0-1	0.0	-1.00
September	0-5	0.0	-5.00
October	3-16	18.8	+3.00
November	2-22	9.1	+8.50
December	2-20	10.0	+13.00
January	0-17	0.0	-17.00
February	2-17	11.8	+2.50
March	3-16	18.8	-1.13
April	1-18	5.6	-12.50

Chases	W-R	Per cent	£1 Level Stake
May	1-8	12.5	-4.00
June	1-10	10.0	+1.00
July	1-6	16.7	+0.50
August	0-2	0.0	-2.00
September	0-6	0.0	-6.00
October	2-23	8.7	-13.50
November	2-35	5.7	-11.63
December	2-42	4.8	-23.50
January	2-25	8.0	-10.00
February	3-21	14.3	-7.50
March	10-46	21.7	+38.83
April	3-34	8.8	-15.25

Totals	W-R	Per cent	£1 Level Stake
May	3-21	14.3	-7.00
June	2-16	12.5	+21.00
July	1-11	9.1	-4.50
August	0-3	0.0	-3.00
September	0-11	0.0	-11.00
October	7-43	16.3	-2.25
November	5-58	8.6	+3.87
December	5-67	7.5	-6.50
January	2-45	4.4	-30.00
February	5-41	12.2	-8.00
March	14-63	22.2	+44.20
April	4-54	7.4	-29.75

DISTANCE

Hurdles	W-R	Per cent	£1 Level Stake
2m-2m3f	6-49	12.2	-8.63
2m4f-2m7f	4-60	6.7	+1.50
3m+	5-43	11.6	-12.50

Chases	W-R	Per cent	£1 Level Stake
2m-2m3f	6-54	11.1	-22.38
2m4f-2m7f	12-99	12.1	+3.00
3m+	9-105	8.6	-33.67

RACE CLASS

	W-R	Per cent	£1 Level Stake
Class 1	0-12	0.0	-12.00
Class 2	3-45	6.7	-25.75
Class 3	9-112	8.0	+2.63
Class 4	26-197	13.2	-17.54
Class 5	6-52	11.5	-15.75
Class 6	4-15	26.7	+35.50

FIRST TIME OUT

	W-R	Per cent	£1 Level Stake
Bumpers	4-16	25.0	+30.25
Hurdles	4-39	10.3	+23.50
Chases	4-36	11.1	-2.50
Totals	12-91	13.2	+51.25

JOCKEYS

	W-R	Per cent	£1 Level Stake
Tjade Collier	21-197	10.7	-23.54
Henry Oliver	8-60	13.3	+19.13
S W Byrne	6-58	10.3	-16.75
Steven Gagan	3-15	20.0	+3.00
Gary Rutherford	3-17	17.6	+21.25
Mr A E Kinirons	3-42	7.1	-15.00
Peter Buchanan	2-4	50.0	+5.50
Peter Toole	1-1	100.0	+4.50
Richard Johnson	1-1	100.0	+7.00

COURSE RECORD

	Total W-R	Non-Hndcps Hurdles	Non-Hndcps Chases	Hndcps Hurdles	Hndcps Chases	NH Flat	Per cent	£1 Level Stake
Carlisle	8-42	0-0	1-12	0-0	7-30	0-0	19.0	+7.96
Hexham	6-25	1-5	1-1	2-8	2-8	0-3	24.0	+19.50
Newcastle	6-36	1-8	1-3	0-5	2-17	2-3	16.7	+21.00
Sedgefield	4-33	0-7	1-4	1-6	1-15	1-1	12.1	-2.00
Catterick	4-38	0-5	0-2	2-9	1-15	1-7	10.5	-16.25
Kelso	3-16	0-2	1-3	2-4	0-7	0-0	18.8	-5.63
Southwell	2-19	0-6	0-0	1-7	1-6	0-0	10.5	+1.00
Aintree	2-21	0-2	0-1	1-9	0-8	1-1	9.5	+8.25
Haydock	2-32	0-5	0-1	0-10	2-16	0-0	6.3	-7.00
Mrket Rsn	2-32	1-6	0-4	0-5	1-16	0-1	6.3	-23.75
Wetherby	2-32	0-5	0-2	1-8	1-17	0-0	6.3	+1.00
Cartmel	1-8	1-3	0-1	0-1	0-3	0-0	12.5	-2.00
Perth	1-8	0-1	0-0	1-2	0-5	0-0	12.5	-2.50
Worcester	1-8	0-1	0-1	0-1	1-4	0-1	12.5	-1.50
Ayr	1-9	0-0	0-1	0-2	1-5	0-1	11.1	+0.50
Bangor	1-9	0-0	0-1	0-1	1-7	0-0	11.1	-5.50
Uttoxeter	1-21	0-4	0-1	0-4	0-10	1-2	4.8	+5.00

NIGEL TWISTON-DAVIES

NAUNTON, GLOUCS

	No. of Hrs	Races Run	1st	2nd	3rd	Unpl	Per cent	£1 Level Stake
NH Flat	*30*	*44*	*6*	*1*	*4*	*33*	*13.6*	*-26.13*
Hurdles	*61*	*227*	*34*	*37*	*20*	*136*	*15.0*	*+15.58*
Chases	*66*	*296*	*43*	*43*	*34*	*176*	*14.5*	*-84.82*
Totals	**125**	**567**	**83**	**81**	**58**	**345**	**14.6**	**-95.37**
07-08	*96*	*523*	*87*	*79*	*51*	*306*	*16.6*	*+6.26*
06-07	*105*	*432*	*61*	*45*	*35*	*291*	*14.1*	*-110.13*

BY MONTH

NH Flat	W-R	Per cent	£1 Level Stake
May	1-5	20.0	-2.13
June	1-2	50.0	-0.50
July	0-1	0.0	-1.00
August	0-0	0.0	0.00
September	2-3	66.7	+2.75
October	1-5	20.0	-2.75
November	0-10	0.0	-10.00
December	0-5	0.0	-5.00
January	0-2	0.0	-2.00
February	0-3	0.0	-3.00
March	0-3	0.0	-3.00
April	1-5	20.0	+0.50

Hurdles	W-R	Per cent	£1 Level Stake
May	5-15	33.3	+9.00
June	1-4	25.0	-1.13
July	3-15	20.0	-8.01
August	3-11	27.3	-4.05
September	4-22	18.2	+36.41
October	4-32	12.5	+0.33
November	5-32	15.6	-12.72
December	0-17	0.0	-17.00
January	1-12	8.3	+3.00
February	2-14	14.3	+0.50
March	2-30	6.7	-14.00
April	4-23	17.4	+23.25

Chases	W-R	Per cent	£1 Level Stake
May	1-11	9.1	-6.50
June	2-9	22.2	-1.67
July	4-15	26.7	-0.63
August	2-9	22.2	-0.50
September	3-17	17.6	-5.67
October	12-38	31.6	+24.85
November	8-51	15.7	-17.50
December	1-24	4.2	-21.13
January	0-21	0.0	-21.00
February	2-27	7.4	-22.46
March	2-35	5.7	-16.00
April	6-39	15.4	+3.38

Totals	W-R	Per cent	£1 Level Stake
May	7-31	22.6	+0.37
June	4-15	26.7	-3.30
July	7-31	22.6	-9.64
August	5-20	25.0	-4.55
September	9-42	21.4	+33.49
October	17-75	22.7	+22.43
November	13-93	14.0	-40.22
December	1-46	2.2	-43.13
January	1-35	2.9	-20.00
February	4-44	9.1	-24.96
March	4-68	5.9	-33.00
April	11-67	16.4	+27.13

DISTANCE

Hurdles	W-R	Per cent	£1 Level Stake
2m-2m3f	16-91	17.6	-4.77
2m4f-2m7f	10-81	12.3	-2.65
3m+	8-55	14.5	+23.00

Chases	W-R	Per cent	£1 Level Stake
2m-2m3f	10-61	16.4	-21.92
2m4f-2m7f	17-97	17.5	-5.88
3m+	16-138	11.6	-57.03

RACE CLASS

	W-R	Per cent	£1 Level Stake
Class 1	5-86	5.8	-45.50
Class 2	7-83	8.4	-12.00
Class 3	24-153	15.7	+2.21
Class 4	33-170	19.4	-12.01
Class 5	9-55	16.4	-22.93
Class 6	5-20	25.0	-5.13

FIRST TIME OUT

	W-R	Per cent	£1 Level Stake
Bumpers	4-30	13.3	-15.88
Hurdles	9-40	22.5	+31.83
Chases	13-55	23.6	+6.93
Totals	26-125	20.8	+22.88

JOCKEYS

	W-R	Per cent	£1 Level Stake
P J Brennan	50-348	14.4	-99.36
David England	23-144	16.0	-9.22
T Molloy	5-35	14.3	+18.85
Timmy Murphy	2-11	18.2	+4.50
Mr S Twiston-Davies	2-11	18.2	-4.13
Mr S Waley-Cohen	1-2	50.0	+10.00

COURSE RECORD

	Total W-R	Non-Hndcps Hurdles	Non-Hndcps Chases	Hndcps Hurdles	Hndcps Chases	NH Flat	Per cent	£1 Level Stake
Uttoxeter	10-37	2-15	1-3	2-5	3-8	2-6	27.0	+28.23
Perth	8-33	3-8	0-5	2-8	2-11	1-1	24.2	-5.47
Cheltenham	8-79	1-15	4-20	2-14	1-29	0-1	10.1	+11.00
Stratford	6-29	0-7	3-6	1-4	1-9	1-3	20.7	-3.75
Worcester	5-18	1-7	1-2	1-3	1-4	1-2	27.8	+1.16
Aintree	5-25	0-2	0-0	0-4	5-18	0-1	20.0	+10.00
Ayr	3-4	0-0	1-1	1-1	1-2	0-0	75.0	+14.38
Warwick	3-8	2-3	0-1	1-1	0-1	0-2	37.5	+10.83
Southwell	3-12	1-4	0-2	1-1	1-4	0-1	25.0	+23.00
Mrket Rsn	3-17	1-4	0-2	0-3	2-8	0-0	17.6	-6.88
Towcester	3-21	1-7	1-3	0-2	1-6	0-3	14.3	+9.33
Bangor	3-23	1-3	1-4	0-6	1-8	0-2	13.0	-16.00
Ludlow	3-32	0-4	2-6	1-9	0-7	0-6	9.4	-20.13
Lingfield	2-4	1-2	0-0	0-0	1-2	0-0	50.0	-0.31
Nton Abbot	2-8	2-2	0-3	0-1	0-1	0-1	25.0	-1.75
Exeter	2-9	1-2	0-0	0-1	1-6	0-0	22.2	-1.17
Carlisle	2-13	0-0	0-6	0-0	2-7	0-0	15.4	-5.00
Wincanton	2-13	0-2	0-1	1-3	1-6	0-1	15.4	+2.00
Huntingdon	2-18	2-5	0-2	0-2	0-7	0-2	11.1	-9.71
Newbury	2-26	0-5	0-1	0-4	2-14	0-2	7.7	-20.38
Hexham	1-1	0-0	0-0	0-0	0-0	1-1	100.0	+1.25
Wetherby	1-4	1-2	0-1	0-0	0-1	0-0	25.0	0.00
Fontwell	1-7	0-2	0-0	0-1	1-3	0-1	14.3	-1.50
Kelso	1-8	0-2	0-1	0-1	1-4	0-0	12.5	-4.00
Hereford	1-13	0-4	0-2	0-2	1-2	0-3	7.7	-10.00

PAUL WEBBER

MOLLINGTON, OXON

	No. of Hrs	Races Run	1st	2nd	3rd	Unpl	Per cent	£1 Level Stake
NH Flat	*20*	*34*	*1*	*2*	*4*	*27*	*2.9*	*-19.00*
Hurdles	*31*	*72*	*8*	*3*	*6*	*55*	*11.1*	*+49.88*
Chases	*19*	*67*	*7*	*12*	*5*	*43*	*10.4*	*-4.00*
Totals	**58**	**173**	**16**	**17**	**15**	**125**	**9.2**	**+26.88**
07-08	*64*	*174*	*12*	*16*	*23*	*123*	*6.9*	*-64.00*
06-07	*60*	*158*	*12*	*22*	*13*	*111*	*7.6*	*-56.25*

BY MONTH

NH Flat	W-R	Per cent	£1 Level Stake
May	0-1	0.0	-1.00
June	0-0	0.0	0.00
July	0-0	0.0	0.00
August	0-0	0.0	0.00
September	0-0	0.0	0.00
October	0-5	0.0	-5.00
November	0-10	0.0	-10.00
December	0-1	0.0	-1.00
January	0-2	0.0	-2.00
February	0-5	0.0	-5.00
March	0-4	0.0	-4.00
April	1-6	16.7	+9.00

Hurdles	W-R	Per cent	£1 Level Stake
May	0-3	0.0	-3.00
June	1-6	16.7	+7.00
July	0-2	0.0	-2.00
August	0-4	0.0	-4.00
September	0-3	0.0	-3.00
October	0-6	0.0	-6.00
November	2-16	12.5	-2.00
December	0-9	0.0	-9.00
January	2-3	66.7	+4.88
February	1-4	25.0	+17.00
March	1-8	12.5	+7.00
April	1-8	12.5	+43.00

Chases	W-R	Per cent	£1 Level Stake
May	0-7	0.0	-7.00
June	0-4	0.0	-4.00
July	0-1	0.0	-1.00
August	0-1	0.0	-1.00
September	0-2	0.0	-2.00
October	0-5	0.0	-5.00
November	2-16	12.5	+18.00
December	3-8	37.5	+13.00
January	0-5	0.0	-5.00
February	1-4	25.0	0.00
March	0-7	0.0	-7.00
April	1-7	14.3	-3.00

Totals	W-R	Per cent	£1 Level Stake
May	0-11	0.0	-11.00
June	1-10	10.0	+3.00
July	0-3	0.0	-3.00
August	0-5	0.0	-5.00
September	0-5	0.0	-5.00
October	0-16	0.0	-16.00
November	4-42	9.5	+6.00
December	3-18	16.7	+3.00
January	2-10	20.0	-2.12
February	2-13	15.4	+12.00
March	1-19	5.3	-4.00
April	3-21	14.3	+49.00

DISTANCE

Hurdles	W-R	Per cent	£1 Level Stake
2m-2m3f	3-46	6.5	-25.13
2m4f-2m7f	3-21	14.3	+20.50
3m+	2-5	40.0	+54.50

Chases	W-R	Per cent	£1 Level Stake
2m-2m3f	3-19	15.8	+11.00
2m4f-2m7f	3-29	10.3	0.00
3m+	1-19	5.3	-15.00

RACE CLASS

	W-R	Per cent	£1 Level Stake
Class 1	2-12	16.7	+47.50
Class 2	2-10	20.0	+16.00
Class 3	5-37	13.5	-8.63
Class 4	6-77	7.8	-6.00
Class 5	1-22	4.5	-7.00
Class 6	0-15	0.0	-15.00

FIRST TIME OUT

	W-R	Per cent	£1 Level Stake
Bumpers	1-20	5.0	-5.00
Hurdles	2-21	9.5	+0.50
Chases	0-17	0.0	-17.00
Totals	3-58	5.2	-21.50

JOCKEYS

	W-R	Per cent	£1 Level Stake
Dominic Elsworth	7-53	13.2	+17.00
W T Kennedy	6-62	9.7	+47.00
A P McCoy	1-3	33.3	-0.13
Timmy Murphy	1-5	20.0	-2.00
Mark Bradburne	1-12	8.3	+3.00

COURSE RECORD

	Total W-R	Non-Hndcps Hurdles	Non-Hndcps Chases	Hndcps Hurdles	Hndcps Chases	NH Flat	Per cent	£1 Level Stake
Kempton	3-12	1-4	0-1	0-1	2-4	0-2	25.0	+12.50
Doncaster	2-5	1-1	0-0	0-0	1-2	0-2	40.0	+2.88
Uttoxeter	2-22	2-9	0-2	0-4	0-5	0-2	9.1	+6.00
Aintree	1-1	0-0	0-0	1-1	0-0	0-0	100.0	+50.00
Catterick	1-2	1-1	0-0	0-0	0-1	0-0	50.0	+3.00
Leicester	1-3	0-0	1-1	0-1	0-1	0-0	33.3	+10.00
Wetherby	1-4	0-2	1-1	0-0	0-1	0-0	25.0	+17.00
Plumpton	1-7	0-1	0-0	0-0	1-2	0-4	14.3	-3.00
Newbury	1-8	0-1	0-1	1-1	0-5	0-0	12.5	-2.50
Huntingdon	1-10	1-4	0-2	0-0	0-3	0-1	10.0	+11.00
Sandown	1-10	0-3	0-1	0-3	1-2	0-1	10.0	-6.00
Ludlow	1-12	0-0	0-5	0-1	0-1	1-5	8.3	+3.00

EVAN WILLIAMS

LLANCARFAN, VALE OF GLAMORGAN

	No. of Hrs	Races Run	1st	2nd	3rd	Unpl	Per cent	£1 Level Stake
NH Flat	10	19	2	3	1	13	10.5	-3.00
Hurdles	97	308	44	43	31	190	14.3	-65.89
Chases	48	170	26	26	20	98	15.3	-32.90
Totals	**124**	**497**	**72**	**72**	**52**	**301**	**14.5**	**-101.79**
07-08	*141*	*538*	*57*	*48*	*67*	*366*	*10.6*	*-261.63*
06-07	*140*	*503*	*65*	*50*	*58*	*330*	*12.9*	*-127.71*

BY MONTH

NH Flat	W-R	Per cent	£1 Level Stake
May	0-0	0.0	0.00
June	0-1	0.0	-1.00
July	0-0	0.0	0.00
August	0-0	0.0	0.00
September	0-3	0.0	-3.00
October	0-3	0.0	-3.00
November	1-2	50.0	+4.00
December	0-2	0.0	-2.00
January	1-2	50.0	+8.00
February	0-1	0.0	-1.00
March	0-3	0.0	-3.00
April	0-2	0.0	-2.00

Hurdles	W-R	Per cent	£1 Level Stake
May	1-19	5.3	-10.00
June	3-22	13.6	-7.75
July	4-26	15.4	-14.03
August	3-15	20.0	-3.00
September	3-24	12.5	-15.11
October	9-36	25.0	+23.97
November	7-28	25.0	+21.75
December	3-30	10.0	-15.50
January	0-17	0.0	-17.00
February	1-25	4.0	-22.00
March	5-39	12.8	-11.25
April	5-27	18.5	+4.03

Chases	W-R	Per cent	£1 Level Stake
May	3-17	17.6	+21.50
June	1-12	8.3	-7.50
July	6-23	26.1	+0.65
August	2-15	13.3	-7.25
September	5-13	38.5	+16.88
October	1-17	5.9	-12.00
November	3-16	18.8	-3.00
December	1-18	5.6	-14.75
January	0-7	0.0	-7.00
February	1-10	10.0	-6.00
March	2-10	20.0	-5.31
April	1-12	8.3	-9.13

Totals	W-R	Per cent	£1 Level Stake
May	4-36	11.1	+11.50
June	4-35	11.4	-16.25
July	10-49	20.4	-13.38
August	5-30	16.7	-10.25
September	8-40	20.0	-1.23
October	10-56	17.9	+8.97
November	11-46	23.9	+22.75
December	4-50	8.0	-32.25
January	1-26	3.8	-16.00
February	2-36	5.6	-29.00
March	7-52	13.5	-19.56
April	6-41	14.6	-7.10

DISTANCE

Hurdles	W-R	Per cent	£1 Level Stake
2m-2m3f	22-193	11.4	-76.29
2m4f-2m7f	19-83	22.9	+18.90
3m+	3-32	9.4	-8.50

Chases	W-R	Per cent	£1 Level Stake
2m-2m3f	12-71	16.9	-5.58
2m4f-2m7f	13-61	21.3	+7.18
3m+	1-38	2.6	-34.50

RACE CLASS

	W-R	Per cent	£1 Level Stake
Class 1	4-31	12.9	-10.38
Class 2	0-22	0.0	-22.00
Class 3	11-94	11.7	-29.36
Class 4	40-243	16.5	-35.31
Class 5	16-96	16.7	+3.00
Class 6	1-11	9.1	-7.75

FIRST TIME OUT

	W-R	Per cent	£1 Level Stake
Bumpers	1-10	10.0	-4.00
Hurdles	12-85	14.1	+2.41
Chases	6-29	20.7	+16.75
Totals	19-124	15.3	+15.16

JOCKEYS

	W-R	Per cent	£1 Level Stake
D P Fahy	31-184	16.8	-24.81
Paul Moloney	24-158	15.2	-17.00
Christian Williams	10-85	11.8	-12.11
A P McCoy	2-6	33.3	-1.60
Harry Skelton	1-1	100.0	+4.50
Robert Thornton	1-4	25.0	0.00
S P Jones	1-5	20.0	-2.90
Mr J E Tudor	1-6	16.7	-3.13
Mr Nick Williams	1-16	6.3	-12.75

COURSE RECORD

	Total W-R	Non-Hndcps Hurdles	Non-Hndcps Chases	Hndcps Hurdles	Hndcps Chases	NH Flat	Per cent	£1 Level Stake
Uttoxeter	9-37	5-18	1-2	0-7	3-10	0-0	24.3	+0.80
Fontwell	8-44	2-15	1-1	3-15	2-11	0-2	18.2	-4.96
Taunton	5-26	1-8	1-2	1-11	0-2	2-3	19.2	-2.52
Worcester	5-26	0-9	3-4	0-4	2-8	0-1	19.2	+23.50
Huntingdon	4-8	2-4	0-1	2-3	0-0	0-0	50.0	+28.40
Fakenham	4-15	4-8	0-2	0-4	0-1	0-0	26.7	-2.15
Plumpton	4-16	2-5	0-0	1-9	1-2	0-0	25.0	+16.50
Stratford	4-23	2-9	0-2	0-1	2-10	0-1	17.4	-11.58
Mrket Rsn	3-18	2-8	0-1	0-1	1-8	0-0	16.7	-4.25
Hereford	3-32	2-11	1-3	0-8	0-6	0-4	9.4	-22.06
Ludlow	3-59	2-20	0-4	1-12	0-19	0-4	5.1	-41.20
Sedgefield	2-7	0-3	0-0	0-2	2-2	0-0	28.6	+2.88
Cheltenham	2-15	2-7	0-1	0-4	0-2	0-1	13.3	+5.00
Southwell	2-17	1-5	1-3	0-3	0-5	0-1	11.8	-13.07
Chepstow	2-34	0-13	0-2	2-11	0-7	0-1	5.9	-25.50
Ayr	1-1	0-0	1-1	0-0	0-0	0-0	100.0	+1.88
Musselbgh	1-1	0-0	1-1	0-0	0-0	0-0	100.0	+3.00
Haydock	1-1	0-0	0-0	1-1	0-0	0-0	100.0	+11.00
Cartmel	1-3	0-0	0-1	1-2	0-0	0-0	33.3	+3.00
Hexham	1-3	1-1	0-1	0-0	0-1	0-0	33.3	+1.00
Exeter	1-4	0-1	0-0	1-3	0-0	0-0	25.0	+2.50
Leicester	1-5	0-0	1-2	0-0	0-3	0-0	20.0	-1.75
Newbury	1-5	0-1	0-0	1-2	0-2	0-0	20.0	-2.25
Wetherby	1-7	0-0	1-2	0-2	0-3	0-0	14.3	-3.50
Ascot	1-8	0-3	1-1	0-1	0-3	0-0	12.5	-4.75
Wincanton	1-11	1-3	0-0	0-5	0-3	0-0	9.1	+8.00

IAN WILLIAMS

PORTWAY, WORCS

	No. of Hrs	Races Run	1st	2nd	3rd	Unpl	Per cent	£1 Level Stake
NH Flat	*6*	*10*	*1*	*0*	*1*	*8*	*10.0*	*+7.00*
Hurdles	*49*	*125*	*10*	*9*	*13*	*93*	*8.0*	*-48.45*
Chases	*15*	*44*	*3*	*4*	*9*	*28*	*6.8*	*-25.00*
Totals	**62**	**179**	**14**	**13**	**23**	**129**	**7.8**	**-66.45**
07-08	*59*	*255*	*20*	*25*	*20*	*190*	*7.8*	*-95.46*
06-07	*82*	*293*	*19*	*21*	*38*	*215*	*6.5*	*-80.63*

BY MONTH

NH Flat	W-R	Per cent	£1 Level Stake
May	0-0	0.0	0.00
June	0-0	0.0	0.00
July	0-0	0.0	0.00
August	0-0	0.0	0.00
September	0-0	0.0	0.00
October	0-1	0.0	-1.00
November	0-0	0.0	0.00
December	0-2	0.0	-2.00
January	0-1	0.0	-1.00
February	0-0	0.0	0.00
March	1-4	25.0	+13.00
April	0-2	0.0	-2.00

Hurdles	W-R	Per cent	£1 Level Stake
May	0-15	0.0	-15.00
June	0-2	0.0	-2.00
July	1-6	16.7	+5.00
August	0-1	0.0	-1.00
September	1-3	33.3	+3.50
October	3-11	27.3	+3.30
November	3-12	25.0	+15.75
December	1-17	5.9	-6.00
January	0-14	0.0	-14.00
February	0-17	0.0	-17.00
March	1-16	6.3	-10.00
April	0-11	0.0	-11.00

Chases	W-R	Per cent	£1 Level Stake
May	0-7	0.0	-7.00
June	0-3	0.0	-3.00
July	0-6	0.0	-6.00
August	0-0	0.0	0.00
September	0-0	0.0	0.00
October	1-4	25.0	+4.00
November	0-3	0.0	-3.00
December	0-4	0.0	-4.00
January	0-5	0.0	-5.00
February	0-3	0.0	-3.00
March	2-4	50.0	+7.00
April	0-5	0.0	-5.00

Totals	W-R	Per cent	£1 Level Stake
May	0-22	0.0	-22.00
June	0-5	0.0	-5.00
July	1-12	8.3	-1.00
August	0-1	0.0	-1.00
September	1-3	33.3	+3.50
October	4-16	25.0	+6.30
November	3-15	20.0	+12.75
December	1-23	4.3	-12.00
January	0-20	0.0	-20.00
February	0-20	0.0	-20.00
March	4-24	16.7	+10.00
April	0-18	0.0	-18.00

DISTANCE

Hurdles	W-R	Per cent	£1 Level Stake
2m-2m3f	4-55	7.3	-32.75
2m4f-2m7f	5-43	11.6	+4.30
3m+	1-27	3.7	-20.00

Chases	W-R	Per cent	£1 Level Stake
2m-2m3f	0-5	0.0	-5.00
2m4f-2m7f	0-13	0.0	-13.00
3m+	3-26	11.5	-7.00

RACE CLASS

	W-R	Per cent	£1 Level Stake
Class 1	0-6	0.0	-6.00
Class 2	0-14	0.0	-14.00
Class 3	6-29	20.7	+11.00
Class 4	5-95	5.3	-46.75
Class 5	3-32	9.4	-7.70
Class 6	0-3	0.0	-3.00

FIRST TIME OUT

	W-R	Per cent	£1 Level Stake
Bumpers	0-6	0.0	-6.00
Hurdles	3-46	6.5	-15.25
Chases	0-10	0.0	-10.00
Totals	3-62	4.8	-31.25

JOCKEYS

	W-R	Per cent	£1 Level Stake
Michael Murphy	4-56	7.1	-32.50
David Dennis	3-59	5.1	-23.00
Robert Thornton	2-2	100.0	+11.75
Dean Coleman	1-3	33.3	+5.00
Charlie Huxley	1-3	33.3	+3.50
Wayne Hutchinson	1-3	33.3	+14.00
Tom Scudamore	1-5	20.0	+1.00
Jason Maguire	1-6	16.7	-4.20

COURSE RECORD

	Total W-R	Non-Hndcps Hurdles	Non-Hndcps Chases	Hndcps Hurdles	Hndcps Chases	NH Flat	Per cent	£1 Level Stake
Uttoxeter	3-20	2-9	0-0	1-6	0-4	0-1	15.0	-1.20
Warwick	2-13	1-5	0-0	0-5	1-3	0-0	15.4	+8.50
Towcester	2-14	1-5	0-0	0-3	0-3	1-3	14.3	+8.50
Kelso	1-1	0-0	0-0	0-0	1-1	0-0	100.0	+5.50
Haydock	1-3	1-1	0-0	0-2	0-0	0-0	33.3	-0.25
Plumpton	1-4	0-1	0-0	1-2	0-1	0-0	25.0	+2.50
Aintree	1-5	0-0	0-0	1-4	0-1	0-0	20.0	+2.00
Mrket Rsn	1-5	0-2	0-1	1-2	0-0	0-0	20.0	+6.00
Sandown	1-5	1-2	0-0	0-2	0-1	0-0	20.0	+3.00
Cheltenham	1-7	0-1	0-0	0-3	1-3	0-0	14.3	+1.00

VENETIA WILLIAMS

KINGS CAPLE, H'FORDS

	No. of Hrs	Races Run	1st	2nd	3rd	Unpl	Per cent	£1 Level Stake
NH Flat	*11*	*16*	*2*	*3*	*2*	*9*	*12.5*	*-7.75*
Hurdles	*66*	*204*	*29*	*28*	*25*	*122*	*14.2*	*-27.96*
Chases	*55*	*204*	*34*	*38*	*15*	*117*	*16.7*	*+114.50*
Totals	**110**	**424**	**65**	**69**	**42**	**248**	**15.3**	**+78.79**
07-08	*125*	*467*	*69*	*60*	*54*	*284*	*14.8*	*-87.71*
06-07	*100*	*412*	*75*	*53*	*41*	*243*	*18.2*	*+27.01*

BY MONTH

NH Flat	W-R	Per cent	£1 Level Stake
May	0-0	0.0	0.00
June	0-0	0.0	0.00
July	0-0	0.0	0.00
August	0-0	0.0	0.00
September	0-0	0.0	0.00
October	0-1	0.0	-1.00
November	0-5	0.0	-5.00
December	1-2	50.0	+2.50
January	1-2	50.0	+1.75
February	0-4	0.0	-4.00
March	0-2	0.0	-2.00
April	0-0	0.0	0.00

Hurdles	W-R	Per cent	£1 Level Stake
May	2-13	15.4	-2.90
June	0-4	0.0	-4.00
July	1-5	20.0	+12.00
August	0-2	0.0	-2.00
September	0-0	0.0	0.00
October	0-10	0.0	-10.00
November	2-24	8.3	-9.50
December	3-32	9.4	-14.75
January	3-23	13.0	+18.00
February	13-45	28.9	+2.57
March	3-29	10.3	-6.00
April	2-17	11.8	-11.38

Chases	W-R	Per cent	£1 Level Stake
May	1-9	11.1	-4.00
June	0-2	0.0	-2.00
July	0-2	0.0	-2.00
August	0-5	0.0	-5.00
September	0-4	0.0	-4.00
October	1-12	8.3	-3.00
November	2-30	6.7	-5.50
December	11-30	36.7	+25.67
January	8-28	28.6	+18.73
February	7-34	20.6	-8.15
March	1-29	3.4	+5.00
April	3-19	15.8	+98.75

Totals	W-R	Per cent	£1 Level Stake
May	3-22	13.6	-6.90
June	0-6	0.0	-6.00
July	1-7	14.3	+10.00
August	0-7	0.0	-7.00
September	0-4	0.0	-4.00
October	1-23	4.3	-14.00
November	4-59	6.8	-20.00
December	15-64	23.4	+13.42
January	12-53	22.6	+38.48
February	20-83	24.1	-9.58
March	4-60	6.7	-3.00
April	5-36	13.9	+87.37

DISTANCE

Hurdles	W-R	Per cent	£1 Level Stake
2m-2m3f	22-119	18.5	+2.30
2m4f-2m7f	4-60	6.7	-27.88
3m+	3-25	12.0	-2.39

Chases	W-R	Per cent	£1 Level Stake
2m-2m3f	6-50	12.0	-1.40
2m4f-2m7f	14-67	20.9	+22.10
3m+	14-87	16.1	+93.80

RACE CLASS

	W-R	Per cent	£1 Level Stake
Class 1	8-45	17.8	+170.25
Class 2	6-63	9.5	-36.25
Class 3	20-126	15.9	-5.27
Class 4	24-155	15.5	-38.89
Class 5	5-24	20.8	-4.15
Class 6	2-11	18.2	-6.89

FIRST TIME OUT

	W-R	Per cent	£1 Level Stake
Bumpers	0-11	0.0	-11.00
Hurdles	7-55	12.7	+10.83
Chases	5-44	11.4	-8.00
Totals	12-110	10.9	-8.17

JOCKEYS

	W-R	Per cent	£1 Level Stake
A Coleman	31-195	15.9	-7.59
Sam Thomas	24-149	16.1	-19.08
William Biddick	6-31	19.4	+23.71
Liam Treadwell	2-21	9.5	+101.00
Tom Scudamore	1-2	50.0	+3.50
Mr C D Thompson	1-7	14.3	-3.75

COURSE RECORD

	Total W-R	Non-Hndcps Hurdles	Non-Hndcps Chases	Hndcps Hurdles	Hndcps Chases	NH Flat	Per cent	£1 Level Stake
Taunton	8-24	4-12	1-1	2-5	1-5	0-1	33.3	+25.06
Towcester	7-31	3-9	1-3	1-6	0-9	2-4	22.6	-6.05
Cheltenham	7-39	0-3	0-2	1-12	6-22	0-0	17.9	+54.25
Bangor	5-22	1-5	2-4	0-4	2-8	0-1	22.7	-3.05
Ludlow	4-9	0-0	0-0	0-0	4-9	0-0	44.4	+24.50
Hereford	4-17	2-6	0-0	1-4	1-6	0-1	23.5	+5.20
Leicester	3-11	1-3	1-2	0-1	1-5	0-0	27.3	-4.38
Sandown	3-19	0-0	0-0	1-9	2-9	0-1	15.8	+9.25
Wincanton	3-23	0-3	1-2	0-7	2-11	0-0	13.0	-15.13
Mrket Rsn	2-2	1-1	0-0	1-1	0-0	0-0	100.0	+2.92
Fontwell	2-11	1-6	0-2	0-2	1-1	0-0	18.2	+1.63
Doncaster	2-15	0-2	1-2	0-2	1-9	0-0	13.3	-10.52
Ascot	2-17	0-2	0-0	1-6	1-9	0-0	11.8	+13.00
Chepstow	2-19	1-7	0-0	0-2	1-7	0-3	10.5	-6.00
Newbury	2-19	0-4	1-1	0-4	1-10	0-0	10.5	-13.34
Perth	1-2	0-0	0-0	1-1	0-1	0-0	50.0	+1.00
Fakenham	1-3	1-2	0-0	0-0	0-1	0-0	33.3	+4.00
Cartmel	1-4	1-2	0-0	0-1	0-1	0-0	25.0	-1.90
Warwick	1-4	1-3	0-0	0-0	0-1	0-0	25.0	-2.38
Haydock	1-9	1-1	0-0	0-1	0-7	0-0	11.1	-5.75
Worcester	1-9	0-3	0-0	1-3	0-3	0-0	11.1	+8.00
Kempton	1-13	0-3	0-1	1-4	0-5	0-0	7.7	-6.00
Folkestone	1-15	0-5	0-1	0-2	1-6	0-1	6.7	-9.50
Aintree	1-23	0-5	0-0	0-7	1-11	0-0	4.3	+78.00

SEASON STATISTICS JUMPS 2008-2009 - JOCKEYS

NAME	WINS-RUNS	2nd	3rd	4th	WIN £	TOTAL £	£1STK
A P McCoy	186–853 22%	136	101	72	£1,511,714	£2,302,676	-78.29
Richard Johnson	132–806 16%	131	118	89	£749,528	£1,400,117	-127.84
Robert Thornton	119–654 18%	99	77	75	£1,005,070	£1,569,871	-177.11
Noel Fehily	89–505 18%	59	56	48	£594,697	£905,176	+39.33
P J Brennan	84–595 14%	88	66	54	£964,054	£1,434,374	-134.72
Denis O'Regan	83–534 16%	73	55	56	£474,527	£805,576	-167.46
Sam Thomas	78–476 16%	76	40	49	£453,523	£844,595	-94.86
Jason Maguire	70–472 15%	69	50	56	£353,682	£574,010	-72.21
R Walsh	69–252 27%	45	27	27	£1,742,946	£2,358,758	-37.10
G Lee	67–612 11%	80	60	59	£478,614	£816,420	-218.54
B J Geraghty	65–245 27%	33	22	20	£1,185,433	£1,585,655	+10.05
Timmy Murphy	63–455 14%	58	47	33	£455,344	£956,971	-126.21
Tom Scudamore	62–573 11%	59	54	62	£559,305	£799,181	-238.48
T J O'Brien	59–514 11%	61	52	58	£391,714	£694,336	-107.57
Christian Williams	59–494 12%	55	59	46	£353,676	£584,949	-62.09
A Coleman	55–448 12%	55	53	42	£463,132	£658,725	-51.25
Brian Hughes	50–490 10%	48	44	36	£217,377	£312,109	-180.18
Jamie Moore	45–503 9%	52	56	52	£337,393	£506,332	-233.22
Dominic Elsworth	41–378 11%	46	43	31	£315,395	£520,201	-56.72
R P Flint	40–210 19%	25	28	26	£240,416	£354,402	+3.44
Jack Doyle	39–274 14%	35	24	17	£277,901	£405,485	-7.03
Paul Moloney	38–361 11%	36	34	31	£272,042	£434,668	-79.37
Felix De Giles	38–275 14%	23	31	22	£175,847	£266,062	-59.62
S E Durack	36–382 9%	26	54	37	£351,739	£560,331	+5.43
D P Fahy	35–224 16%	35	30	22	£157,945	£250,024	-10.81
W Hutchinson	33–265 12%	22	32	35	£259,679	£398,403	-54.01
Dougie Costello	32–400 8%	47	43	40	£166,567	£302,265	-160.85
David England	32–282 11%	28	23	28	£174,955	£265,313	-56.85
Mark Bradburne	28–368 8%	37	31	49	£185,472	£356,252	-84.50
Richard McGrath	28–383 7%	43	38	32	£140,008	£275,879	-131.87
Andrew Tinkler	28–269 10%	21	26	17	£166,006	£228,560	-84.19
Peter Buchanan	28–322 9%	21	27	31	£145,106	£210,203	-112.53
Harry Skelton	27–175 15%	15	15	21	£211,871	£271,947	+25.07
W T Kennedy	27–311 9%	23	28	27	£171,668	£244,833	+2.04
Wilson Renwick	27–338 8%	24	39	25	£138,424	£225,185	-69.59
Tom Siddall	27–320 8%	21	31	29	£135,523	£204,328	-10.85
C I Gillies	27–244 11%	22	28	22	£110,330	£162,327	+22.35
Robert Walford	25–188 13%	23	12	18	£154,684	£207,883	-21.90
D J Condon	24–218 11%	17	15	20	£199,644	£294,927	-72.50
Brian Harding	24–343 7%	24	25	25	£125,999	£203,734	-100.30
Liam Treadwell	23–241 10%	32	24	18	£633,417	£752,570	+36.24
Daryl Jacob	23–347 7%	43	41	40	£130,864	£311,778	-46.08
Barry Keniry	23–324 7%	25	28	33	£116,112	£182,668	-104.69
Tjade Collier	23–244 9%	21	22	21	£106,894	£166,640	-51.54
Mr O Greenall	23–177 13%	12	15	14	£94,187	£121,759	-33.97
Sean Quinlan	22–247 9%	18	17	14	£79,318	£121,212	-63.83
Danny Cook	22–145 15%	9	13	12	£74,891	£115,537	+77.53
James Reveley	21–203 10%	29	33	22	£239,039	£349,012	-45.47
Nick Scholfield	21–219 10%	20	18	20	£158,249	£268,947	-76.79

SEASON STATISTICS JUMPS 2008-2009 – TRAINERS

NAME	WINS-RUNS	2nd	3rd	4th	WIN £	TOTAL £	£1STK
P F Nicholls	155–614 25%	101	60	56	£2,338,821	£3,473,329	-70.02
N J Henderson	115–499 23%	68	48	35	£1,548,584	£2,122,857	+2.01
A King	136–781 17%	115	102	87	£1,159,476	£1,888,035	-216.97
Miss V Williams	65–424 15%	69	42	37	£1,126,218	£1,409,141	+78.79
P J Hobbs	103–576 18%	87	61	66	£725,183	£1,371,896	-64.03
N A T'ston-Davies	83–568 15%	81	59	54	£907,587	£1,354,003	-96.36
D E Pipe	76–662 11%	58	66	51	£687,964	£1,293,981	-205.59
Jonjo O'Neill	97–623 16%	63	60	51	£662,799	£1,084,837	-64.07
J H Johnson	83–495 17%	61	51	41	£404,263	£717,102	-146.29
P Bowen	44–392 11%	38	42	47	£460,369	£680,805	-83.58
C J Mann	63–299 21%	46	41	34	£384,990	£640,960	+39.14
Evan Williams	72–497 14%	72	52	46	£381,872	£625,689	-101.80
D McCain Jnr	62–483 13%	73	55	61	£317,962	£569,275	-96.12
Ferdy Murphy	45–428 11%	57	36	45	£303,295	£524,919	-172.99
T R George	37–228 16%	41	17	23	£304,545	£473,383	-64.26
G L Moore	47–416 11%	42	42	48	£319,514	£446,986	-123.35
H D Daly	31–282 11%	31	44	32	£192,927	£411,919	-56.22
Mrs S J Smith	48–433 11%	47	51	41	£217,014	£390,452	-32.92
N G Richards	38–270 14%	30	19	27	£265,781	£367,718	-21.51
Miss E C Lavelle	29–194 15%	22	16	19	£238,087	£362,144	-2.75
J M Jefferson	30–223 13%	36	27	34	£220,313	£360,444	-39.97
Tim Vaughan	55–322 17%	40	36	34	£207,226	£326,979	-20.04
W P Mullins	3–27 11%	1	3	2	£221,659	£312,617	-17.25
R H & S Alner	25–234 11%	23	26	31	£172,525	£259,240	-5.38
Miss L V Russell	31–277 11%	23	31	35	£178,734	£257,798	+16.10
Carl Llewellyn	17–191 9%	18	17	9	£205,441	£255,054	-13.93
K G Reveley	15–190 8%	22	25	15	£161,740	£252,302	-85.55
C L Tizzard	19–237 8%	19	24	34	£165,730	£251,457	-80.50
Mrs L Wadham	18–133 14%	20	17	9	£142,866	£241,198	-8.44
O Sherwood	24–207 12%	25	30	17	£152,269	£227,105	-65.77
Andrew Turnell	20–154 13%	14	14	15	£147,106	£221,587	-5.55
R H Buckler	12–137 9%	12	21	17	£147,533	£219,613	+8.00
Nick Williams	10–81 12%	12	12	9	£100,377	£207,155	-35.80
P R Webber	16–173 9%	17	15	19	£150,970	£206,431	+26.88
Miss H C Knight	15–206 7%	26	16	16	£86,784	£198,671	-60.25
N J Gifford	25–171 15%	21	30	10	£111,846	£197,500	-22.42
V R A Dartnall	21–129 16%	12	14	8	£157,632	£194,306	+3.81
Mrs A M Thorpe	24–239 10%	33	28	24	£94,570	£189,133	-24.77
B G Powell	22–408 5%	31	35	33	£96,139	£175,997	-208.69
W K Goldsworthy	12–113 11%	15	17	11	£92,074	£173,224	+39.95
J J Quinn	15–110 14%	14	18	11	£109,509	£168,009	+26.38
D T Hughes	1–17 6%	1	3	1	£67,596	£161,661	-8.50
C Byrnes	2–13 15%	0	1	0	£153,927	£157,184	+3.00
P Monteith	19–174 11%	15	23	20	£83,090	£151,799	-32.50
Noel Meade	2–14 14%	0	0	0	£132,229	£148,845	+7.00
R Lee	20–129 16%	13	16	13	£100,133	£145,814	+39.00
C E Longsdon	17–175 10%	17	19	23	£87,982	£144,206	+13.27
Gordon Elliott	24–82 29%	16	9	8	£101,317	£136,780	+4.61

SEASON STATISTICS JUMPS 2008-2009 – OWNERS

NAME	WINS-RUNS	2nd	3rd	4th	WIN £	TOTAL £
John P McManus	88–545 16%	59	50	44	£796,682	£1,207,177
Clive D Smith	8–16 50%	2	3	0	£776,388	£797,590
The Stewart Family	21–85 25%	10	4	9	£402,000	£741,698
Mrs Vida Bingham	2–7 29%	2	0	0	£563,980	£574,376
D A Johnson	24–193 12%	22	16	10	£200,126	£554,760
Sir Robert Ogden	7–102 7%	14	12	15	£241,462	£544,190
Trevor Hemmings	32–306 10%	39	37	33	£207,171	£509,407
Andrea & Graham Wylie	61–343 18%	49	34	33	£251,765	£503,796
Mr & Mrs R K Hughes	13–47 28%	6	5	6	£215,452	£278,303
Walters Plant/Egan Waste	4–16 25%	2	3	0	£199,454	£259,609
Raymond Tooth	3–16 19%	0	2	3	£248,638	£259,572
Alan Peterson	11–47 23%	10	7	6	£111,029	£229,422
Our Friends In The North	5–14 36%	1	0	0	£220,071	£224,993
R Stanley & Y Reynolds II	3–5 60%	0	0	0	£221,199	£222,359
Mrs M Findlay & P Barber	8–20 40%	2	1	1	£92,052	£214,660
McNeill Racing	10–28 36%	6	4	1	£157,125	£193,204
Mrs Diana L Whateley	13–54 24%	5	5	9	£116,719	£190,256
David Sewell	9–26 35%	3	5	5	£155,270	£173,046
Mrs Judy Wilson	4–10 40%	2	2	1	£81,744	£155,134
Mr & Mrs R A Green	12–88 14%	11	7	5	£124,835	£151,864
Mrs J Morgan	5–12 42%	4	0	1	£92,246	£151,851
Seamus Murphy	4–6 67%	0	0	0	£144,418	£144,998
Mr & Mrs William Rucker	3–20 15%	1	3	3	£83,689	£141,113
J Hales	6–20 30%	5	2	3	£84,354	£137,531
J Lewis, M Jooste, M King	9–16 56%	1	1	0	£125,804	£135,259
Peter Spiller	2–4 50%	0	0	0	£134,063	£134,063
Paul Green	6–36 17%	8	4	2	£80,365	£127,170
P K Barber/Mrs M Findlay	7–22 32%	7	2	1	£74,077	£122,420
Terry Warner	16–48 33%	7	2	5	£99,343	£122,317
Malcolm C Denmark	5–45 11%	2	3	2	£111,768	£118,532
Walters Plant Hire Ltd	11–52 21%	9	7	5	£96,894	£114,571
H R Mould	7–45 16%	4	5	5	£70,430	£112,875
Mr & Mrs John Poynton	2–10 20%	3	1	0	£26,300	£111,212
Power Panels Ltd	6–20 30%	3	2	2	£79,589	£107,173
D Hughes. M Evans Ptnrs	4–29 14%	5	6	2	£48,390	£104,599
Simon W Clarke	3–11 27%	1	3	0	£76,525	£104,420
Paul Duffy Diamond Ptnrs	5–16 31%	2	3	1	£70,268	£102,351
Paul Beck	5–33 15%	3	2	2	£74,346	£99,069
Gigginstown House Stud	2–23 9%	3	3	2	£72,665	£98,011
R E Dimond	2–8 25%	0	1	0	£91,484	£97,019
Goat Racing Syndicate	1–1 100%	0	0	0	£96,917	£96,917
Top Of The Hill Syndicate	1–1 100%	0	0	0	£96,917	£96,917

Fixtures for 2009-2010

NOVEMBER 2009

1	Sunday	Carlisle, Huntingdon, Lingfield (AWT)
2	Monday	Plumpton, Wolverhampton (AWT)
3	Tuesday	Catterick, Exeter, Kempton (AWT)
4	Wednesday	Chepstow, *Kempton (AWT), Nottingham, Warwick
5	Thursday	Haydock Park, Lingfield (AWT), Towcester
6	Friday	Fontwell Park, Friday, Hexham, Southwell (AWT), Wolverhampton (AWT)
7	Saturday	Doncaster, Kelso, Sandown Park, Wincanton
8	Sunday	Hereford,Market Rasen, Ffos Las
9	Monday	Carlisle, Southwell, Wolverhampton (AWT)
10	Tuesday	Exeter, Lingfield Park, Sedgefield
11	Wednesday	Bangor-On-Dee, *Kempton (AWT), Southwell (AWT), Warwick
12	Thursday	Ludlow, Southwell (AWT), Taunton, Wolverhampton (AWT)
13	Friday	Cheltenham, Lingfield (AWT), Newcastle, Wolverhampton (AWT)
14	Saturday	Cheltenham, Lingfield (AWT), Uttoxeter, Wetherby, *Wolverhampton (AWT)
15	Sunday	Cheltenham, Fontwell Park, Market Rasen
16	Monday	Leicester, Plumpton, Wolverhampton (AWT)
17	Tuesday	Fakenham, Folkestone, Southwell (AWT)
18	Wednesday	Hexham, *Kempton (AWT), Lingfield (AWT), Market Rasen
19	Thursday	Hereford, Huntingdon, Kempton (AWT), Wincanton
20	Friday	Ascot, Exeter, Kelso, Wolverhampton (AWT)
21	Saturday	Ascot, Haydock Park, Huntingdon, Kempton (AWT), Lingfield (AWT), *Wolverhampton (AWT)
22	Sunday	Musselburgh, Aintree, Towcester,
23	Monday	Kempton Park, Ludlow, Ffos Las
24	Tuesday	Lingfield, Sedgefield, Southwell (AWT)
25	Wednesday	Chepstow, *Kempton (AWT), Lingfield (AWT), Wetherby
26	Thursday	Kempton (AWT), Newbury, Taunton, Uttoxeter
27	Friday	Musselburgh, Lingfield (AWT), Newbury, *Wolverhampton (AWT)
28	Saturday	Lingfield (AWT), Newbury, Newcastle, Towcester, *Wolverhampton (AWT)
29	Sunday	Carlisle, Kempton (AWT), Leicester
30	Monday	Fakenham, Folkestone, Wolverhampton (AWT)

DECEMBER 2009

1	Tuesday	Hereford, Lingfield (AWT), Southwell
2	Wednesday	Ayr, Catterick, Kempton (AWT), Plumpton
3	Thursday	Leicester, Market Rasen, Wincanton, Wolverhampton (AWT)
4	Friday	Exeter, Lingfield (AWT), Sandown Park, *Wolverhampton (AWT)
5	Saturday	Chepstow, Sandown Park, Southwell (AWT), Wetherby, *Wolverhampton (AWT)
6	Sunday	Kelso, Lingfield (AWT), Warwick, Musselburgh
7	Monday	Lingfield (AWT), Wolverhampton (AWT)
8	Tuesday	Fontwell Park, Sedgefield, Southwell (AWT)
9	Wednesday	Hexham, *Kempton (AWT), Leicester, Lingfield (AWT)
10	Thursday	Huntingdon, Kempton (AWT), Ludlow, Taunton
11	Friday	Cheltenham, Doncaster, Southwell (AWT), Wolverhampton (AWT)
12	Saturday	Cheltenham, Doncaster, Lingfield, Southwell (AWT), *Wolverhampton (AWT)
13	Sunday	Hereford, Kempton (AWT), Ayr, Plumpton
14	Monday	Wolverhampton (AWT)
15	Tuesday	Catterick, Folkestone, Southwell (AWT)
16	Wednesday	Bangor-On-Dee, *Kempton (AWT), Lingfield (AWT), Newbury
17	Thursday	Exeter, Ludlow, Southwell (AWT), Wolverhampton (AWT)
18	Friday	Ascot, Southwell (AWT), Uttoxeter, *Wolverhampton (AWT)
19	Saturday	Ascot, Haydock Park, Lingfield (AWT), Newcastle
20	Sunday	Carlisle, Kempton (AWT), Musselburgh
21	Monday	Kempton (AWT), Ffos Las
22	Tuesday	Bangor-On-Dee, Southwell (AWT)
26	Saturday	Huntingdon, Kempton Park, Market Rasen, Sedgefield, Towcester, Wetherby, Wincanton, Wolverhampton (AWT)
27	Sunday	Kempton Park, Southwell (AWT), Wetherby
28	Monday	Catterick, Chepstow, Leicester, Wolverhampton (AWT)
29	Tuesday	Musselburgh, Newbury, Southwell (AWT)
30	Wednesday	Haydock Park, Kempton (AWT), Lingfield (AWT), Taunton
31	Thursday	Lingfield (AWT), Uttoxeter, Warwick

JANUARY 2010

1	Friday	Catterick, Cheltenham, Exeter, Musselburgh, Fakenham, Southwell (AWT)
2	Saturday	Ayr, Folkestone, Sandown Park, Southwell (AWT)
3	Sunday	Kempton (AWT), Plumpton, Lingfield Park
4	Monday	Wetherby, Wolverhampton (AWT)
5	Tuesday	Leicester, Southwell (AWT), Taunton
6	Wednesday	Hexham, *Kempton (AWT), Lingfield (AWT), Southwell
7	Thursday	Huntingdon, *Kempton (AWT), Ludlow, Southwell (AWT)
8	Friday	Bangor-On-Dee, Fontwell Park, Lingfield (AWT), *Wolverhampton (AWT)
9	Saturday	Lingfield (AWT), Sedgefield, Wincanton, Ffos Las
10	Sunday	Hereford, Southwell (AWT)
11	Monday	Ayr, Taunton, Wolverhampton (AWT)
12	Tuesday	Leicester, Newcastle, Southwell (AWT)
13	Wednesday	Doncaster, Kelso, *Kempton (AWT), Lingfield (AWT)
14	Thursday	Catterick, Southwell (AWT), Towcester, Wolverhampton (AWT)
15	Friday	Musselburgh, Huntingdon, Lingfield (AWT), *Wolverhampton (AWT)
16	Saturday	Kempton Park, Lingfield (AWT), Warwick, Wetherby
17	Sunday	Wolverhampton (AWT), Ffos Las
18	Monday	Fakenham, Plumpton, Wolverhampton (AWT)
19	Tuesday	Folkestone, Southwell, Wolverhampton (AWT)
20	Wednesday	*Kempton (AWT), Lingfield (AWT), Newbury
21	Thursday	Ludlow, Southwell (AWT), Taunton, *Wolverhampton (AWT)
22	Friday	Catterick, Chepstow, Lingfield (AWT), *Wolverhampton (AWT)
23	Saturday	Ascot, Haydock Park, Lingfield (AWT), Wincanton
24	Sunday	Kempton (AWT), Market Rasen, Towcester
25	Monday	Fontwell Park, Lingfield Park, Wolverhampton (AWT)
26	Tuesday	Leicester, Sedgefield, Southwell (AWT)
27	Wednesday	Musselburgh, Huntingdon, *Kempton (AWT), Lingfield (AWT)
28	Thursday	*Kempton (AWT), Southwell (AWT), Warwick, Ffos Las
29	Friday	Doncaster, Lingfield (AWT), Newbury, *Wolverhampton (AWT)
30	Saturday	Cheltenham, Doncaster, Lingfield (AWT), Uttoxeter
31	Sunday	Hereford, Kempton (AWT)

FEBRUARY 2010

1	Monday	Kempton Park, Ludlow, Wolverhampton (AWT)
2	Tuesday	Folkestone, Southwell (AWT), Taunton
3	Wednesday	Exeter, *Kempton (AWT), Leicester, Lingfield (AWT),
4	Thursday	Southwell (AWT), Towcester, Wincanton, *Wolverhampton (AWT)
5	Friday	Catterick Bridge, Chepstow, Lingfield (AWT), Wolverhampton (AWT)
6	Saturday	Doncaster, Lingfield (AWT), Sandown Park, Wetherby
7	Sunday	Musselburgh, Fontwell Park, Southwell (AWT)
8	Monday	Lingfield Park, Southwell, Wolverhampton (AWT)
9	Tuesday	Market Rasen, Sedgefield, Southwell (AWT)
10	Wednesday	Carlisle, *Kempton (AWT), Lingfield (AWT), Ludlow
11	Thursday	Huntingdon, *Kempton (AWT), Southwell (AWT)
12	Friday	Bangor-On-Dee, Kempton Park, Southwell (AWT), *Wolverhampton (AWT)
13	Saturday	Ayr, Lingfield (AWT), Newbury, Warwick, *Wolverhampton (AWT)
14	Sunday	Exeter, Hereford, Kempton (AWT)
15	Monday	Catterick, Plumpton, Wolverhampton (AWT)
16	Tuesday	Folkestone, Newcastle, Southwell (AWT)
17	Wednesday	Musselburgh, *Kempton (AWT), Leicester, Lingfield (AWT)
18	Thursday	Kelso, *Kempton (AWT), Southwell (AWT), Ffos Las
19	Friday	Fakenham, Lingfield (AWT), Sandown Park, *Wolverhampton (AWT)
20	Saturday	Ascot, Haydock Park, Lingfield (AWT), Uttoxeter, Wincanton
21	Sunday	Sedgefield, Southwell (AWT)
22	Monday	Carlisle, Market Rasen, Wolverhampton (AWT)
23	Tuesday	Lingfield (AWT), Southwell, Taunton
24	Wednesday	Doncaster, *Kempton (AWT), Lingfield (AWT), Ludlow
25	Thursday	Ayr, Huntingdon, *Kempton (AWT), Southwell (AWT)
26	Friday	Sandown Park, Southwell (AWT), Warwick, *Wolverhampton (AWT)
27	Saturday	Chepstow, Kempton Park, Lingfield (AWT), Newcastle
28	Sunday	Fontwell Park, Kempton (AWT), Towcester